For Janet —

SOUTHERN *Beauty*

RACE, RITUAL, AND MEMORY IN THE MODERN SOUTH

ELIZABETH BRONWYN BOYD

*The University of
Georgia Press
Athens*

Elizabeth Bronwyn Boyd

© 2022 by the University of Georgia Press
Athens, Georgia 30602
www.ugapress.org
All rights reserved

Designed by Kaelin Chappell Broaddus
Set in 11/13.5 Corundum Text Book by Kaelin Chappell Broaddus

Most University of Georgia Press titles are
available from popular e-book vendors.

Printed digitally

Library of Congress Cataloging-in-Publication Data

Names: Boyd, Elizabeth Bronwyn, 1960– author.
Title: Southern beauty : race, ritual, and memory in the modern South /
Elizabeth Bronwyn Boyd.
Description: Athens : The University of Georgia Press, [2022]
| Includes bibliographical references and index.
Identifiers: LCCN 2021061980 | ISBN 9780820362311 (hardback) |
ISBN 9780820362328 (paperback) | ISBN 9780820362304 (ebook)
Subjects: LCSH: Women—Southern States. | Femininity—Southern States. |
Sex role—Southern States. | Racism—Southern States. |
Beauty contests—Southern States. | Debutante balls—Southern
States. | College sorority members—Southern States.
Classification: LCC HQ1438.A13 B69 2022 | DDC 305.40975—dc23/eng/20220404
LC record available at https://lccn.loc.gov/2021061980

FOR

Bronwyn Clare Redvers-Lee

AND

Peter Redvers-Lee

CONTENTS

PREFACE

I THINK IT WAS THE SCREAMING. IT WAS THE LATE 1980S, AND I HAD moved to Oxford, Mississippi, to pursue a master's degree in southern studies at the University of Mississippi, or Ole Miss, as it is known colloquially. Partial funding for this endeavor came in the form of a graduate assistantship that charged a small cadre of students with proofreading the original *Encyclopedia of Southern Culture* (UNC Press, 1989). Reading aloud to one another in pairs as we marked up the manuscript, we would lounge about the common rooms of Barnard Observatory, home to the Center for the Study of Southern Culture and characterized in those days by peeling paint, creaky floorboards, and faded cabbage-rose wallpaper. Nice weather found us out on the porch, where we couldn't help but observe the comings and goings of Sorority Row. It was there that I first witnessed the resounding, ecstatic cries and hyperfeminine motions of sorority rush.

The scene came as a bit of a shock. Though, having grown up in the state capital of Jackson, the move to Mississippi was a return for me, I had forgotten the extent to which a regionally specific and competitive femininity charged nearly every milieu. Or perhaps I had blotted it out or assumed that things had changed. But here it was: highly structured and highly visible, high volume and high stakes. The scene playing out before me was perhaps a heightened expression of the sort, but it was also part and parcel of a ubiquitous regional institution: southern beauty culture. This regional realm of feminine competency emphasized looks, lineage, grooming, and manners, all measured by performance. Nearly a decade earlier, hoping to escape the rah-rah nature of campus life at a big state university, I had purposely chosen a smallish liberal arts college in south-central Texas, where the only sport of note was *tennis*. Yet here I was, drawn back to ground zero of southern beauty culture in my quest to understand and interpret the South. The irony of our poring over the *Encyclopedia*'s serious scholarship on "History and Manners," "Women's Life," and "Mythic South" with sorority-rush door songs as a soundtrack was not lost on me. Yet what I first experienced as amusing happenstance was, in retrospect, serendipity. Like any spectacle, sorority rush was fascinating, nearly impossible not to watch. But I increasingly also found it compelling, a possible key to unraveling relationships of region, race, and identity with which I had just begun to grapple. A number of scholars were exploring such questions, and I had a hunch that gender rituals somehow played a role. Whiteness as a category of analysis was also ascendant, with the racialization of region an intellectual problem. If southern identity was persistently coded as White, what did femininity have to do with it? I would not seriously undertake the subject for several more years, but my interest was piqued and I returned to questions of gender performance, race, and region again and again.

Eventually faced with selecting a dissertation project, I set about crafting a methodology capable of producing answers. Twenty-five years earlier Laura Nader had called for a critical repatriated anthropology, urging scholars to "study up"—to consider "the colonizers rather than the colonized, the culture of power rather than the culture of the powerless, the culture of affluence rather than the culture of poverty."[1] Back on home ground, I embarked on a study of gender rituals of White southerners in hopes of discerning their role in constructing and conserving notions of region. My attention was quickly drawn to three feminine rituals that figure prominently in the lives of many southern women: sorority rush, the beauty pageant, and the debutante ball. Historically, all three performances featured participants making regional claims in the process of securing social status.

My research model was necessarily eclectic, designed to illuminate wide-ranging but related questions from multiple vantage points. Oral history interviews allowed me to probe the motivations and reflections of participants past and present. Sorority members in Mississippi and Alabama; beauty pageant contenders in Mississippi, Alabama, and Tennessee; and alumnae of the Confederate Pageant at Natchez, Mississippi, shared their candid impressions and ruminations. Others connected to the rituals—coaches, directors, club officers, university administrators, advisers, dance teachers, tailors, and judges, to name only a few—also lent their thoughts. All told, I conducted recorded interviews with sixty-one participants between 1997 and 2006 and conversed more casually with many more; all related papers, recordings, and transcripts remain in my possession. Ethnographic research made possible up-close, fly-on-the-wall observation, which in turn informed my view from a distance, allowing me to discern the cultural meanings rituals inscribed on the southern landscape. Backstage access to rehearsals and preliminary competitions of beauty pageants of various sorts in Texas, Mississippi, Tennessee, and Alabama gave me the knowledge to make sense of final nights of competition and the larger pageant world. My understanding of sorority rush was exponentially enhanced by the experience of being "in the house" as the rites unfolded at the University of Mississippi in 1996 and 1997 and at the University of Alabama in 2002. Attending performances of the Confederate Pageant of the Natchez Pilgrimage in 1998 and 2000, I witnessed a public performance for tourists layered with purely local meanings. Paying attention to pop culture over time showed me the continued significance of the southern beauty figure across genres and geographies, despite claims to the contrary. Archival research required some creativity, as few collections were processed and cataloged in such a way as to suggest their relevance to my concerns. Research in archival collections in Louisiana, Mississippi, Alabama, North Carolina, South Carolina, and Illinois yielded rich historical detail about the role of gender rituals in commemorative life. Extensive reading in secondary literature—on collective memory, Whiteness, nostalgia, segregation, performance, region, ritual, elites, and campus culture—allowed me to put varied primary sources into context.

In retrospect, my methodology not only fit my questions; it fit me. The child of southerners (but not Mississippians) and of educators, I had grown up in a bookish, left-leaning family without the typical extended web of Mississippi relations. The result was a sense at times of being in but not completely of the culture. Growing up during and coming of age in the immediate aftermath of the civil rights movement in a place where the local and national news were sometimes one and the same (I was among the students who desegregated the local public schools) was truly a formative experience—the reason I grew up to study, teach, and write about the South. The child of intellectuals in an anti-intellectual climate, of antiracist Whites in a racist society, of Episcopalians in a sea of southern Baptists, and of liberals in a state controlled by conservatives, my perspective was perhaps inevitably one of both participant and observer. Of course, only in hindsight do I see clearly that I was both part and parcel, a thorough product of the local culture and also of my family's place in and stance toward it. This dual perspective (by no means unique to me) would become explicit upon my return to Mississippi to pursue a graduate degree in southern studies. In his autobiography *North toward Home*, Willie Morris notes that "Mississippi may have been the only state in the Union (or certainly one of a half dozen in the

South) which had produced a genuine set of exiles, almost in the European sense: alienated from home yet forever drawn back to it, seeking some form of personal liberty elsewhere yet obsessed with the texture and the complexity of the place from which they had departed as few Americans from other states could ever be."[2] Adopting ethnographic methods (a decision made easily after an early career in journalism), I peered back into the culture that looked so familiar and so foreign to me at the same time.

Like many scholarly studies, this one took longer to complete than anticipated. Oral history work means constantly creating sources, a time-consuming endeavor. The capricious nature of academic employment also prolonged my work. But any disadvantages to taking a leisurely route to publication were outweighed by silver linings. Over the course of my research, the burgeoning field of memory studies virtually exploded, and the ability to incorporate this research benefited my project. The longer germination period that necessitated incorporating new developments and fresh evidence into my analysis also provided built-in opportunities to reassess my arguments at critical cultural junctures. Working with contemporary and living sources is not for the faint of heart, and there were moments when I feared my analysis would not hold. Yet close inspection of altered rituals and apparent cultural shifts often revealed superficial changes that did not transform central meanings. In fact, the persistence and consistency of meaning produced by even reworked gender rituals only underscored my thesis. Radical change (a sign of hope!) occurred only where radical honesty prevailed. If there is a metasubject of this book, it is what ethnography can reveal of a culture determined to conceal. I conclude this project simultaneously relieved to find my arguments sound and aghast to find my concerns relevant—reassuring for the scholar but regrettable for the southerner, who, with the publication of this book, hopes to inspire dialogue about gendered rituals, memory, race, and privilege.

Takoma Park, Maryland
June 2021

ACKNOWLEDGMENTS

WHEN I CONSIDER HOW MANY PEOPLE, ORGANIZATIONS, AND INSTI-
tutions assisted me in creating this work, I am humbled. It is with pure joy
that I recognize and thank them. My first thanks go to my informants, without whom this book would not exist. Participants in sorority rush, beauty
pageants, and the Confederate Pageant of the Natchez (Miss.) Pilgrimage
gave freely of their time and thoughts, and I am grateful. Although not all
are quoted, each interview subject added to my layered understanding of the
rituals in question.

This project began as a master's paper at the University of Mississippi
and followed me to the University of Texas at Austin, where Desley Deacon directed my doctoral dissertation with wisdom, skill, and grace. I thank
her and the other members of my committee: Bill Stott, Jim Sidbury, Bob
Abzug, Steve Hoelscher, and Charles Reagan Wilson, who returned to the
forty acres just for the occasion.

Friendships formed in graduate school represent a special bond. I am
grateful for those of Katie Blount (née Drayne), David Nelson, Lauri Law-
son, Shelley Sallee, Lisa Rhodes, Kathleen Banks Nutter, and the late Jane
Elkind Bowers, who continued sending me a steady stream of clippings and
"hastily scrawled notes" full of tone even after moving out West. You were
there for me in all the ways that matter most, and my gratitude is everlasting.

The Center for the Study of Southern Culture at the University of Mississippi provided the critical milieu that made my study possible. My life
there and in the larger community was enriched by Ann Abadie, Kirsten
Dellinger, Robbie Ethridge, Bill Ferris, Sue Grayzel, Jeff Jackson, Katie
McKee, Ted Ownby, Tom Rankin, and David Wharton. Ed Kamara provided me space at the Blues Archive for conducting interviews. The gender
studies reading group read early pages of this work, providing useful criticism and a welcome sisterhood. Charles Reagan Wilson remains my every-

thing: he provided the example, the support, the advice, and the faith in my project that inspired my persistence. Thank you, mentor and friend.

Nancy Bercaw deserves more thanks than I can adequately express. She not only accompanied me to beauty pageants in the hills of north Mississippi but read drafts, invited talks, and generally walked alongside me on the twisting road to publication. Many know her as a gifted scholar and curator; she is an even better friend. Scott Kreeger, perhaps just as much: he heard it all but remained in the wings, keeping us all well fed and watered along the way.

Katherine Drayne Blount inspired the Natchez chapter by sending me a newspaper clipping about pilgrimage hostesses, with incisive commentary scrawled in the margin. Mimi and Ron Miller, of the Historic Natchez Foundation, provided introductions and a place to conduct interviews, stories, and documents, along with decadent breakfasts. Members of the Natchez Garden Club, the Pilgrimage Garden Club, and other local citizens were generous with their time and reflections.

At Vanderbilt University Larry J. Griffin and Dale Cockrell gave me an institutional home in the American and Southern studies program, where they proved generous mentors and exemplars of decent leadership. Allison Pingree gave freely of the gift of presence. Sheri Sellmeyer, Barry Kolar, Sherry Loller, and the Spanish class gang made sure I maintained a social life outside of Vandy. Alice Randall offered me a seat at the table with the ladies who lunch. My students at Vanderbilt and at the University of Illinois at Urbana–Champaign indulged my interests in public memory and sharpened my analysis. In Emory, Virginia, Julia Wilson invited me to teach and present, while Elisabeth and John Iskra kept me sane and entertained. In Silver Spring, Maryland, the Reverend Lael Sorensen proved a kindred spirit and confidante.

Research is expensive; there is never enough time and rarely enough money. I am grateful to the institutions and organizations that provided me research support: University of Texas at Austin's American Studies Department; University of Texas's women's studies program; American Association of University Women, Austin chapter; Sallie Bingham Center for Research on Women's History and Culture, Duke University; Deep South Regional Humanities Center, Tulane University; Institute for Southern Studies, University of South Carolina; and American Studies Department, University of Maryland–College Park. A visiting fellowship at Humanities Research Center, Australian National University, broadened my perspective on "Biography, Memory, and Commemoration," while Desley Deacon, Sarah Gleeson-White, and Rosanne Kennedy kept me well entertained down under. The Illinois Program for Research in the Humanities, University of Illinois at Urbana–Champaign gave me a room of my own and congenial colleagues with whom to explore the topic of "Beauty." Catharine Gray and Ricky Baldwin and their sons; Dana Rabin and Craig Koslofsy and their children; and members of the Chapel of St. John the Divine made my midwestern sojourn all the warmer.

Librarians and archivists make research possible. I am grateful for those at Alabama Department of Archives and History; Chattanooga Public Library; Duke University; Georgia State University; Historic Natchez Foundation; Historic New Orleans Collection; Library of Congress; Mississippi Department of Archives and History; National Museum of African American History and Culture; National Museum of American History; Newcomb College Center for Research on Women; South Caroliniana Library; Tennessee State Library and Archives; Tulane University; J. S. Hoole Special Collections Library, University of Alabama; University of Illinois at Urbana–Champaign; Archives and Special Collections, University of Mississippi; University of North Carolina at Chapel Hill; and Vanderbilt University.

Lisa Eveleigh urged me to submit a conference paper on sorority rush to *Southern Cultures*, where it was published as "Sister Act: Sorority Rush as Feminine Performance," and I am forever grateful. Thanks go to the University of North Carolina Press for allowing me to republish a version of it here. At the University of Georgia Press, Walter Biggins relit a fire under me at a crucial point of revision. Nathaniel Holly adopted a long-standing project and shepherded its completion with grace, skill, and good humor. This book is better for both of them. A constellation of reviewers provided critical suggestions for revision. Jon Davies and Susan Silver detangled my documentation and troubleshot my prose.

My parents, George Wilson Boyd and Josephine Richards Boyd, did not live to see the publication of this book but championed my early research. Shirley Lee aided my research in North Carolina, and she and the late Vernon Lee welcomed me for a conference in South Africa. My siblings supported me in more ways than perhaps they realize. Thanks for the love and the laughter. Bronwyn Redvers-Lee has lived with this project for her entire life, and Peter Redvers-Lee even longer. Their continued faith in me and support for my work means the world to me. This book is dedicated to them.

SOUTHERN
Beauty

INTRODUCTION

Power Play

THE DECISION WAS WIDELY DENOUNCED AS OVER THE TOP. AFTER
University of Oklahoma members of Sigma Alpha Epsilon, a fraternity with
southern roots, were caught on video in 2015 chanting a racist song with
references to lynching, Greek leaders and campus officials at the University of Georgia announced a prohibition of hoopskirts. The reaction among
many White UGA students and onlookers ranged from irritation to disbelief. The costume of choice for such campus events as Kappa Alpha's Old
South Week and SAE's Magnolia Ball had *nothing to do* with racial intolerance, critics claimed. It was *just fashion,* and the crinoline embargo was yet
another kowtow to political correctness. Contemplating attendance at such
events without their sartorial standby, collegians wondered aloud, "What
did the hoop have to do with the hate?"[1]

But at least one UGA administrator understood all too well the ability
of southern symbols to suggest and even celebrate structures of inequality.
Relegating the hoopskirt to mothballs required only a single meeting with
Greek student leaders, who, concerned with inviting negative attention,
came to agree that such attire was "not appropriate in the context of some
events." If there was dissention among their ranks, their silence concealed
it. Ironically, the same campus leaders who brokered the ban limited its impact by quelling discussion of their decision. After a flash of national publicity, the story failed to gain traction, and other schools did not rush to enact similar proscriptions. Choosing silence over discussion, campus leaders
shut down a potent symbol at UGA but made no call for its curtailment else-

where. In the end the episode was a testament to the continuing power of southern symbols—but also to the power of silence.[2]

The southern beauty was alive and well on the landscape of the twenty-first-century U.S. South—and so was a particular silence. All across the region young White women routinely turned in renditions of femininity more in keeping with nineteenth-century gender ideals—and most did not even require a hoopskirt. In popular performances that gestured toward the southern past, the southern beauty performed a choreography of exclusion, consolidating privilege and reiterating race in a near absence of scrutiny. These largely visual displays were all the more effective for failing to inspire debate.

Observers willing to look, not merely listen, must have been surprised by what they saw. Triumphal claims of a postracial age were stopped short by performances that told a different story. Amid calls for diversity and vocal support for the social changes brought about by the civil rights movement, the southern beauty starred in rituals designed to thwart these very changes. Even as lingering Confederate symbols were retired from civic life, the southern beauty carried on, delivering signature performances of White nostalgia. Nurtured by tacit acceptance, the southern beauty controlled the crises of social equality (feminism, multiculturalism) with stealth and style. She was rarely questioned. Her task was simplified by the complacency of observers. Failing (or refusing) to recognize the racial work of such performances, witnesses colluded through their silence.

In the decades spanning the late twentieth century and the early twenty-first, the southern beauty maintained an elusive yet powerful presence in U.S. culture. In turns demure and flirtatious, she at once evoked iconic symbols of region—the southern lady and her junior counterpart, the southern belle—and signaled them once more. From Carolina cotillions and azalea trail maids to campus competitions and society balls, young White women regularly demonstrated their ability to "do" southern womanhood convincingly and on cue.

Simultaneously hard to pin down and instantly recognizable, the southern beauty surfaced both in everyday behaviors and periodic rituals—and starred in moments of cultural crisis. Day to day she emerged more in stylized gestures and manners and in standards of grooming and etiquette than in any particular look. With her easy grace, steady patter of pleasantries, and ingrained response to every social occasion, she was fitting in every way. In the realm of ritual, she was central to traditions of hospitality—to the holiday dinners, tailgate parties, pilgrimage tours, and bridal teas (to name only a few) organized by women and designed to spotlight and uphold certain standards of womanhood. The look of May Day celebrations, Southeastern Conference tailgating parties, and the Kentucky Derby were so easily called to mind because of the repeated patterned actions of southern women. In a few formal rituals, such as those explored here—sorority rush, the beauty pageant, and an Old South tourist production—the regional expectations associated with White femininity were blatantly displayed and measured on the body. Such public displays were both ephemeral and arresting: a crystallized, coherent, and *current* articulation of White southern womanhood.

Chances are, no one ever noticed. That is precisely the point. The southern beauty enjoyed such wide acceptance that the curiosity and consequences of her style were routinely overlooked. Perhaps the only thing as predictable as the southern beauty's presence was the standard claim of her utter insignificance. Though some observers no doubt found her irritating—a gender throwback—many others, when they noticed her at all, saw only a familiar, endearing figure. No one paid her much mind. The southern beauty was such an accepted character and known quantity that she was considered common knowledge—one of the things just about everybody knew about the South.

But was this lack of perception by accident, design, or deep-seated denial of the beauty's racial work? The U.S. public's distraught overdue reckoning with Confederate symbols after the 2015 mass murder of nine African American churchgoers in Charleston, South Carolina, at the hands of a White supremacist suggests the last. The killer so blatantly linked his racist views with the Confederate banner, and the victims' families responded with such radical forgiveness, that the American people were finally forced to look squarely at their past and at symbols of region and habits of nostalgia long evaded. The national conversation that followed was unprecedented, a catharsis of collective guilt and shame. In every medium critics, journalists, and historians joined average observers in confirming slavery as the root cause of the Civil War and in exposing a long history of complicity in denying or downplaying this fact. In the face of the pure racial violence in Charleston, the "heritage not hate" apology long attached to Confederate symbols no longer held— nor did the entrenched accommodationist public memory that had enabled it. For some, owning up to the truth about pet racial fictions was excruciating, a true reckoning. For others the price for having knowingly overlooked them for so long was deep compunction. Still others refused to yield and dug in their heels; historical facts were no match for beliefs.

But if the pain, regret, and denial were acute, the corresponding action was swift: within a matter of weeks, a variety of Confederate symbols were removed, relocated, renamed, and retired. Those not promptly vanquished were subjected to vigorous debate. For some the long overdue dialogue sparked a rush of release, a collective exhalation. When activist Bree Newsome first climbed the flagpole outside the South Carolina statehouse and removed the Confederate battle flag, and later the New Orleans City Council removed monuments to Confederate heroes from sites across the city, supporters celebrated the actions as nothing short of deliverance. But the sense of relief came coupled with remorse over how long honesty had taken. Why had it taken these horrific murders for the nation to admit its deep investment in obfuscation? Why had it taken so long for so many to choose honesty over the jealous protection of privilege?[3]

The turn toward atonement coincided with surges of activism by Black Lives Matter, the Black liberation movement formed in 2012 to protest the extrajudicial killing of Black people by police and vigilantes and expanded to address the general dehumanization of Black people by the state. The two movements were antiracist and shared a common demand to look squarely at the past. Both called for the public to recognize the persistence of racist incidents over time as evidence of a deep and systemic racial divide, not some disconnected series of isolated events. Police violence against Blacks and acts of Confederate remembrance among Whites represented two sides of the same racist coin, the one obviously brutal, the other only seemingly benign. Both surfaced from the same deep source of White supremacy.[4]

But the renouncement of Confederate symbols was soon overshadowed by real-life social concerns. To a nation gripped by racial turmoil—roiled by extrajudicial police killings of Black citizens, inequitable incarceration rates, and voter ID and other laws aimed at disenfranchising African Americans and other minorities—efforts to come clean about collective memory and Confederate and other southern symbols paled on the ground. How meaningful was furling the Confederate banner—much less divesting the collegiate belle of her signature garment—in a political climate marked by anti-immigrant backlash, right-wing obsession over a majority-minority future, student protest of institutional racism on college campuses, and the GOP candidacy of bigot and birther Donald Trump? Disenfranchising laws and prejudice would remain even after flags came down and skirts were put away. In this volatile milieu what *did* the hoop have to do with the hate? Columnist Sally Jenkins perhaps best made the connection. Writing in the

Washington Post, she proclaimed, "We will have truthfully reckoned with our racial history when high school and college students quit going to Heritage Balls wearing butternut military tunics and sashes and understand that Jeff Davis and Bobby Lee should have spent the rest of their natural lives in work camps, breaking rocks with shovels, instead of on their verandas— and the fact that they didn't was a profound miscarriage." Never found far from such displays of Old South nostalgia was the serene southern beauty. She was also a frequent bystander at scenes of crude racism. Pictured aboard that infamous SAE bus, silently observing the raucous racist chanting of the brothers, sat a quintessential southern beauty.[5]

This book is an attempt to explain the long presence of this unlikely figure—and the widespread studied attempts over time to ignore her. The fact that the southern lady and her younger counterpart, the southern belle, enjoyed a heyday in the nineteenth century is small surprise, given the agenda of White supremacy they supported. The fact that their legacy, the southern beauty, has maintained a strong and largely unexamined presence well into the twenty-first century is more curious and proof of persistent cultural power. Yet, while scholars have generally agreed about the southern lady's historical origins, construction, and use, and many acknowledge the lingering presence of lady and belle ideals, no one has clarified exactly *how* they managed to survive into the present century in the face of great cultural change. Nor *why*. How and why the southern beauty abides is the subject of this book.[6]

In the pages that follow, I explore three popular feminine rituals: sorority rush, the beauty pageant, and an Old South tourist production. All feature a southern beauty with distinct traces of the lady and belle figures. I explore these rituals for their accomplishment of cultural memory work over time— for the role they played in promoting particular remembrances of the southern past. The introduction suggests my central argument, offers a brief discussion of the ways of cultural memory, and provides a historical overview of the southern beauty's role in constructing region. Chapter 1 goes behind the scenes of sorority rush at two flagship universities in the Deep South to examine how this feminine ritual of exclusion, so absorbed with lineage and looks, effectively reinscribed notions of race, region, and social place. Chapter 2 explores southerners' success and investment in beauty pageants, familiar productions in which highly competitive contestants enacted region by displaying and measuring innocence and deference. Chapter 3 visits Natchez, Mississippi, where between 1932 and 2014 the women of the local garden clubs staged an Old South tourist production that doubled as a debutante ball, performing nostalgia and choreography of social structure in one fell swoop. An epilogue revisits southern beauty rituals for signs of continuity and change, takes note of related memory work, and suggests the cultural consequences of performances frequently dismissed as "just tradition."

My research combines firsthand observation, archival research, and recorded interviews with participants. Ethnographic research spanning the final decade of the twentieth century and the first of the twenty-first is considered in light of secondary literature on memory, performance, gender, and southern history. The southern beauty's efficacy in sustaining a racialized understanding of region over time—especially during decades otherwise associated with inclusion and a nascent multiculturalism—represents the crux of the project. More recent developments that challenge or disrupt this phenomenon are noted as promising signs of hope, with the caveat that they are not definitive. Any temptation to declare the southern beauty or her influence defunct on the basis of apparent progressive breakthroughs must be cautioned against, as this only risks replicating the dismissive memory pattern in question. Nostalgia about the past and wishful thinking about the future are kissing cousins, and critics call related pronouncements—of the end of White supremacy, of the advent of postracialism—"always premature," the product of denial regarding the intransigence of structural racism. Antiredistributive Whiteness simultaneously voices support for multiculturalism while eschewing any structural change to the racial order. In a worried time Whiteness is recast in terms of vulnerability and victimhood, and "pro White" racial pride is communicated through cultural cues, "dog whistle" speech, and gestures. Far from "post-" or in the past, race structures the present and menaces the future.[7]

I propose that the southern beauty remained a regular feature on the landscape because she fulfilled an imaginative need for some southerners and others. In a long modern age in which identification on the basis of region seemed always poised to disappear, the southern beauty remained a site of nostalgia, a focal point for imagining community across time and space. For many White southerners she was sweet reminder of a bygone South, a cue for recalling past times and imagined places where common values and clear social hierarchies were a source of comfort and privilege.[8] For those who experienced the present in terms of loss, the southern beauty was a living memento of better days. White southern identity had always been a cultural memory project and right into the twenty-first century it remained so, with the southern beauty the region's most potent, persistent symbol and effective memory mechanism.

Literary critic Patricia Yaeger might have dubbed her "hidden in plain sight"—one of those everyday mechanisms that maintain social hierarchies so seamlessly they rarely draw recognition, despite their public nature. So much a part of the warp and weft of southern life (so "natural," so "traditional"), the southern beauty enacted region while going largely unnoticed by participants and observers alike. Ubiquity was part of her power, a secret to her success. Standout strange but widely ignored, highly visible but easily missed, the southern beauty signified southernness so continually and so successfully that she was scarcely noticed. That this rendition clearly raced region—reiterated a southern = White equation with each gentle gesture— was a fact as obvious as it was overlooked. The beauty succeeded where other symbols faltered because the same fluff that constituted her power also concealed it. Undetected, she went unsuspected.[9]

In truth an entire economy of unknowing, of willed "not seeing" the race and gender practices so clearly known by heart, operated among White southerners, with racial obliviousness the comforting result. Refraining from recognizing (much less scrutinizing) the "unseen everyday"—those mundane, repetitive actions that built White supremacy into the very structures of White southern life without drawing attention to themselves—White southerners continually reproduced their race privilege and, with it, exclusive understandings of southernness. The southern beauty was "unseen everyday." Between the 1920s and the 1970s White southern women quietly engineered, normalized, and sustained White supremacy by weaving it into the fabric of everyday life. Policing one another—the voter registrars, social workers, PTA volunteers, and textbook adoption committee members who maintained segregation behind the scenes but also the organizers of local pageants, commemorations, and rituals that celebrated and perpetuated standards of White southern womanhood in public—they ensured that de facto White supremacy would persist long after the demise of de jure segregation. By tying privilege and status to coming-of-age gender rituals, perpetuation of the productions and their meanings was ensured. In that sense the southern beauty represented a signature achievement: well into the twenty-first century, a seemingly outdated gender figure maintained a significant presence on the southern landscape and in the international imagination. In everyday gestures and fantastic displays, the southern beauty constructed region not intermittently or covertly but continually and right in front of our eyes.[10]

Literary critics Anne Goodwyn Jones and Susan Donaldson have suggested that "gender in the end may be as important an analytic category for making sense of the South as race itself traditionally has been acknowledged to be," noting that "in the South, gender and race haunt one another as they haunt the region's bodies."[11] Yet analysis of southern symbols has concentrated on those closely identified with the Confederacy (flags, monuments), with less notice paid to modern gender signs, despite their racial work. The study of southern memory, where it has incorporated gender, skews to the masculine and material. Meanwhile, works exploring the feminine have largely focused on the distant past, and studies of performativity have rarely considered the South. Perhaps least considered of all are those late twentieth-century and more recent feminine rituals that shored up age-old racial hierarchies. Where many studies have explored representations, my focus is on performance. The ability of thoroughly modern White southern women to perform nostalgia while escaping notice is a paradox I find all the more compelling. I propose that scrutiny of gender performance is crucial to understanding tenacious relationships of memory, race, and region.[12]

Regions might seem stable and constant, securely rooted in lineage, locale, and history. But in truth the South, like any region, required constant production. Over time the southern beauty proved this production's most reliable actor. Just as race was widely understood as a social construction and gender as conveyed through a "stylized repetition of acts," so too did region depend on repeat performance and a steady trafficking in difference. The South was continually produced in a common theater of consumption in which actors and audiences, buyers and sellers, confirmed that the region really *was* different, really *was* a distinct culture and place. Some of the consumption was literal and material—the exchange of goods that by design or association unmistakably signaled region. The circulation of deviled-egg plates and julep cups, praline receipts and seersucker suits, was not only pleasurable and predictable but also meaningful: it was one way that southerners reinscribed region. But the consumption was also visual and performative. The costume and patterned feminine motions associated with customs of leisure and hospitality—from christening celebrations to sporting events—were as important to producing region as more obvious spectacles. Woven into the fabric of everyday life, feminine performance accentuated difference and sustained region without calling attention to itself.[13]

Black and White southerners in the modern South shared a common history, but they often remembered it in such drastically different ways that racial reconciliation remained elusive. Black southerners understood the end of the Civil War in unmistakable terms of freedom: liberation and jubilee. They recognized Emancipation as a watershed moment in a long arc of progress, a milestone in an unfinished quest for equality. Many White southerners, though, could only look back on this same moment with a sense of loss and defeat. For every progressive White southerner with a sense of historical consciousness, for whom regional identity was located in collectively remembered crucibles of racial reckoning and transformative change, was another for whom family and community memories got in the way, for whom time-honored tales of Confederate bravery, honor, and loss crowded the mind and competed for the heart. More complicated still were those whose allegiances were continually tugged in both directions. For them White southernness was a persistent paradox: a simultaneous source of solace and pride, discomfort and regret.[14]

Writers have called for southerners of all races to recognize the commonalities of their experience.[15] Only by viewing the past through a shared lens of tragedy would southerners Black and White see themselves in each other. Only by acknowledging that their future together is inextricable from their ability to share the past could southerners hope to create a regional identity of common definition. But for White southerners brought up on cherished myths and oft-told tales, revising or enlarging the racial boundaries of regional identity threatened all touchstones of self. When family stories were inextricable from regional myths, calls to question and revise collective understandings of the southern past shook the very foundations of identity. "If the past is essential for one's identity," writes David Goldfield, "then renouncing, forgetting or ignoring that past shatters the self."[16] For many decades the result was a confederacy of silence, a tacit agreement equal parts etiquette, obstinacy, and shame.[17] It was a pact shattered by the murders in Charleston.

Yet, even as remorseful White southerners breathed a sigh of relief and joined the push for changes to the nation's commemorative culture, others resolutely pushed back. The initial surge to remove Confederate symbols from civic spaces was soon met by backlash and litigation. The fierce resistance fit a familiar pattern: eras of African American progress and moments of Black agency had always prompted a racist backlash, and the age of Black Lives Matter and the first Black presidency was no different. Opposition to retiring Confederate symbols joined discriminatory legislation in Mississippi and North Carolina targeting transgender persons, state laws designed to prevent minority voting, the celebration of Confederate Heritage Month in seven states, and the misogynistic and xenophobic presidential candidacy of Donald Trump to produce a political climate one national magazine dubbed "Confederate Spring." The following November Trump would prevail by appealing to alienated White voters, including men plagued by "aggrieved entitlement"—the sense that the unearned economic, political, and cultural privileges White men had enjoyed for centuries were under attack by minorities, women, and immigrants. White identity politics clearly resonated with a wide swath of the U.S. electorate. But they did nothing less than embolden White nationalists. On August 12, 2017, two hundred self-proclaimed White supremacists descended on Charlottesville, Virginia, in response to city officials' plans to remove a bronze statue of Confederate general Robert E. Lee from a downtown park. Marching through the University of Virginia campus, these Unite the Right protestors chanted, "Our blood, our soil!" and "Jews will not replace us!" By the end of a day marked by violent skirmishes, nineteen counterprotesters had been injured and antiracist activist Heather Heyer was dead. For anyone needing proof that the Charleston massacre had been no fluke, the fatal violence in Charlottesville provided it.[18]

Yet even as raucous and violent protests against dismantling monuments and retiring flags drew headlines, quieter symbols of White southernness carried on unabated. Where less is spoken, more is performed. For every contested southern landscape was another that continued to serve as a stage for acts of region too volatile for words. In ritual gender performances and routine feminine gestures, young White women continued to make the racial claims of region that could no longer be spoken.

There is a certain irony about the southern beauty's ability to escape critical notice considering the established importance of both women and performance to White southerners' understanding of themselves. Regional identity depends on collective memory, and collective memory on performance, and at the heart of the southern memory work—past and present—are women.

Collective, or cultural, memory—those shared remembrances that foster the sense of a common past—produces and sustains identity by fostering a "sense of sameness over time and space." Individuals acquire, order, and recall their memories according to group membership and in turn locate a sense of self. Interpreting personal stories in light of broad historical narratives, individuals root themselves in the world. If turn-of-the-century White southerners considered themselves members of a fellowship transcending time, space, gender, and class, it was because they continued to remember in common, to recall the southern past in shared ways.[19]

But if regional identification is a product of remembrance, it is also one of forgetting. Memories are malleable and memories change. Collective forgetting—or "collective amnesia"—is crucial to remembering in common. Through selective remembrance individuals smooth off the sharp edges of the past, the better for making personal stories mesh with accepted group stories and contemporary concerns. Embracing and blending some details while shedding or altering others, people shape the past into something that suits their current mindset. Societies do much the same, reconstructing their pasts with current concerns in mind. When they dwell on certain historical details but overlook others, an acceptable version of the past takes shape, one that typically justifies the existing social order.[20]

Performance in particular facilitates remembering. Ritual performances—commemorative performances and repetitive bodily practices—convey and sustain our images and recollected knowledge of the past. In fact, commemorative ceremonies are only as successful as they are performative. The conspicuous repetition of iconic gestures is key to remembering in common, with performances that are "stylized, stereotyped, and repetitive" not only encouraging but shaping collective memory. Such acts are successful because they do more than merely remind participants of mythic events: they literally represent them. Such representations do not merely imply continuity with the past but explicitly claim it.[21]

Joseph Roach suggests that habitual patterned movements operate in partnership with showy public rituals to invent and reproduce culture. In spectacle and ritual participants reiterate and confirm their self-definitions by stepping into the roles of departed predecessors and seamlessly repeating them. These cultural heirs emphatically demonstrate who they are—and who they are not. The goal of timelessness demands a steady succession of stand-ins: any gaps in the dramatic facade would expose the suggested permanence as pure fabrication. In stylized movements writ large, participants perform a preferred past for all to see. In turn gestures associated with such grand displays settle deep in the body, creating powerful mnemonic reserves. These reserves then surface in ingrained bodily habits, skills, mannerisms, and responses—in etiquette—effectively reinscribing cultural claims of status and place. The overall result is a near lock on collective memory and myths of origins that is difficult to dislodge. Readily visible but nearly imperceptible, ritual and everyday performance work in concert to assert social authority and privilege.[22]

Women, meanwhile, have historically served as both vessels and keepers of memory, as passive repositories and active caretakers of cultural dreams and national imaginaries. Whether sculpted in stone, reproduced on paper, or carved into the mastheads of ships, images of women stood in for the hopes and ideals of nations. Real women, meanwhile, assumed the duty of minding the collective past. It was certainly so in the South. While men gravitated to history, populating the membership rolls of military roundtables and societies, women coalesced around heritage, assuming the vague but vital task of caring for the southern past. Women tended to family memory: They wrote the letters, researched the genealogy, preserved the diaries, displayed the photographs, kept the scrapbooks, saved the mementos, and charted the lineage inside the family Bibles. They organized the gatherings—the holiday celebrations and family reunions—central to maintaining connection with one another and the past. And they ventured outside the household to assume leadership of activities that defined and protected the southern past. Erecting monuments, preserving historic sites, and creating heritage displays, White southern women shaped and safeguarded the "true history" of the region.[23]

Realizing the power of performance to consolidate memory, women harnessed it at every turn. After the Civil War White southern women staged elaborate pageants, tableaux, and other public spectacles designed to demonstrate the superiority and sanctity of an idealized southern past. Often as not, women starred in these productions—they understood full well the efficacy of gender performance to facilitating and swaying memory. In historical pageants, Confederate memorial rituals, and monument unveilings, White women and girls took center stage, emulating antebellum gender traditions. Not content with static displays, women performed region and embodied it in dramatic gestures.[24]

Bolstering regional cohesion through performance was nothing new for White southerners. In the decades leading up to the Civil War, defensive White southerners had rallied to create a nation (the Confederacy) and an identity (southernness) out of the cultural stuff at hand. Beleaguered by the issue of slavery, southerners played up supposed cultural differences from the North and manufactured others in their desire for unity and coherence.

COLUMBIA'S 150th BIRTHDAY CELEBRATION

SPIRIT OF COLUMBIA

MARCH 22-26 1936

THE SESQUICENTENNIAL OF THE FOUNDING OF THE CAPITAL OF SOUTH CAROLINA

HISTORICAL PAGEANT of South Carolina's Capital

2000 IN CAST

STADIUM

MARCH 23, 24 and 25

Parades — Dances — Horse Show and Races Polo — Singing Festival — Etc.

General Admission 50 Cents . . . . . Children 25 Cents

Columbia, South Carolina, celebrated its sesquicentennial in 1936 with a historical pageant featuring the Spirit of Columbia and a cast of two thousand. COURTESY OF THE BROADSIDES FROM THE COLONIAL ERA TO THE PRESENT COLLECTION, SOUTH CAROLINIANA LIBRARY, UNIVERSITY OF SOUTH CAROLINA, COLUMBIA.

The fact that the South had little distinctive about it that did not stem from slavery did not stop White southerners from crafting a dreamy myth of difference. Evoking Greek antiquity and Lord Byron, European nationalists and romantic fiction, slaveholders scrambled to produce a picture of themselves as a unified but misunderstood people—a culture of honor in conflict with the modern world.[25]

Central to this story was the notion that White southerners could trace their different values, habits, and politics to aristocratic Cavalier ancestors of Norman descent. This noble lineage, in sharp contrast to the middling Puritan "Roundhead" ancestry of northerners, was credited with southerners' purported gallant nature and sense of refinement. In the face of creeping materialism, the planter-aristocrat, with his code of honor and languorous ways, and his feminine counterpart, the pampered lady, were appealing figures. Popular representations aided the southern cause, from the chival-

Dorothy Zimmerman, as "Spring," crowns Irma Sweeney as the May queen at
the May Day festival at the Neighborhood House, May 2, 1925, Washington, D.C.
PHOTOGRAPH 97519624, LIBRARY OF CONGRESS, WASHINGTON, D.C.

ric novels of Sir Walter Scott to the Cavalier romances published in *Godey's
Lady's Book*. Harkening back to hierarchal societies of early modern Europe,
southerners invented an image of themselves as a glorious civilization frankly
superior to the dangerous democracy of the North.[26]

So successful was the South at selling this story that it even convinced
itself. In gendered spectacles and romantic rituals, White southerners bol-
stered their fictive backstory with performative proof that they were the
equal, merely transplanted cousins of European aristocracy. Jousting tournaments, May Day celebrations, and Twelfth Night parties—all chivalric
celebrations culminating in the crowning of a local maiden queen—offered
opportunities for life to imitate art, and southerners relished such occasions. Inspired by medieval pageantry and possessing all the flourishes of
horsemanship, royal dress, and military pomp, these rites were irresistible to
White southerners eager to legitimate aristocratic pretensions. Held before
and after the war and primarily, although not exclusively, in the South, these
rituals romanticized social hierarchy by celebrating gender ideals. Perform-

ing difference, southerners convinced themselves and observers that their way of life was gracious, honorable, and truly a world apart.[27]

Such an ambitious, imaginative project demanded a convincing rationale, and southerners found it in the southern lady ideal. Rooted in patriarchy and nurtured by proslavery ideology, the southern lady was the fabrication of White, slaveholding men, who looked to her to rationalize their "peculiar institution." Pious and passive, delicate and dependent, the southern lady was envisioned as a vessel of morality and exemplar of devotion. Modest, graceful, and obedient, she found her greatest happiness in pleasing her husband, bringing up his heirs, and managing his household. The picture of innocence, she took no interest in intellectual pursuits. Physically weak, she depended on male protection. She was, in short, "her culture's idea of religious, moral, sexual, racial, and social perfection."[28]

She was always, of course, more mythological than real. The whole idea of southern womanhood, notes Sara Evans, "revealed more about the needs of white planters than about the actual lives of women, white or black."[29] Indeed, the image must have rankled many a plantation mistress. Elite women put in long, demanding days managing the work of enslaved persons and manufacturing goods for the entire household, a schedule and responsibility that flew in the face of their reputation for pampered living.[30] The lady image also provided cover for mistresses' domestic dominance and violence. White women were complicit in abuses of power under slavery, a fact often diminished in histories—another silence.[31]

But if the lady ideal served as both prescription and decoy in antebellum days, it assumed its greatest power after the war, particularly after Reconstruction. Whereas hierarchies of race and class had been rather easily maintained under slavery—with White patriarchs enjoying authority over households of women, children, and slaves—the dissolution of the institution saw the lady ideal take on new tasks. As mistresses fought to reestablish and buttress claims to race and class privilege in the face of Black political and economic advances, the White home was reimagined as a highly gendered and racialized sanctuary—the domain of ladies whose social standing was defined in part by having Black help. Black women whose actions exposed the instability of this domestic set piece therefore infuriated White women; they felt that freedwomen parading about in public in finery mocked them, just as it presaged a reconfiguration of race and gender ideologies. Gender performance cut both ways.[32]

Cast-iron coin bank in the form of
"Mammy," circa 1925.
GIFT OF THE JAMES M. CASELLI AND
JONATHAN MARK SCHARER COLLECTION,
NATIONAL MUSEUM OF AFRICAN
AMERICAN HISTORY AND CULTURE,
SMITHSONIAN, WASHINGTON, D.C.

Increasingly, the lady ideal was deployed to rationalize not only social hierarchies but racial violence. In the 1890s, threatened by the political and social advances of the "New Negro" and facing an uncertain economy, White southerners enacted Jim Crow laws and institutionalized lynching in the name of defending White womanhood. Asserting the purity of southern womanhood as natural and irreproachable, White southern men also stressed the constant threat of rape represented by supposedly bestial Black men—a dramatic recasting of the docile Sambo figure of the remembered plantation family. By perpetuating this rape myth, White men justified their brutality of Black men and attempted to rein in White women who dared challenge patriarchal norms. Real White women were not in any particular need of protection, but White southern men kept the southern lady image trapped on a pedestal of ever-increasing elevation, her virtue in need of vigilant safeguarding. They knew that the lady ideal was the symbolic linchpin without which the whole system crumbled.[33]

But there would be little chance of that. In the post-Reconstruction South, the lady served as principal emblem of a comprehensive landscape of segregation. White southerners performed region and reproduced privilege

Music publishers based in northern cities promoted White southern nostalgia with pieces like this one, published in 1917.

in a theater of everyday life, with the entire commonplace culture—architecture, popular culture, everyday objects—setting the stage for White supremacy. Race and class tensions inspired a sweeping revival of the classical architectural style associated with antebellum landmarks. The southern colonial in particular littered the landscape, asserting continuity with a glorious past through symmetry, scale, and massive columns. Inside, the Black domestic reprised the role of Mammy, allowing the middle-class White homemaker to pass as a southern lady. Domestic goods too reiterated the racial order, with contrasting images of White leisure and Black toil pointing up "natural" race difference. The packaging of domestic consumer products—from food and beverages to matchboxes and laundry powder—was alternately emblazoned with stately mansions and sharecropper shacks, genteel Whites and hapless Blacks. Toothy mammies in bright head rags grinned idiotically from cookie jars and spoon rests, cookbooks and pancake mixes, while the southern belle's unmistakable shape embellished linens, dinnerware, soda bottles, and even table lamps. Ironwork "pickaninnies" and lawn jockeys decorated front lawns. Segregation had a soundtrack too: "Coon songs" and plantation rhapsodies alike, with their stock images and lyrical longing for "the land of cotton," appealed to White nostalgia. Ubiquitous elements of the southern scene asserted White southerners' definition of the past.[34]

Against such a comprehensive backdrop—with White supremacy built into the landscape, the mindscape, and even the soundscape—reiterating race and class privilege was as simple as going through the motions of White southern life. Jim Crow laws and racial violence provided the legal and extralegal framing for segregation, but everyday customs and ritual practices played a central role in reiterating race—and were all the more effective for their seeming unimportance. With an integral supremacist set and crucial props in place, southerners staged Whiteness in steady routine. One result was an easy equation of region and race, a prevailing understanding (among those it privileged) of southernness as Whiteness. This White southernness was most efficiently produced in repetitive performances that suggested a natural and continuous link with a splendid plantation past. The look and arrangement of public spaces—with buildings, monuments, streets, and schools commemorating the Confederacy on practically every corner—amounted to "visual representations of White southern history." But it was in everyday performances that White southerners made this message repeatedly relevant. Not only in blatant public spectacles but also in semipublic and private occasions, White southerners enacted region by performing the remembered past.[35]

"White southerners," writes Goldfield, "found that there were traditions, unlike slavery, that they could carry on after the war, that provided a direct behavioral link to a hallowed past. . . . The Old South could shine through in the 'old forms.'" Etiquette—accepted manners of conducting everything from everyday conversations to elaborate entertainments—consequently assumed new importance in the New South. Once merely the customary way of doing things in a highly stratified society, form in the New South became both a means and a measure of place. Rituals as routine as visiting and as special as weddings offered occasions for demonstrating continuity with a South perfected by memory. Through precise execution of the old forms, White southerners sustained the fiction that life in the modern South was indistinguishable from that of old. While Black freedom, enfranchisement, and growing consumer agency presented irrefutable evidence of political and economic change, rituals offered equally compelling proof of the constancy of place. "Old forms carried not only grace and civility forward to the New South," writes Goldfield, "but also the social relations implied in those forms." By continuing the old ways in a radically changed

Capt. Joseph Baker and Elise Davis Hayes, 1938 Chattanooga Cotton Ball.
CHATTANOOGA COTTON BALL COLLECTION, CHATTANOOGA PUBLIC LIBRARY.

context, beleaguered White southerners reiterated time-honored, hierarchical relationships of gender and race that had long supported White supremacy in general and White male dominance in particular. With reiteration came restoration. By literally minding their manners, White southerners at once honored the Lost Cause and sustained Old South social relations in the New. Failure of form, conversely, threatened to expose supposedly "natural" social hierarchies as pure fiction. This would never do. White southerners consequently made a fetish of form and ostracized those who flouted it. White southerners, desperate for the New South to function at least socially like the Old, followed form with new interest. They behaved.[36]

Etiquette created culture, mandating the bodily discipline and emotional restraint that resulted in polished social performances.[37] An exacting if unspoken etiquette governed even the simplest rituals. Patterns of speech and conversation, conventions of gesture and comportment, and habits of hospitality comprised the etiquette. "I lived in a world where social arrangements were taken for granted and assumed to be timeless," recalls historian Drew Gilpin Faust of her childhood in 1950s Virginia. "There were formalized ways of organizing almost every aspect of human relationships and interactions—how you placed your fork and knife on the plate when you had finished eating, what you did with a fingerbowl; who walked through a door first, whose name was spoken first in an introduction, how others were addressed—black adults with just a first name, whites as 'Mr.' or 'Mrs.'—whose hand you shook and whose you didn't, who ate in the dining room and who in the kitchen."[38] For White southerners navigating the confounding uncertainties of the modern South, knowledge of the intricate grammar of this etiquette and the ability to seamlessly perform it served as both exacting yardstick and comforting touchstone of place. White southerners' easy, constant performance of rule-bound social rituals continually produced region by reassuring them that the South as they understood it was essentially unchanged. These same rituals simultaneously served as a gauge of social standing, as proof of place.

Semipublic rites like resort promenading, debutante presentations, and campus May Day celebrations had always been exclusive by nature, choreographed for only partial public visibility. But in the early decades of the twentieth century, new spectacles emerged that placed feminine display of region in full view. As Lost Cause commemorative events dwindled with the passing of the last Confederate veterans, public performances of White femininity increasingly assumed the mantle of regional representation. In beauty pageants, agricultural festivals, sporting events, tourist productions, parades, and fairs, White southern women commanded the spotlight as symbols of regional pride. For White southerners accustomed to holding up the lady as distillation of regional values, it was a small move to relocate the ideal woman from pedestal to pageantry.[39]

These new productions combined commercial and civic boosterism with continued concerns about gender, race, and social place.[40] Corpus Christi, Texas, for example, refashioned Splash Days, a simple beauty revue begun in 1917, into a three-day, merchant-sponsored celebration dubbed Buccaneer Days after the city's swashbuckling past. By 1937 the winning contestant of Miss Buc Days reigned over a parade, a historical pageant, and a ball and stood for everything best and brightest about the city—its hopes, its dreams, its heritage.[41]

Queen competitions at agricultural fairs in the 1930s promoted sex appeal and commerce in one fell swoop with beauties who were counted on to draw interest in surplus yields. Publicity photographs of scantily clad contestants frolicking in the fields or caressing the crops employed a daring modern sensuality to lure buyers. More wholesome depictions invoked agrarian

Contestants in the Chilton County, Alabama, Peach Festival Queen Pageant, circa 1940–50.
ALABAMA PHOTOGRAPHS AND PICTURES COLLECTION, ALABAMA DEPARTMENT OF ARCHIVES AND HISTORY,
MONTGOMERY.

innocence, appealing to wistfulness for an idyllic South. Draped in tobacco
leaves, cloaked in cotton, or picking a peach, the harvest queen contestant
embodied the land and its bounty. In the process she emerged a valuable regional commodity in her own right, pretty proof that superior feminine specimens sprang from southern soil. Agricultural trade-board marketing campaigns featuring the White harvest queens did double duty, masking the
tenant labor (Black and White) essential to crop production while reaffirm-
ing the region's social and economic order.[42]

Yet when agricultural celebrations came to town, the rituals sometimes
revealed more than organizers intended. The Memphis Cotton Carnival,
founded by business leaders in 1931 to promote the region's "white gold," featured a Cotton Carnival queen who reigned over masked balls, float parades,
and midway rides. But the same pageantry that celebrated cotton production exposed its underside too. After early festivals either excluded Blacks or
featured them in demeaning roles, Black Memphians formed their own Cotton Makers' Jubilee in 1935 that operated much the same as its White counterpart. The result was that each spring Black and White Memphians staged

A view of the Cotton Carnival parade in Memphis, Tennessee, May 10, 1950.
COURTESY OF THE DEPARTMENT OF CONSERVATION PHOTOGRAPH COLLECTION,
FILE 87, BOX 55, TENNESSEE STATE LIBRARY AND ARCHIVES, NASHVILLE.

a celebration of cotton that mirrored the region's stark racial divide. Taking
part in simultaneous but separate private events and in mass public events
conducted according to the intricate rules of segregation, Memphians performed choreography of Jim Crow with an archetypal southern beauty at
the center of the show.[43]

The Maid of Cotton beauty pageant inaugurated in Memphis in 1939 also
used the bodies of young White women to communicate commercial and
social concerns. The brainchild of the National Cotton Council, the Memphis Cotton Carnival, and the Cotton Exchanges of Memphis, New York,
and New Orleans, the pageant promoted the versatility and value of cotton. Open to young women born in one of the seventeen southern cotton-
growing states, the pageant evaluated contestants on the basis of beauty,
personality, poise, good manners, and intelligence; a family background in
cotton production was considered especially helpful. Contestants vied to
serve as fashion and goodwill ambassadors of the cotton industry in a five-
month, all-expense paid tour of U.S. cities—an itinerary that was expanded
globally in the 1950s. Appearing in 100 percent cotton regalia at county fairs,

parades, and other public events; starring in fashion shows; and delivering speeches in all-cotton outfits, the maids were the appealing personification of the cotton industry wherever they went. Like earlier rural commodity queens, the urban Maid of Cotton showcased the crop itself on her body. Thoroughly modern advertising campaigns appealed far and wide to nostalgia as a means of stoking and justifying habits of consumption. National Cotton Council print advertisements depicting the 1941 Maid of Cotton, Alice Beasley, dressed in a cotton riding outfit in front of a columned mansion, for example, shrewdly targeted White fantasies of wealth and privilege by evoking the plantation lady ideal. Promotional campaigns that presented the thoroughly modern maids as southern belles with Old South pedigrees pursued female consumers and feminized and racialized the land, all while obscuring the means of production.[44]

Across the South it was much the same: young White beauties served as centerpieces of leisure activities that celebrated and validated a distinctive, segregated way of life. Some celebrations made modern claims about southern society, highlighting the technological and industrial advances present in even deeply rural locales. But they also looked backward, enshrining nostalgic notions of the southern past. In either case the southern beauty proved the perfect emblem, both motif of place and its rationale.[45]

Tourist campaigns staged and sold a romanticized Old South. At the depths of the Depression, towns and cities appealed to tourists weary of northern climes with promises of uncommon architecture, natural beauty, and, above all, gracious hospitality awaiting them down south. On home and garden tours across the region, hosts in heirloom hoopskirts drove the popularity and profitability of a burgeoning pilgrimage movement that showcased a carefully curated southern past. The same history of racial inequality that plagued the South in many quarters proved its premier drawing card with tourists. Against an unsettling national backdrop of economic deprivation, rising ethnic diversity, and shifting labor relations, the chance to experience southern gentility—to luxuriate in plantation grandeur, savor local delicacies, and enjoy essentially unreconstructed social relations—held enormous appeal. Promising experiences of privilege and order in the face of disarray, southern home and garden tours offered an opportunity to step back into another world. On garden-club tours from the Shenandoah Valley to New Orleans and from the hills of northern Mississippi to the Carolina coast, tourists could look fondly backward, savoring the textures and comforts of a storied past.[46]

Crowning of azalea queen actor Debra Paget (*center*) at the 1959 Azalea Festival,
Wilmington, N.C. Nancy Stovall, teenage princess (*second from left*);
Ronald Reagan, master of ceremonies (*third from left*); and Luther Hodges,
governor (*third from right*) are among those present.
HUGH MORTON COLLECTION, WILSON LIBRARY, UNIVERSITY OF NORTH CAROLINA, CHAPEL HILL.

By midcentury, as segregation increasingly drew national opposition,
obvious, predictable icons had become bankable memory mechanisms for
tourists longing to feel southern. When Cypress Gardens, a central Florida
tourist attraction known for its tranquil grounds and exhilarating water-ski
shows, installed southern-belle hostesses at the gates in 1940, they proved
such a draw that the proprietors soon opened a belle photography conces-
sion besides. Visitors could don hoopskirts for keepsake portraits of themselves promenading among the flowers.[47] In 1948, the year Dixiecrats se-
ceded from the Democratic Party over opposition to civil rights, the first
annual Azalea Festival in Wilmington, North Carolina, put an absolute fantasia of southern gentility on display, naming Hollywood celebrities azalea
queen and master of ceremonies and inviting collegiate May queens from
across the state to stand about the city's mansions and gardens in faux antebellum finery.[48] Instantly recognizable and imminently reproducible, the
southern beauty on display at midcentury tourist sites was a modern sign for
modern times—a silent symbol of unapologetic southern Whiteness.

In the 1950s White southern youth embraced both the future and the past.
OLE MISS, 1959, SPECIAL COLLECTIONS, UNIVERSITY OF MISSISSIPPI LIBRARIES, OXFORD.

By the 1950s, as teenagers across the country drove an irrepressible youth culture of music, dancing, movies, and cars, White southern youth exhibited a divided response. White southern teens swooned over Elvis, listened to rhythm and blues over thoroughly integrated airwaves, and preferred Black bands for their campus parties, but they also looked backward, embracing deeply held notions of race and region. The danceable "race music" broadcast over radio stations across the South drew teens together across racial lines at juke joints and nominally segregated shows, creating a sense of possibility that hung in the air alongside the sounds of rock and roll. But to ardent segregationists the possibility in the air was always miscegenation. Inciting fears of "mixed marriages" and mongrelization, White supremacists seized control of public discussions about race; an integrated youth culture would not emerge at the expense of White feminine respectability. Without that, the segregationist rationale did not hold. Just as Black and White youth cultures appeared headed for convergence, White supremacists em-

Lynda Lee Mead, Miss America
1960 (*left*), with Mary Ann
Mobley, Miss America 1959.
UNIVERSITY ARCHIVES PHOTOGRAPHS
COLLECTION, SPECIAL COLLECTIONS,
UNIVERSITY OF MISSISSIPPI LIBRARIES,
OXFORD.

phasized the image of White southern womanhood with new fervor. Pete
Daniel has referred to this moment of missed potential—when Black and
White southerners appeared poised to forge alliances, but White suprema-
cists instead carried the day—as a lost revolution.[49]

With the rise of massive resistance, the pop culture spotlight focused more
narrowly and thus more brightly on the southern beauty. A full century after her antebellum heyday, the southern lady experienced perhaps her finest
hour. Upheld once more as the reason behind "our southern way of life," she
remained a focal point for White southerners' resistance to racial equality.
If vocal and violent White defiance defined massive resistance, silent and serene defiance defined the passive resistance of the southern beauty.

Midcentury university campuses in particular served as stages for gendered spectacles of White supremacy. Alternating displays of Whiteness
with parodies of Blackness, collegians reiterated southern Whiteness. Sorority rituals, beauty pageants, campus-newspaper photo features, and annual sporting traditions continually reproduced the southern lady, repeatedly holding her up as a powerful sign. If 1954 was the year of *Brown vs.
Board of Education*, the landmark Supreme Court decision abolishing legal
segregation, the years that followed were those of Mary Ann Mobley and

"African Bush Wuggies" at a Delta Delta Delta rush party, University of Alabama, 1955. *COROLLA*, 1955, SPECIAL COLLECTIONS, UNIVERSITY OF ALABAMA LIBRARIES, TUSCALOOSA.

Lynda Lee Mead, sorority sisters at the University of Mississippi and the state's back-to-back Miss Americas, who, with their deft passing of the national beauty torch, drew attention to the campus and the state as strongholds of White southern womanhood.[50]

White sorority houses set the scene, gradually undergoing architectural transformations that constituted visual, spatial acts of resistance to social change. Architectural additions and renovation projects gave campus Greeks a visual language for suggesting links to a romantic plantation past. Adding columns, verandas, "plantation" shutters, and rocking chairs in abundance, sororities claimed connection to the Old South. White-clad Mammy figures sweeping up out front (in reality, domestic employees in uniform) completed the look. Such "home improvements" turned what were once loose collections of architecturally disparate, single-family homes into a visually unified icon: the aggressively "antebellum" Sorority Row that continues to dominate southern campuses today.[51]

With such faux plantation houses as backdrops, collegians regularly incorporated Blackface spoofs into their campus parties and traditions. Blackface "plantation parties," "sharecroppers' balls," and "slave auctions" were common amusements, with talent shows, Greek Week, Dixie Week, and

Old South all opportunities for Blacking up. When some thirty members of Delta Gamma fraternity crowded the stage in Blackface and top hats for a 1948 Stunt Night skit at Ole Miss, they took part in a widespread and popular practice. Rushees approaching the Delta Gamma house in 1951 found the front door "magically opened by two little colored boys dressed as slaves of by-gone days," to reveal a staircase filled with "lovely southern belles dressed in hoop skirts and organdy." Football rivalries occasioned Blackface writ large on lawn decorations of the competitive sort. When the Louisiana State University Tigers arrived at Ole Miss for a 1953 matchup, they were met by outsized cardboard cutouts of "Little Black Sambo" on sorority-house lawns; the Zetas asserted that the Rebels would "melt the Bengals to Butter." At the University of South Carolina, a Pi Phi Shakespeare satire featuring Blackface took top honors at Stunt Night 1957, and the Chi O's mechanized "Brer Tarpin's done got hooked" won the Panhellenic 1958 display cup. Nothing approached Blackface for magnifying White privilege.[52]

The racist "hijinks" pointed up a prevailing reverence for White southern womanhood rooted in resistance to social change. Operating in tandem with minstrel mischiefs were campus productions that elevated the southern beauty as regional icon and rationale, along with student publications that celebrated and contrasted the two displays. Beauty pageants and revues, fraternity sweetheart ceremonies, homecoming traditions, and May Day festivities all showcased serene beauties who silently validated segregation with their every move and gesture to the southern past. Saucy images also appealed to regional chauvinism. Cheesecake photos of "Kentucky Kernel Kuties," "Bama Belles," "Loveliest of the Plains," "Bantam Beauties," and "Campus Cuties" regularly appeared on the front page of campus newspapers. Striking improbable poses in abbreviated attire, these campus pinups supported regional claims of pulchritude.[53]

The anxious decade that saw segregation under threat witnessed not only an upsurge in defiant race and gender play but also a corresponding rush to commemorate and circulate the moment. The 1951 *Corolla* yearbook celebrated "Dixie Doin's"—"sharecropper shenanagans [*sic*]," Kappa Alpha secession, Confederate uniforms, hoopskirts, and an Old South ball—while the same year's *Ole Miss* paid tribute to

> One Thousand Southern Belles.
> Magnolia-Scented Memories.
> Delicate Charm.

The Rustle of Hoop-Skirts and Lace.
Winsome Smiles.
The Beauty of Southern Women.

Some productions twinned the beauty and the Blackface for an unmis-takable message. The University of South Carolina's 1956 and 1957 May Day Coronations held to tradition with elaborate pageants on the Horse-shoe. *South Land*, set in the "Garden of a Southern Plantation" in 1861, fea-tured children in Blackface dancing to "Dixie," costumed adults performing a Virginia reel, battle scenes from the *War between the States*, and a reading of *Lee's Farewell Address*. The festivities peaked when the university presi-dent crowned the May queen, who enjoyed a traditional maypole dance per-formed by her court.[54]

By 1958 the *Corolla* featured an image of two female students in Black-face feigning fright over Autherine Lucy's desegregation of the university in 1956. After the Rho Chapter of the Kappa Alpha Order celebrated 1961 by hosting all the Kappa Alpha chapters in South Carolina for the annual Old South Weekend, the *Garnet and Black* documented the party that began on Friday night with a "Sharecropper's Shindig," continued through a Se-cession Ceremony and Mint Julep Party on Saturday, and climaxed with an Old South Ball "enjoyed 'til the wee hours of dawn." Pairing performances of Old South gentility with Blackface mockery and Aunt Jemima send-ups with ubiquitous campus beauties, midcentury campus culture demonstrated an unmistakable stance: White southern collegians steadfastly supported White supremacy and would use their campus productions to construct and preserve it.

The arrogance couldn't last. The Civil Rights Act of 1964 signaled the be-ginning of the end of blatant expressions of racial hatred, and over time bald assertions of either race supremacy or degradation became verboten. In the segregated South White supremacists had expressed their racial views with-out thought of retribution. In speeches, sermons, songs, newspaper columns, political cartoons, and campus shows, they had argued for White over Black in no uncertain terms. But in the desegregating South overt racism gradu-ally became untenable. To be sure, ardent segregationists first reacted to the end of Jim Crow by quickly recreating all-White spaces: White-flight neigh-borhoods and Whites-only private academies, where they and their children could retreat from integration. But in time, alongside real if halting gains in race relations, came a widespread understanding that racial isolation was not sustainable and straightforward racism no longer acceptable. Racist attitudes and beliefs did not disappear, but in the 1970s, 1980s, and 1990s, they went steadily underground, forming an undercurrent of bitterness susceptible to disruption.[55]

Resentment also roiled other waters. Women activists' subordination within the civil rights movement gave rise to the second-wave feminist movement of the 1970s, with women nationwide reaching across racial lines in gender solidarity. But in the U.S. South most White women showed little intention of abandoning the lady's bargain that promised them race and class advantage in exchange for gender subordination. They were resentful, too, finding the prominence accorded African American women (including civil rights veterans) at International Women's Year state meetings of 1977, for example, threatening or infuriating or both. The White supremacist myth of the southern lady—financially supported, removed from public life, and in need of protection from Black men—had been used to justify everything from slavery to lynching to segregation. It silenced women and demonized Black men, while veiling White male power as chivalry. Still, White southern women were loath to abandon the narrative that was the source of their power and their privilege. The feminist movement's intense identification with the civil rights movement inspired supporters of both movements but incensed many White southerners.[56]

Faced with the prospect of gender equality and a perceived loss of protections, White southern women instead rallied to the cause of antifeminism, lining up behind conservative activist Phyllis Schlafly to protest the Equal Rights Amendment (Schlafly's "Stop ERA" campaign stood for "stop taking our privileges"). In the South—a bastion of traditional gender roles and of evangelical and fundamentalist Protestantism—Schlafly's portrayal of women's equality as a threat to the family resonated. The family, after all, was sacred: the locus of parental rights and the site of a sort of White supremacist maternalism, where "good White women" taught and enforced racial separation at home and in the larger public sphere. White southern, especially religious, women practically leaped off their pedestals and into public life to organize for "family values" and to protest against their own liberation.[57]

They had a lot of support. White supremacists also saw the women's movement as an extension of the civil rights movement and they mobilized against the Equal Rights Amendment in part to retaliate. The massive and powerful Southern Baptist Convention experienced a conservative takeover in 1979 and promptly abandoned its initial moderate support of the women's rights movement. Within a few years it would officially remind women of the biblical injunction to be subservient to their husbands. Just as it had become unacceptable to be overtly racist, by the late 1970s blatant, public exclamations of antifeminism were widely accepted—and accomplished some of the same racial work. Ultimately, White southern women would form the racist backbone of a new Right conservatism, as the GOP abandoned four decades of support for the Equal Rights Amendment to chase the votes of antifeminist White southerners.[58]

Threatened at every turn, White southerners regrouped and saved face by reverting to form: they minded their manners. But they also exhibited something of a cultural lag, a reluctant acquiescence. As they struggled to acclimate to a changing larger society, White southerners met iconic representations of Dixie with enthusiasm and fondness, expressing a deep-seated nostalgia and resistance that increasingly went unspoken. Threatened by the prospect of race and gender equality but hard-pressed for a suitable response, White southerners showed fresh appreciation for the familiar. Cherished performances of southern beauty enjoyed steady popularity. Even as the legal, material, and built environments of segregation were gradually dismantled, gender performance persisted, a sly if unexamined signal of racial sentiment. Protected from protest by her ostensible fluff, the southern beauty enacted White southernness in plain sight.

Nostalgia is a funny thing. As much as it may seem wrapped up in the past, it is also always about the present. Nostalgia thrives on transition, on the rude discontinuities of history, on dislocations of all sorts, on cultural trauma and social shock. Disappointment in the present improves the view of the past.[59]

An endangered sense of identity in particular prompts the wistful backward glance. When events or ideas in the present rock the very foundations of identity—especially those time-honored understandings of the past that define our place in the world—nostalgia rushes in. Promoting reconnection with an ideal past (while brushing aside the issue of its authenticity), nostalgia restores the cornerstone of identity.[60]

But nostalgia is as much about forgetting as remembering, as much a product of collective amnesia as of recalling in common. Muting or filtering out unpleasant parts of the past and swaddling what is left in a tender, redeeming aura, nostalgia eliminates the shame, guilt, or embarrassment that can come with frank remembering. Paradoxically, an idyllic past comforts so effectively precisely because it is irrevocably past—impossible to recreate or resurrect. The disappointed, nostalgic soul longs not to recreate the past in actuality but to momentarily connect with it in reverie. Such longing for something absent—something far away or presumably present in an earlier age—is thus in the end surely harmless.[61]

Or is it? Fred Davis notes that under the proper conditions, symbols from the past "can trigger wave upon wave of nostalgic feeling in millions of persons at the same time." Especially when the symbol in question is "of a highly public, widely shared, and familiar character," a condition of widespread, collective nostalgia can result.[62] An agent of nostalgia more widely recognized or public in nature than the southern beauty is difficult to imagine. To assume that the collective nostalgia prompted by the modern southern beauty was either harmless or apolitical is a bit of willed "not seeing" that deserves scrutiny.

It is hard to imagine a group more dismayed, dislocated, and, above all, disappointed than resistant White southerners in the immediate aftermath of the civil rights movement. *Brown v. Board of Education* may have signaled the beginning of the end of the strict segregation Gov. George Wallace called "our southern way of life," but the Voting Rights Act of 1965 sounded the death knell of Whites-only political power in the South and with it the abrupt end of mythologies that had informed White southern worldviews for generations. With civil rights activists providing daily proof that White superiority was neither natural nor logical, White southerners were forced to recognize unwelcome facts. Ideas they had been reared to believe obvious, natural truths—Black deference, contentment, and incompetence; "good race relations"; White benevolence—were instead revealed as radical falsehoods, the shaky foundation of an unsustainable social structure. The result was shock and a lack of conceptual tools for grappling with it. The only world White southerners had ever known had collapsed, and one utterly incomprehensible had appeared in its place. Disbelief prevailed, accompanied by emotional reactions ranging from anger, amazement, resentment, and denial to bafflement, resignation, and nascent understanding. But one thing was clear: their world had been turned inside out and upside down. And there would be no going back.[63]

White southerners reacted to the end of massive resistance with dismay and loss. Over time they comprehended the sea change in southern life, Black and White—some with grace, some with rancor, some with grudging acquiescence. But they all lived through it. For many what small solace was to be found existed in the continuities of everyday life, in those common-place customs that formed the fabric of White southern life. "When change came, it was a partial and messy process," notes Jason Sokol, whose history of White southerners during the age of civil rights is a chronicle of complex responses and deep disappointment. "Few southerners achieved, much less desired, a clean break from the past. The intensity and form of discrimination often changed, not the fact of its existence."[64] To Whites with wounded pride stranded in a hostile and unfamiliar present, the sense of a permanent and timeless southern past carried enormous appeal.[65] Enacting rituals of re-membrance that produced a common past was one way of maintaining some sense of self. White southerners anxious over the prospect of racial equality stopped shouting but continued performing.

In his study of community festivals in the U.S. South on the threshold of the twenty-first century, Rodger Lyle Brown found annual rituals manufac-tured in attempts to perpetuate societies under economic and cultural stress. At the watermelon festivals, tobacco days, and cotton carnivals that dot-ted the calendar and the landscape, southerners gathered on neglected Main Streets and courthouse squares to celebrate their local, often agricultural, histories. But the action at the local fair was never merely play but the rit-ual enactment of collective memory and display of community. At the small-town southern fair, the most active participants of all were typically those most determined to recall a bygone way of life—White southerners. In fact, the small-town southern fair was almost exclusively the production of White communities, among whom Brown detected a subtext of mourning. Run-ning beneath the simple goodness of handicrafts and kettle corn was an un-dercurrent of anxiety over the loss of social and economic place. In the wake of traditional communities built around shared values and common produc-tion, the folksy annual fair assumed special duty as a site of memory. With the radical restructuring of U.S. cultural and economic life since the mid-twentieth century—with Main Street long abandoned to big-box retailing, the family farm replaced by agribusiness, and old hierarchies of race and gen-der privilege destabilized by feminism, multiculturalism, and the civil rights movement—only conspicuous displays could satisfy the demand for regional identity. And so White southerners routinely gathered to perform their pre-ferred versions of the past in public. Stepping into the roles of predecessors, they conjured up an imagined place and golden time when their interests were in favor and their privilege intact.[66]

In the decades following the civil rights movement, such conspicuous displays of White southernness gradually became the motions of choice for Whites longing to feel southern. With political defiance no longer tenable, pop culture emerged to support a new southern strategy, one based on appealing images and gestures rather than a rhetoric of hatred. In the absence of code words and incendiary symbols, the southern beauty stepped in at festivals, parades, broadcasts, and sporting events to convey unobjectionable but unmistakable messages of race and region. As White southerners abandoned the Democratic Party en masse for the GOP in what became known as the "Great White Switch," the southern beauty made only familiar moves as she stood in and stood up for White southerners.[67]

This is not to suggest that White southerners consciously longed for the days of formal segregation. Dramatic change in both race relations and social justice was surely the major story of the twentieth-century South. Rather, there was a sense of loss that went unspoken, and at times unrecognized, but not undemonstrated. Over time women consistently acted out both claims and defenses of social place. In routine gestures and prominent displays, young White southern women deployed powerful mnemonic reserves, enacting region and maintaining a particular southern story, even if some failed to realize it. As Jennifer Eichstedt and Stephen Small note in their book on representations of slavery in southern plantation museums, "the continuation of racially oppressive institutions and practices does not rely primarily on the intentions of some group of people we can identify as 'racist.' . . . racialized disadvantage and advantage continue to be created even by well-intentioned people." Racialization occurs "in various locations, linked by shared and often overlapping ideologies and representations, to produce and reproduce racialized inequality and oppression." Varieties of southern beauty performance enacted by well-meaning young women in a range of scenarios, locations, and eras fit this description. Defining region through a repertoire of gender performance, the southern beauty starred in a "racialized regime of representation" that articulated and reaffirmed the mythic life of White southerners.[68]

Patricia Yaeger notes that in southern women's writing, place is "always a site where trauma has been absorbed into the landscape."[69] On the landscape of the U.S. South, sorority girls, beauty queens, and debutantes performed familiar feminine motions, continually constructing region and facilitating a sense of place right before our eyes. What sorts of trauma did their frivolity obscure?

A sense of longing lingered in the South, a nostalgia for bygone days and a wistfulness for an imagined past forever out of reach. It was not something openly acknowledged; called to account, White southerners embraced diversity, at least publicly and officially. But the popular, the frivolous, the collegiate, the touristic, and the just-for-fun told a different story. *Southern Beauty* offers a glimpse of that action.

CHAPTER 1

Sister Act

THE SCENE INSIDE FULTON CHAPEL WAS ALMOST ENOUGH TO MAKE one forget that it was two o'clock on a late summer afternoon in Mississippi. Despite the sweltering heat, the melting humidity, and the lack of air conditioning, the atmosphere inside was one not of languidness but of high anxiety. Here some 665 incoming female students were seated in groups of 70. They were chattering; they were excited; they were nervous. It was the opening scene of sorority rush, and at the University of Mississippi—known affectionately by most Whites as "Ole Miss"—rush was serious business.[1]

In the next few days these young women (or girls, as they referred to themselves and one another) would submit to a process of evaluation that would determine the course of their social life for the next four years. For some the stakes would be for life. But for the moment they were all equal— at least, equally nervous—as they checked out the competition.

If the air was filled with tension, the scene revealed nothing but composure and preparation. Here the rule was flawless skin, tasteful manicures, and healthy, glossy hair that had just been trimmed, highlighted, and deep-conditioned. Perfect vision and contact lenses prevailed. All hair was at least shoulder length. The clothing was "studied casual"—shorts, sundresses, new sandals. A few false eyelashes. Full makeup, expertly done.

The view was also one of almost panoramic Whiteness. Fidgeting in tiered theater seats were banks of beauties, terraced profusion of blondes, redheads, and brunettes. Although the university had made considerable racial progress since the crisis over James Meredith's integration of the campus in 1962, sorority rush near the turn of the twenty-first century remained largely segregated, a diversity holdout. In a state 37 percent African American, Blacks at Mississippi's flagship university made up only 17 percent of the student body.[2] The number who had attempted to pierce this particular sorority citadel of privilege was miniscule; the number who had been successful was even smaller. Rather, most still concentrated on gaining admission to the historically and predominately African American sororities on campus, which conducted their own series of intake events at a completely different time of year. The situation was replicated across the region. With their modest houses, different criteria for membership, and separate calendar, the Black sororities—highly influential in their own realm—made little impression on the campus social powerhouse: the White Greek system. Certainly they were of little interest to those assembled in Fulton Chapel, who awaited a long-anticipated moment—the chance to rush in Ole Miss's legendary system of social exclusion. From the ranks of eager and ambitious young women, configurations of power and privilege would be reinscribed. The gathered were expectant. On the brink of division, yet still one, they realized the portent of the moment.

Roaming the crowd were the rush counselors, twenty-five knowledgeable rising seniors who had given up their sorority affiliations for the week to help guide and advise the new rushees. They held meetings, said "yea" or "nay" to dresses, and shepherded the rushees around from house to house. For them this convocation—the official opening of rush—was old hat. Dressed in Panhellenic T-shirts, khaki shorts, and athletic shoes, they roamed the auditorium with an air of purpose and self-assurance. Not for them the rushee's complete makeup, incongruously paired with casual shorts and sandals. They wore day makeup, tastefully blended. And they hauled around enormous backpacks to carry the rushees' essentials.

A couple of hours later, the rushees gathered at the back of Brown dorm. The casual clothes of the afternoon had been replaced by demure, long, swingy sundresses (the small-town Tennessee girls); contemporary, short-sleeved suits (the Dallas girls); matching, slightly out-of-date pants suits (the Delta girls); and bright floral, sixties pop-art sundresses (the Jackson girls). And everywhere, as if it had washed up in an Irish tide, was a virtual sea of linen. Not linen-blend or "linen-like" but sure-enough, my-family-can-afford-it linen. Suit-weight and handkerchief. The genuine article. The shoe of the hour was chunky, brown or black, and generously strapped. The girls had stuffed their essentials—keys, lipstick, all manner of cosmetic expertise—in labeled, plastic bags, to be carted up and down Sorority Row for them by the rush counselors.

Outside the Theta house the rushees learned the pattern of the evening. Waiting in the stifling heat, they suddenly heard what sounded like war whoops and pounding coming from inside the front door. At the strike of five, the Thetas, two hundred strong, threw back the door and appeared in formation, crowding the door from floor to sill with Theta faces, radiating Theta love, and singing a Theta song. Then they burst from the door, each calling a particular rushee's name: "Caitlin! Ashley! Brooke!" The Thetas were dressed in different shades of the same scoop-necked shift; together they created a linen rainbow. Taking the rushees by the hand and scooting them indoors, the Thetas proceeded to "rush" them—to woo them with party chatter and giant, unrelenting smiles—for exactly twenty minutes.

Inside the Theta house it was cool and tasteful: apricot walls, country French reproduction furniture, floral arrangements in front of every gilt mirror, oriental-style rugs. After a frenetic few minutes of socializing, the girls were herded into the meeting room for a slideshow highlighting Theta life and its many advantages: formals with fraternity men, parties and more parties, "sisterhood." Then more high-volume meeting and greeting took place in the front rooms and on to the next house, but not before the Thetas once again crowded the doorway, this time to sing good-bye.

Sorority rush is a feminine stratification ritual performed each year at scores of college campuses across the country. Consisting of a series of increasingly selective "get acquainted" parties, rush is a proving ground of competitive femininity cloaked in the guise of gracious hospitality and collegiate spirit. If at first glance rush appears all fresh-scrubbed good looks, lilting laughter, and nonstop smiles, a closer look reveals something else entirely: a two-way scrutiny session in which women evaluate one another based on looks, status, and feminine competency.

As the twentieth century gave way to the twenty-first, rush remained a daunting social obstacle course wherever it was enacted, but nowhere were the expectations higher, the standards more stringent, or the consequences as crucial as in the South, where many a feminine future still depended on a few days in autumn. At Southeastern Conference schools, between 20 and 54 percent of female students routinely went Greek—but there was a qualitative difference too.[3] As schools in other parts of the country gradually adopted more relaxed rush procedures—featuring casual get-togethers, foreshortened rush schedules, and bidding practices geared toward inclusion rather than exclusivity—the large southern schools were slower to change, hanging on to old forms and arcane formalities that made a southern rush

Zeta Tau Alpha greets new members at the University of Georgia, 2017.
PHOTO BY DUSTIN CHAMBERS.

increasingly distinctive. Participants understood that time-honored social meanings—about race and place, region and identity—resulted from the process, with established rush practices the best at producing and sustaining these meanings. Demonstrating continuity, spotlighting difference, and measuring minutiae of insider knowledge, formal rush excelled at reinscribing long-standing social arrangements. The southern investment in keeping rush formal (or "frilly") signaled widespread commitment to existing structures of privilege. At the start of the twenty-first century, feminine performance remained the central production site of region, with sorority rush the standout act.

By charging girls on the brink of womanhood with the task of constructing region and linking this duty to annual gender rituals crucial to social success, White southerners had nearly guaranteed the perpetuation of a racialized regional imaginary. The practice may be traced to the slaveholding South, where nascent college sororities reinscribed hierarchies of race and class. Sorority rush had its beginnings in the literary societies college women formed in the latter half of the nineteenth century in imitation of those found at men's schools. The men's clubs of the era organized the presentation of speeches on political and philosophical issues of the day and in the process became settings for shaping and judging status. In a society with high illiteracy rates, oratory was a prized skill, and the literary clubs emerged as incubators of campus leadership. As alumni went on to positions of prominence, club meeting halls were outfitted with trappings of refinement conducive to socializing: fine furniture, gilt-framed portraits of key members, impressive libraries. Providing a space for the cultivation of political viewpoints, sociability, and genteel manners outside of college jurisdiction, male literary societies became the prevailing social arbiters on campus.[4]

The women's literary societies operated a bit differently—featuring softer "conversations"—but easily matched the men's as sites for displaying and evaluating gendered argument and behavior and then assigning status accordingly. With myriad behavioral rules and conversational topics chosen to inculcate ladylike behavior ("Which is most pleasing, beauty or grandeur?"; "Which should be most censored—dancing or novel reading?"), the women's literary societies enforced separate-spheres ideology and served as a self-policing gender gauge.[5]

Out of such literary societies grew Greek letter sororities, with the very first arising in the South. The Adelphian Society (later Alpha Delta Pi) was formed in 1851 in Georgia at the nation's first female college, Wesleyan, with the Philomathean Society (later Phi Mu) established on the same campus the following year. Literary activities still represented a major component of the early clubs, but membership was by invitation, and exclusion a chief means of group definition. As Christie Anne Farnham notes in her history of antebellum southern women's education, the charter members of the Adelphian Society "formed not only an exclusive set based on their own characteristics—[Mary] Evans reported that 'the highest standard of scholarship was an open sesame of our ranks'—but also by virtue of the prominence of their fathers." Ostensibly secret, the Greek letter societies were highly visible socially, and sorority members soon came to identify themselves in contradistinction to nonmembers.[6] Like the men's literary societies on which they were patterned, private sororities met the needs of college women seeking to set themselves apart from the typical female student.

From the beginning socialization in ladylike behavior was a major focus of southern sororities. The bylaws of the Adelphian Society, for example, required the president to see that all members "be especially attentive to propriety and decorum in all of their deportment." They also required the president to prohibit "all low, cant phrases and unlady-like expressions and actions." In a culture committed to traditional views of honor that forbade White women's working outside the home except in cases of dire necessity, southern sororities emphasized the belle ideal that would give members an edge in the marriage market. Realizing their circumscribed agency in courtship, southern college women found in sororities a venue for empowerment, a place for developing the set of stylized behaviors ("being fascinating") that would help them as they contemplated constrained choices in marriage.[7] With their selective membership practices, secret rituals, and commitment to nineteenth-century gender conventions, sororities confirmed members' sense of superiority while drawing a distinct boundary between members of the group and those outside it. In short, southern sororities reflected the hierarchical nature of southern society.[8] As Farnham notes, "It is not surprising that the first sorority would begin in the slave South, where hierarchy was an integral part of the social fabric and distancing oneself from social inferiors was an imperative of the lady of chivalry."[9]

What remains surprising is the longevity of the ritual and steadfastness of its meanings. Accentuating hierarchies of race and class was imperative in the antebellum South, but 150 years later, in an era characterized by claims of equity and calls for diversity, southern college students still prioritized performances that almost guaranteed opposite results. Ethnography revealed what participants repeatedly denied or failed to grasp: ritual trains certain people to naturally embody and routinely enact superiority and privilege.

As a laboratory of White southern womanhood, sorority rush remained unsurpassed well into the twenty-first century. At Ole Miss and schools like it, the annual performance represented a pinnacle of sorts, an apex of feminine enactment with its own regional meanings, yardsticks, and habits. In a mere five days of careful choreography, time-honored gender standards were upheld and celebrated, as intertwined ideas about family and femininity, race and place, were mapped on the bodies of young women. Demanding the performance of a fairly specific rendition of White womanhood, rush momentarily resurrected the southern lady—strong yet demure, chaste but fertile, ethereal yet grounded, knowing but silent—in all her contradictory mythological splendor. In the process regional feminine ideals were maintained, class and race structures were reaffirmed, and the Old South existed ephemerally in the New.

Rush demanded a particular feminine performance that combined attributes of the lady with those of her iconographic counterpart: the belle.[10] That the belle's polished surfaces—her high-wattage allure, her conversational dexterity—should prove useful during rush was not surprising. But her true advantage was found beneath the gloss, in her strategic mind, self-

ish nature, and determined heart. During rush it might have been easy to assume that somewhere along the way the two figures had become fused in the
popular imagination, with a single, hyperfeminine persona the result. But to
give the participants credit, the late-model rushee was a situational construction, a pragmatic feminine character with the deft ability to display the appropriate lady or belle characteristics in turn, as circumstances demanded.
As if instinctively understanding rush for what it was, a crucial rite of passage between the carefree ways of youth and the more serious demands of
southern womanhood, the able rushee navigated expectations on cue, alternately exhibiting the bright sparkle of the belle and the sincere empathy
of the lady. Meanwhile, behind the scenes both active and rushee operated
from decidedly belle-like positions: cold calculation and opportunism. The
successful rushee was the one who performed the pertness of the belle while
evidencing the promise of the lady. In the final analysis rush came down on
the side of the lady, for a lady would never embarrass her sisters.

It should come as no surprise that such stylized performance would reach
its zenith at Ole Miss, where an extended public debate over the university's
symbols stretched into the new century. Long after the Confederate flag, the
song "Dixie," and the planter-gentleman mascot, Colonel Reb, had been officially discontinued by university officials in the interest of improving public
perceptions, these contentious signs continued to surface and endure scrutiny. On a campus forever haunted by the integration crisis of 1962, the social progress was indisputable but also hard-won and campus symbols ever
explosive.[11] When a chancellor-led campaign to improve the reputation of
the university caused Confederate flags to all but disappear from the football stadium, that potent symbol migrated to the bodies of young women,
who continued to sport it in the form of whole-flag wraparound skirts and
Greek T-shirts incorporating the insignia. When in 2010 the university introduced a new mascot, the Rebel Black Bear, to replace Colonel Reb, some
seven years retired, some students and alumni spearheaded legislation to return him and other Old South symbols to public life. Officially gone but not
forgotten, the flag and Colonel Reb never so much went away as went underground, where in some circles they enjoyed the cachet of renegade booty:
their visibility curtailed, their circulation improved, with femininity and the
flag, masculinity and the mascot, explicit, corporal mechanisms of White
southern remembrance.[12]

The symbols controversy exemplified "hidden in plain sight," the long-
standing phenomenon of southerners' inability—or refusal—to acknowl-

Sorority event at Georgia State University, circa 1970s.
COURTESY OF SPECIAL COLLECTIONS AND ARCHIVES, GEORGIA STATE UNIVERSITY LIBRARY, ATLANTA.

edge the cultural mechanisms they saw so clearly working before them.[13] In the modern South, mechanisms responsible for maintaining race and gender hierarchies often accomplished their work so seamlessly they rarely drew recognition, despite their public nature. So persuasive yet so pervasive, they went largely unnoticed. Perhaps least recognized of all were those rituals that shored up conservative notions about race in the process of reiterating prescriptive gender ideals. For all the ink spilled and the breath spent on the South's racial symbols, little public debate attended its gender signs, much less the link between the two.

Sorority rush hid much in plain sight. Not far from the athletic fields thrived a symbol sport of another sort. Across the Grove on Sorority Row, on the Capstone at Alabama, and the Horseshoe at South Carolina, the southern lady returned each year for a cameo appearance, which in its precision and predictability offered comforting reassurance. Gone for the week were the baseball caps and Birkenstocks that typified the sorority girl's class-day wardrobe. In their place appeared demure, churchy frocks that in their dated modesty spoke volumes about collective longings for innocence. Out of character with day-to-day college life, the scene was in sync perhaps with only rush itself—and with a persistent regional anxiety about a forever changed South. The dramatic contrast between the performative style of the everyday and that of rush, if not purposely exaggerated, nevertheless took on heightened significance, visible evidence that for many rush remained a sacred space, a ritual link between nineteenth-century ideals and twenty-first-century imaginations. With acting feminine and acting southern twin criteria, rush was a two-act performance and accepted standards of breeding, grooming, lineage, appearance, and class the markers the successful rushee was required to not only possess but tastefully display. What with rushees and actives attempting to assess each other's social value while demonstrating their own, and rushees trying to land themselves in a "good house" to make their families proud, a lot of cultural work went on behind the lipstick and laughter.

But don't for a second equate such romantic ritual with self-conscious Confederate commemoration. That scent wafting down Sorority Row was not magnolia blossoms but dry-cleaning. And out in the street was not a horse-drawn carriage in sight, just late-model BMWs and sport utility vehicles as far as the eye could see. Nostalgic longings were best pursued with contemporary technology and postmodern techniques. Hopeful rushees burned up their devices checking in with Mom and the hometown crowd, while harried actives put the finishing touches on digital presentations and synced software for voting. But for all the cutting edge communication, a facade of innocence clung to the process, an air of mystery and a pretense of discretion utterly at odds with the rampant virtual sharing of information. For here were the columned mansions, the wide verandas, the plantation shutters, the shady oaks. For just as antebellum society had once placed a gender icon—the southern lady—at the center of its racial and economic rationale, then measured status and place through so many movements and approximations of etiquette, so too did sorority rush demand proof of a particular feminine competency, then sorted out the campus pecking order on the basis of execution. Rush was a command performance, and the ability to "do" White southern womanhood was still suddenly, strangely, in high demand. Tara might have been bought out by agribusiness, but, for a few days each fall, sorority rush was surely a living symbol, a romantic ritual that conserved much more than it changed. Once again being received in the right houses depended on lineage, on pure blood, on being able to claim—and visually represent—a direct line of honorable descent. Perhaps most of all, this was what made rush at Ole Miss so "hard core," "cut throat," even "brutal," as participants described it. According to a junior Tri Delta from Houston, Texas, friends back home going through rush at the University of Texas had been warned ahead of time that theirs was a "hard rush" and that only one other in the country was known to be tougher—that at Ole Miss.[14] Well into the twenty-first century, a southern rush, although in many respects similar to rituals taking place on far-flung campuses, was distinguishable in both obvious and subtle ways.

The texts, settings, and performance of rush emphasized feminine competency and its necessity to social success. The rush party's multiple texts— including the lyrics of sorority songs, skit scripts, the one-on-one party talk between active and rushee, and the sorority president's monologue—all articulated a singular rite of homosocial wooing ultimately in service of heterosexual romance. The physical setting of rush—especially the antebellum mansion-like architecture of the southern sorority house and its ultrafeminine decor—held out the promise of inhabiting a real, grownup woman's home. When the fledgling woman joined a sorority, her feminine, domestic destiny was promised; cachet was granted.

In this realm of feminine intimacies, older, seemingly glamorous and sophisticated actives sought out new members who appeared to possess a high level of feminine competence, performed through clothing, cosmetic know-how, manners, and sociability. Girls likely to prove an "asset to the house" would contribute positively to the overall public profile of the group by being any or all of the following: cute, popular, a campus leader, a beauty, an athlete, a good student, or a member of an established, prominent family.[15] Rushees, in turn, sought out a group in which they felt "comfortable" but in which they could also imagine improving themselves—a group the rushee considered "like me, only better."

Throughout it all the performance of authenticity was central, as each sorority endeavored to posit itself as the one group that "really did" value diversity and where a new member "really could" find a home. In turn the rushee strived to appear as sincerely interested in one sorority as the next, in effect not showing her hand. Both active and rushee played roles in a ritual that, through its annual performance, reinscribed a conservative, prescriptive rendition of gender.

For all its appearances of spontaneity, sorority rush was, as *Look* magazine once put it, "as premeditated as an electrocution."[16] Throughout the spring and summer, incoming women students received information about Greek life and the specifics of rush. For many this information was simply a long-awaited formality; those with Greek sisters and aunts and cousins—the legacies—had been hearing about rush all their lives. Over the summer the ambitious rushee obtained recommendation letters from alumnae of each and every house. The clothes shopping got serious. A formal application was made that focused on grades, high school activities, the claim to legacy status, and letters of recommendation from family and friends.

Times were when an additional, informal layer of persuasion took place over the summer. Before the National Panhellenic Conference put a stop to the practice, an entire series of prerush overtures preceded the main event. Actives spent their spare winter moments writing personal cards and letters to high school girls, inviting them to open houses, alumna teas, casual dinners, and, most flattering of all, weekends with them at the sorority house. Much of this informal visiting, whether on campus or in hometowns, took place during "summer rush"—the sororities' last-gasp chance to track their quarry free of the rules of formal rush. But updated restrictions meant fewer opportunities for such unrestrained courting and more reliance on nuance: on the ability to read the signs and between the lines of the two-way romance that is rush.

Once the official action began, the sorority hopeful attended three or four rounds of increasingly selective parties. Each night sorority actives met late into the evening to discuss the rushees, vote, and make their cuts. The next morning the rushees learned which sororities had invited them back to their next party and had the option to accept or decline the invitations. Accepting the maximum number of parties allowed was the smart girl's strategy; by so "playing the game," she was typically guaranteed a bid at the end of the week. Declining any invitation put her at risk of getting "cut out of rush"—a fate equaling social oblivion on some heavily Greek southern campuses. According to campus legend, many a rushee dealt such a blow had promptly packed her bags, withdrawn from school, and rushed again on a less competitive campus.

After the final round of parties, all rushees still "in the game" gathered to make their final decisions. Weighing their hopes, their odds, and their own performance, rushees marked their first, second, and third choices for sorority membership. According to Greek life offices, rushees had quite a say. But it was hardly final. If they hadn't read the signals right, if they'd played hard to get or given out the wrong vibes, they might not rank high enough on their preferred sorority's bid list and were in for deep disappointment. Matched mathematically by unforgiving software, this emotional process full of romance, innuendo, and desire met abruptly up with numerical reality. As an algorithm of status, sorority rush was devastatingly efficient.

The factors at issue during rush—looks, family, status, femininity, sociability—made their appearance along a performative axis balancing innocence and knowledge. Both actives and would-be members attempted to perform innocence while acquiring knowledge. Both parties tried to find out more about the other, while keeping the revelations selective. Both endeavored to see the other's hand, without showing their own. In this parlor game knowledge was power. But so was innocence. The dichotomy was evident in the simplest mechanics of rush.

"I felt really intimidated [the first day] because all the sorority girls knew exactly what was going to happen," recalled one Phi Mu. "You kind of knew even then which sororities knew which girls. I kind of caught on that day. They don't know who the heck I am, and they know that girl in my rush group."[17] Even "known" rushees could find the experience unsettling. A Phi Mu at Alabama with extensive family ties found "it weird when they knew stuff about you. I had a rec for each house, so they knew about me coming in. But I remember finding that really weird, that they had memorized certain things about me."[18]

A freshman met up with this imbalance in knowledge even earlier—at the local Walmart the week before rush. Stocking up on dorm-life essentials, she encountered group after group of letter-wearing sorority girls, who met her friendly glances with only silent, knowing stares. The sudden realization that "they know exactly who I am and where I'm from and everything about me, and I have no idea who any of them are" was enough to warn her away from appearing in public that week without first getting "dolled up." At the parties, she continued, "You're sitting there talking, and you know that they're critiquing you, and they know that you're critiquing them. It's their objective to make you think that you are the one that they want, out of everyone in the room."[19]

Once a rushee got used to all the attention, ignorance on the part of actives could seem a poor substitute for knowledge. "They all knew my name," recalled a Tri Delt of her first visits to the house. "It was overwhelming. Then . . . you go to one house, and they [had to] look at your name tag, you're kinda [unimpressed]. At one house they mispronounced my name, and I was like, Oh, well, they obviously don't *know* me."[20] Rushees wise to the ways of rush were known to flip their name tags over to test a particular sorority's level of interest. Actives wryly referred to them as "professional

Kappa Kappa Gamma actives clap and sing in front of their house at
the University of Alabama, 1965.
SPECIAL COLLECTIONS, UNIVERSITY OF ALABAMA LIBRARIES, TUSCALOOSA.

rushees" or the "rush experts." But a little knowledge could be dangerous.
Flaunting shrewdness about a ritual dedicated to pretenses of naiveté had
been known to backfire on bid night.[21]

The rotation groups employed during the rush parties represented a classic split between knowledgeable active and naive rushee. In an effort to
make party circulation appear natural—and rushees feel cherished—actives
performed a tightly choreographed version of musical chairs, moving from
seated rushee to rushee. Designed to create an illusion of popularity and
adoration, the goal of this maneuver, called "bumping," was to make each
rushee feel as if she were the center of attention. Like most illusions, this one
required precision timing and considerable practice. All the rushee saw was
a nonstop stream of actives surrounding her, like bees to a flower. What she

was not to see was that her treatment was not so special after all. As with so many aspects of rush, noted one Phi Mu, "the rushee's really not supposed to know what's happening."[22]

"We know where you're going to be sitting, who's going to break on you, who's going to come over to talk to you, and who's going to come after them," noted an Alabama active. "To that degree it *is* a performance." But for all the carefully sequenced movements, conversations remained unscripted—or at least attempted to appear so. "When you're talking to someone, you should never be performing," said the same active. "It should be real. Of course, you're trying to customize your conversation in terms of what you know about them. But I don't think anybody's fake when they are talking to a rushee because they want to know if she is going to fit in in the end."[23]

This convincing performance of sincerity and spontaneity while surreptitiously gathering intelligence was called effective rushing. It was perfected through deep preparation. The customization of conversations, for instance, if not fake, was certainly calculated, a time-tested technique designed to solicit new information about a girl while reflecting well on the house. Top houses snared top rushees not by some fluke but through meticulous groundwork. It came down to really knowing the girls. During the week before rush, actives engaged in painstaking planning: memorizing biographical data and photos of rushees, using existing intelligence to tailor individual conversations and physical approaches, and carefully matching each rushee with the active most likely to woo her effectively, given all available information. Effective rushers knew exactly what they were going to say to their assigned rushee before the parties even started.[24]

"You have to try to get into the psyche of the girl," explained an Alabama Phi Mu. The active assigned to rush a quiet girl, for example, would be given strict instructions to allow her some breathing space. But for a girl who loved attention, "We would swarm them; that's what we call it. Swarm them. We got all over them."[25] Only later, after the final good-byes of the evening, did the actives sit down and coolly record the rushees' every comment, preference, and quirk, keeping the detailed notes of salespeople on commission. Effective rushing came down to really knowing the girls.

Come the final and most formal night of rush, the tension was palpable: a lot was on the line. For the sororities collective reputations and campus pecking orders were at stake. For the rushees, social futures hung in the balance. Absolutely nothing was left to chance. "We call it 'putting the knife in and turning it,'" laughed an active from Alabama, who likened the moment to sealing the deal with a valuable business client. "You've gotta close her."[26]

The competition was fierce because the sororities all wanted the same thing. They called it "the package." Top rushees (about 10 percent of the total) had the GPA, the looks, the activities, the personality, the wardrobe, the poise, the money, the family, and that special oomph capable of sending an entire houseful of college women over the edge with desire. Through securing them sororities strengthened and consolidated their power. It was a power of near-literal attractiveness, with strong houses acting like giant social magnets, pulling toward them the most prominent leaders, the most visible socialites, the top award winners, and, through them, access to the most attractive fraternity men. Due to the stakes involved, landing top rushees was either a point of pride (put nicely) or a blood sport. When inside knowledge was exhausted, it came down to reading the girls.

Actives looked for a certain look. Put-together. Cute but conservative. At ease. Attractive but not flashy. Not too much makeup. Not attempting to look older. Not sexy. Definitely not sexy. "I don't want to see anything that I shouldn't be seeing during rush," noted one Alabama active. "Because what we are looking for is a lady."[27] Sororities also avoided gendered extremes of appearance: both tomboy roughness and bouffant femininity could be deal-breakers during rush. When a likeable but nose ring–sporting rushee from Chicago was cut from a top house, an Alabama active recalled her sorority sister from California as the only one aghast; everyone else had considered it a foregone conclusion. Fealty to mainstream beauty standards was one price of membership in a top sorority.[28]

Overdone makeup and sartorial discomfort were off-putting to actives not because of some aversion to artifice (far from it) but because they might signal more serious sins of omission. Despite the safeguards of recommendations, the intelligence gathered by hometown "poop groups," and other forms of surveillance, mistakes were occasionally made and bids offered to young women who would ultimately compromise the reputation of the sorority. While a rushee's reputation was easily ascertained, her propensity to greet the freedoms of college life with wantonness was less predictable, and so actives kept a vigilant eye out for signs that something might be concealed or amiss. With the reputation of an entire house depending on that of each and every member, transparency became a goal and kind of holy grail—the last, best hope for illumining real goodness, beauty, and truth.

At the Alpha Omicron Pi house at Ole Miss, the presence of Santa and

Mrs. Claus, numerous lighted Christmas trees, boughs of holly and ivy, and plenty of elves attested to members' claims that their house was "the only thing close to the feeling you get at Christmas."[29] (It also suggested that non-Christian rushees were not anticipated.) Like all the other sororities, the AOPis made claims of authenticity that by definition posited their competition as fake. In the battle for authenticity, two rush scripts were consistently employed: the "home away from home" script (or the narrative of the "lost rushee") and the "diversity" script.

In the first, the lost rushee was away from home for the first time. Stripped of her identity and bewildered by university life, she entered rush in search of a home. Only through sorority membership would the fledgling girl-woman acquire the knowledge necessary to social success. The lost rushee knew she'd come home when she got that Christmasy feeling at AOPi.

Closely related to this script was the narrative of diversity. In this disingenuous script each sorority—an exclusive organization by nature—attempted to "out-diverse" the others with claims of inclusiveness, sincerity, and acceptance. It was only at their house that you could really be yourself. At the AOPi house the diversity skit featured four drum majors, one dancing to her own beat. "You're trying to sell authenticity," said one Phi Mu active. "I try to keep it all authentic. Because I have girls in my sorority who don't. They lie about everything. They . . . tell the rushees, 'Oh, I had the hardest decision to make, and my mother was here, and da-da-da.' You know, trying to get the legacies to come over. And they lie, lie, lie."[30]

At the Kappa Delta house, 250 young women with some of the largest smiles in Mississippi emerged from the columned mansion, dressed in little girls' pinafores, Peter Pan collars, white tights, and ballet slippers, tossing pigtails over their shoulders. It was the Munchkins, and they were positively squealing with little-girl delight. In probably the most professionally performed skit on the sorority circuit, the KDs posited Dorothy as the "Lost Rushee."

But the naiveté stopped there; this definitely wasn't Kansas. The KDs had some crucial messages to get across as Dorothy skipped down the yellow-brick road toward KD sisterhood. The hierarchy of campus status placed the KDs a solid but constant third, behind Chi O and Tri Delta. Strong in activities, grades, and pledge numbers, they nevertheless suffered from a party-girl reputation that kept the highest prestige just out of reach. They were known as being a little bit *wild*.

But was that so bad? Not to see the KDs do it. Like the Chi Os, the KDs were hip. But, their skit demonstrated, they were a lot more fun. After a sweet, fairy-tale introduction, the Wicked Witch of the West ripped into a raucous R & B rendition of "R-e-d-s-h-o-e" to the tune of Aretha Franklin's "Respect." When Dorothy was timid about setting off for Ole Miss and wondered how she would ever find her place in campus life, Auntie Em reassured her that she'd find a home at KD, where she'd also find entrée to the important parts of college: "There'll be the boys, the new friends, the boys, the professors, and, most of all, the boys!"[31]

The KDs weren't lacking in the class department either. When Dorothy met the "Dollypop girls," they were Dolly Parton send-ups with huge balloons for breasts and a countrified appearance. Smacking gum, they suggested that Dorothy would find her place "at the shoppin' mall." In this class-based put-down of some other, unnamed sororities, Dorothy confided, sotto voce, "I don't think they're the group of girls for me." This, the script pointed out, was no house full of hayseeds.[32]

At the Pi Phi house, actives dressed in sporty gym shorts and dainty tennis shoes sank at the feet of rushees perched on chintz sofas and wing chairs. The actives gazed up into their guests' eyes with visible love and adoration. All around the room this was the picture: a rushee attempting to talk and sit in a ladylike manner; a beaming, adoring active wooing her from below. They positively drank each other in.[33]

And it was not just happening at Pi Phi either. For what was rush if not a whirlwind romance among women? Until 1994, in fact, a fourth party was part of the rush schedule. Held the first night of rush, "Ice Water Tea" had been a frenetic, ten-minute party at which rushees were literally swept off their feet as actives attempted to introduce favored rushees to as many sorority sisters as possible.[34] Largely homosocial in nature, the sparking that went on during rush represented a courtship of sorts, but one with a dual dimension. While the primary act of persuasion was a performance conducted between women, the secondary audience was surely the heterosexual romance waiting in the wings. Through successful romance with the right women, the right men would also be delivered.

Men were ever-present during rush but rarely mentioned. When they were, it was in the most programmatic fashion. Guys appeared in the multimedia presentations sororities presented as evidence that theirs was an active and popular group on campus. And men were the unspoken presence behind the tabletop display of photographs on view at many houses during rush: the tableaux of homecoming queens, Pike calendar girls, fraternity little sisters, and the like. Ostensibly evidence of members' campus accomplishments, these feminine shrines pointed the lost rushee along a path to success reached only through heterosexual romance. "It kind of isn't!" exclaimed one Tri Delt when asked if trying to impress women during rush was different than trying to impress a man. "It kind of isn't! There are no men around, and we're not trying to impress men; we're trying to impress other women."[35]

But if "talkin' about guys" was considered tacky during rush, masculinity was hardly absent. In fact, it was necessary to the performance. During the Chi O skit party—based on a *Jungle Book* theme—a battalion of jockish actives decked out in camouflage T-shirts and military-like khaki shorts rushed back and forth from kitchen to chapter room, serving as the rushees' personal waiters. At the end of the party, the room was suddenly hushed, as the Chi Os gathered to whisper a song: "Tie a little ring around your finger / Chi O, Chi O / Any little thing to make you linger / Chi O, Chi O." During the singing of the song, some heavy-duty wooing was going on; actives knelt before the rushees, pleading with them to let them tie a ring of ribbon around their fingers while they told them about what Chi O meant to them. The obvious referent for this scene was the prototypical, heterosexual marriage proposal, with kneeling supplicant and coy, noncommittal feminine object.[36]

At the Tri Delta house, short-haired actives played the male roles in a fifties rock-and-roll skit from the musical *Grease*. Here the gender play was more obvious, with drawn-on mustaches and chest hair, low-slung jeans, and lots of swagger. Laughed one mannish active to another, "Remember when I came through? They had put you on me, and, I swear, I thought you were a guy!" At the AOPi house, a *Brady Bunch* skit featured actives impersonating the TV show's teenage male characters. They sauntered through the aisles, pointed out favored rushees, and mock-whispered, "I'm checkin' you out!"[37]

Masculine appearance, then, had its place in rush, as long as it remained cloaked in play. In a similar way racial spoofing was okay as long as it was clearly an act. Just as the wailing, Aretha Franklin–ish witch at KD got the biggest laughs and applause, the Tri Delts' Motown skit, complete with Supremes, got the biggest hoots. With plenty of laughing at themselves and one another as they let loose, gyrated, and shouted, there was an insider-joke quality to it all, as if to say, "Isn't this funny? This is what the Blacks do!" In the Kappas' circus-themed skit, clowns with brightly colored, Afro-like wigs and large, painted lips took the stage. What began as an improvisational,

Members of Zeta Tau Alpha entertain at a University of Alabama rush party, 1955.
COROLLA, 1955, SPECIAL COLLECTIONS, UNIVERSITY OF ALABAMA LIBRARIES, TUSCALOOSA.

standup-comedy routine quickly deteriorated into shucking and jiving in a surreal approximation of Black vernacular. Within the safe seclusion of the sorority house, the already chosen felt free to play around with cultures not their own. In contrast, the members' elite, chosen status stood out in sharp relief. Up until 1979 the Chi Os performed a skit in Blackface at their annual party. (The "Chi Omega choo-choo" skit featured a Blackface mammy emcee.)[38]

In fact, it was the sororities with the highest campus status and the best track record of delivering the marriageable male goods that ventured the furthest in race and gender play, as if their privilege rendered them immune from scrutiny. Veering too close to realism, however, was dangerous. In a realm where one sorority was cautioned before every party to "Remember, we're all Phi Mu Ladies," actually looking like a boy could spell trouble. One Phi Mu recalled the "problem" her chapter had had the year the friend of an active came through rush looking too masculine for some tastes. "She'd come in looking kind of real boyish, and she didn't wear any makeup, and she was a real tall, tall, big, big girl," she said. "And it was really hard because she had a friend in the sorority, and I think we ended up cutting her. Someone stood up and said, 'Well, she kinda looks like, you know, she's not very attractive, and she kinda looks like a boy or whatever.'"[39]

The comforting insularity of the mainline southern sorority house was disrupted by the dark rushee on the doorstep. Even at the dawn of the twenty-first century, the African American hopeful threatened the premise and the promise of sorority membership as White southerners had long understood them. Anticipations of a golden time of race and class privilege received in exchange for performing revered renditions of womanhood were shattered by the worthy Black candidate waiting just outside. With natural race difference exposed as false, the pact of securing social position through gendered rituals of exclusion was suddenly absurd. The Black rushee at the door was literally, historically, and imaginatively upsetting—a living, breathing invalidation of certain understandings of southernness.

Sororities consequently reacted with defensive regret, falling back on age-old platitudes about freedom of association. For many years this approach had worked: White southern sororities remained segregated decades after the desegregation of southern universities (and, indeed, southern fraternities). Adamant that desegregation not be forced on them, sororities had maintained a passive approach to widening the pool of rush registrants, most never moving beyond the informational pamphlet universities bulk-mailed to all new female students. "Everyone has always been given the opportunity," officials sighed, echoing the same lame lament long offered to explain workplace hiring inequities of every sort.[40] But where equal opportunity law spelled out the fact that it was not enough to crack open the gates of access—active recruitment and mentoring were required to address entrenched patterns of discrimination—sororities preserved the status quo and expressed few qualms about their racial makeup. Members were quick and vocal about espousing ideals of diversity but slow and vague about their responsibility and action plans for realizing such goals. Compelled to contemplate radical change, actives dissembled, their imaginations seemingly immobilized, as if they literally could not conceive of social equality in place of the privilege they had all but convinced themselves was the product of healthy competition and personal choice. Deflecting their gaze from the structures of unearned favor that benefited them, sorority members engaged in not seeing and not knowing, in the blissful ignorance that was the bargain of privilege.

Where less is spoken, more is performed. Faced with the unthinkable, sororities fell back on manners. The same precision performance and exacting evaluation of etiquette that had produced these strongholds of advantage also protected them. African American students rushing traditionally White southern sororities experienced the same polished welcome and rapt attention as everyone else and so were baffled as well as disappointed when they were abruptly cut from every house in the second or third round. When Melody Twilley was denied a bid at the University of Alabama in 2000 and again in 2001, she was initially flabbergasted: bright, attractive, upper-middle class, and a native Alabamian, she was *just like* the other rushees. Only her race set her apart. "At Skit [the third round], I only went to one house," Twilley told reporters. "But I felt so at home at that house." "This is elite ritual practice," explained anthropologist Susan Harding of rush. "It's tacky to be verbally racist, but perfectly acceptable to discriminate through your behavior, through your choices. Elite racism is implicit, acted-out, behaved—not expressed in language."[41]

It was a tribute to sororities' politesse that a rushee like Twilley could be blindsided by rejection, when so many forces worked to assure it. Between the dread of being ostracized by fraternities ("If we had a Black girl in our sorority, none of the fraternities would want to do anything with us") and the sway of alumnae urging all deliberate speed ("Let someone else go first!"), voices advocating for inclusion were typically drowned out by those tinged with fear. Add voting procedures that allowed blackballing, the high price tag of participation, and structural disadvantages like the lack of legacy status, and it was a wonder that any non-White rushee darkened the doorstep of a mainline southern sorority house for good. Individual consciences might have gnawed, but etiquette masked any hint of sisterly discord; a house divided would not stand. Decorum silenced dissent and allowed contentious decisions to masquerade as consensus. Custom concealed. Closing ranks around the already chosen, sororities minded their manners, making their membership decisions appear the inevitable result of a just process, tempered by tradition.[42]

Yet even the most venerable traditions are contrived, and what is fabricated can be refashioned. But the cost could be dear. The tradition of White privilege reinscribed each year through the ritual of rush experienced an identity crisis of sorts, underwent a kind of trauma, when presented with potential new members like Kimbrely Dandridge. An African American journalism major from Como, Mississippi, Dandridge bucked the odds and roused the ire of White and Black students alike when she went through the traditionally White rush system at Ole Miss in 2010 and pledged Phi Mu. Criticized and shunned by African American friends for not going through the mostly Black rush system that had rejected her the previous year on a technicality and cut by the sororities of White friends who had initially encouraged her to rush, Dandridge found herself an anomaly in a peculiar institution she considered "stuck in the old days." Recognizing Greek segregation as both institutional and visible (the gigantic sorority mansions on campus were filled with White women, while African American sororities were located off campus, out of sight), Dandridge also experienced personal racism when she was not initially accepted by some members of her own organization strictly due to her race. Still, the first-generation college student and former president of the Black Student Union maintained a positive attitude. "Every day that I walk into the [Phi Mu] house, people begin to accept it a little more," Dandridge told a reporter. "Being a Phi Mu is not about color."[43]

Dandridge and her supportive Phi Mu sisters took the high road and were soon rewarded when she was elected president of the Associated Student Body on a unity platform. University officials were elated: fifty years after James Meredith's integration of the university, an African American woman held the top student office, the first to do so. The symbolism was lost on no one, but, like a true politician, Dandridge insisted her status as a "first" was important only in terms of paving the way for others to follow. Out of the limelight, though, Dandridge offered a pointed critique of the segregated Greek systems, arguing the two should be combined. "I want it to be where we don't have a Black system and a White system," Dandridge told a fellow journalism student. "I want there to be *a* Greek system where it's everybody together. I don't feel like the Greek systems right now are promoting diversity."[44]

That Ole Miss would be among the first southern universities to break the sorority color line was paradoxical; that it happened at Phi Mu was not surprising. Highly conscious of its segregationist past, the university had strived to move beyond it and yet, inevitably, remained encumbered by it. Official desires to chart a bold new course were hampered by relationships with alumni loathe to be dictated to in "private" matters like Greek rush—that most public of rituals. Yet membership in Phi Mu, unlike many Greek organizations, was based on a simple majority vote: although peer and alumna pressure might exist, so long as 51 percent of active members voted in the affirmative, a bid would be extended.[45] (In organizations that allowed "blackballing," a single negative vote was enough to prevent extending an invitation for membership.) The membership of Dandridge and candidates like her elsewhere was an undeniable mark of progress, but whether it represented substantive or symbolic change remained to be seen. Dandridge's lone bid from Phi Mu came after she was cut late in the game by two other houses, where alumnae persuaded actives that they "*weren't ready for a Black girl yet.*"[46]

Dandridge's overall experience resonated the racial anguish that had periodically disturbed sorority rush across the region. Alpha Gamma Deltas at the University of Georgia were suspended in 2000 on allegations of racial discrimination after Allison Davis blew the whistle on her sisters' blatant discussion of a rushee's race and subsequent swift rejection of her. After Christina Houston revealed that she had broken the University of Alabama color barrier in 2000, pledging Gamma Phi Beta as a mixed-race student without attracting notice a full year before Melody Twilley failed in a widely publicized second attempt, widespread discomfort surfaced on campus: What was the significance of racial difference when no one realized the difference? When Carla Ferguson pledged the same chapter in 2003, university officials expressed hope that the occasion would usher in a gradual dismantling of Greek apartheid. But her admission sparked no transformation of rush patterns.[47]

It would be another full decade before sorority segregation was meaningfully addressed, and, when change finally came, there was nothing gradual—or definitive—about it. The year was 2013, and once again an African American rushee possessed an impeccable resumé. Once again chapter rush officials quietly removed her name from consideration prior to final balloting. Once again an in-house whistleblower called them into question, asking, "Aren't we even going to discuss the Black girl?" But this time her sisters stood with her. What happened next was unprecedented. After the

Members of Gamma Phi Beta wave to potential new members
at the University of Georgia, 2017.
PHOTO BY DUSTIN CHAMBERS.

Crimson-White, the student newspaper, published the informer's account of
pressure from alumnae to cut the candidate on account of her race despite
a collective wish to pledge her, members of the university community decided they had had enough. Fed up with decades of prevarication on the issue by sorority members and administrators alike, they stood up. And they
marched. Several hundred students and faculty gathered at daybreak on a
mid-September morning to trek to the Rose Administration Building to call
for an end to segregation in the Greek system. Dubbing their protest "The
Final Stand in the Schoolhouse Door" (an irony, given that Gov. George
Wallace's original "Stand" fifty years earlier had been to protect segregation,
not dismantle it), they demanded a response from university administrators
they considered complicit with the problem. Officials who routinely parsed
the racial makeup of the student body, athletic teams, scholarship recipients,
and even particular fields of study had deliberately failed to track the racial
diversity of Greek houses—another silence. Racial bias in sororities and fraternities had been tolerated by intentionally ignorant administrations for decades—the university's open secret.[48]

So it was with some surprise that protesters and observers met President
Judy Bonner's prompt order that sororities extend recruitment for the rest

of the year to admit additional new members through "continuous open bidding," a mechanism that allowed the extension of invitations after the close of the official rush period. The move, said Bonner, was intended to "remove barriers" to membership that had contributed to a segregation status quo. It was an abrupt reversal of the administration's long-standing "hands-off" stance to Greek recruitment. Bonner's edict stopped short of insisting organizations accept particular new members (and contained no enforcement mechanism should groups fail to broaden their ranks) but was clearly aimed at eradicating discrimination and promoting diversity. And it was plain that she meant business. Under the watchful eye of Bonner, the national media, and the U.S. Attorney's office, the traditionally White sororities hurried to comply. Only nine days later seventy-two new invitations had been extended, including eleven to African American students. Four African American and two other minority students ultimately accepted bids.[49]

The mood on Sorority Row was jubilant and spectators reacted with a mixture of delight and embarrassed relief. But if the change was sudden and welcomed by many, it was not necessarily durable. While some sorority chapters had successfully overcome alumnae and peer resistance and demanded change, others had shown reluctance, and in the end the historic feat was accomplished only by fiat. Whether chapters would continue to diversify and whether they would do so voluntarily remained to be seen. Minority pledges had entered the big house of old-line sorority membership through the back door of open bidding; would the same clubs receive them through the front door of formal rush? And, if so, would there prove a racial tipping point beyond which traditionally White sororities would not budge? These were houses, after all, customarily filled by the daughters and granddaughters of cotton planters, not cotton pickers. Institutions are slow to change, and there was little reason to assume that sororities—organizations traditionally based on exclusion—would suddenly become inclusive. As sociologist Matthew W. Hughey suggests, such desegregation is best viewed as a problematic beginning rather than a successful end; merely removing an obstacle to membership does not promote integration. The presence of a few Black members, notes Hughey, does not necessarily change the cultural logic of the institution. For transformational change to occur, sororities would have to supplant the prevailing logic of elitism and adopt new yardsticks for evaluating potential new members. They would need to ditch the belle aesthetic that disadvantaged the minority candidate and ultimately subordinated the power of the entire membership to fraternity men. And they would need to speak up. The institutional racism perpetuated by sorority rush had been nurtured and protected by a culture of collusive silence. From the dissembling of actives unwilling to examine their own privilege to the studied ignorance of administrators reticent to track the racial makeup of Greek organizations to the bullying of alumnae banning discussions of minority candidates, silence had been the friend of bigotry. President Bonner spoke up—and acted—only after her administration was publicly shamed.[50]

Within the desegregated sorority house, would the fictive bonds of kinship prove stronger than the ties of White southern memory—links that encouraged nostalgic connections but came laden with old trepidations and taboos? White sorority members explained their hesitancy to pledge Black students in terms of the limitations it would place on their ability to swap (or host parties with particular fraternities) and the possible decline in status that could result. Within a campus culture that emphasized dating and mating (Greek swaps that matched up individual members for the evening were not unusual), a deep-seated fear of miscegenation was the elephant in the chapter room. "Most kids in the Greek system [here] have strange boundaries," said Samantha Perry, a former member of Alpha Delta Pi at Alabama. "Their mentality is like, 'I'm not racist, I have Black friends—but I don't want to recognize them as a sister or a brother.'" To do so called into question the unquestionable. Bedrock understandings of self built on notions of racial purity and bound up with tender remembrances of the southern past dissolved under honest scrutiny. Yet challenging them required a reconfiguring and a reimagining that was painful compared with the comfort and rewards of not knowing.[51]

At the Ole Miss Chi O house, the decor was that of an English hunt club, complete with plate racks on the walls, polished mahogany furniture, plush carpets, and glossy maroon walls. In the meeting room oversized plantation shutters shielded the windows and crystal chandeliers twinkled overhead. These were the moneyed Mississippi Delta girls, and their privilege was quietly evident. If the KDs pointedly verbalized their claims to sophistication and status, the Chi Os didn't have to; each year they took their membership largely from legacies and from Mississippi girls they already knew quite a bit about. Place—in all its permutations—played a significant role in rush.

As in most rushes, of utmost importance were where rushees were from and who they knew. But make no mistake: this was a southern rush, and place didn't stop with hometowns and heritage. In everything from architecture to adornment, place was performed during rush, allowing actives to place rushees, and rushees to learn their place. "She didn't realize that they were *so* into southern girls," a Phi Mu from California said of her mom, herself an Ole Miss alumna. "She didn't realize how hard it was going to be on me, coming in and people not knowing you. Because a lot of these girls in the sororities *know* these girls from when they start ninth grade or from when they're *born*."[52] "Just the fact that I wasn't from Mississippi was a minus," claimed a freshman from Louisiana, who said she didn't stand a chance against the Jackson girls who knew all the Chi Os and Tri Delts. As she remembered it, "Half of them are like quadruple legacies. They come up; they'd gone to high school with all these girls, so they know them."[53]

But the high school connection could be a curse as well as a blessing. A Theta from Georgia recalled her dismay at learning the Jackson girls had spent their high school years in vigilant protection of their reputations, lest the Ole Miss sorority girls caught wind of any drinking bouts (or worse). "These girls were prepping and training for rush as of their sophomore year [of high school]," said the Theta. "And if the girls at the university found out about [any questionable behavior], they would be screwed."[54]

To remedy her situation the California Phi Mu had "kind of made it known that I had southern roots, some sort of connection to the South." She had also sent her mother on a recognizance mission to Mississippi boutiques. "I expected to get into a sorority here, which is stupid," she recalled. "I expected to be treated good because I was from someplace they're not. . . . As opposed to being treated like I was, which was, 'Hmmm, well, we don't really know who she is.'"[55]

How did they know who they were? In a nutshell, by using a system of rushing that emphasized hometowns, insider knowledge, and maintenance of lineage. Active members hoping to promote rushees from their hometown advertised them within the sorority house through posters featuring photographs of the favored rushee and lists of her interests and attributes. But having a friend in the house wasn't enough. Alumnae chapters, in-house "poop groups," and a vast network of family and friends were called on to verify applicants' reputations and class status. "Trust your sister," was an adage sororities turned to when in doubt.[56] Furthermore, all hometowns were not created equal. In an effort to consolidate alumnae support, individual

Emotions run high for University of Alabama sorority students, circa 1970.
SPECIAL COLLECTIONS, UNIVERSITY OF ALABAMA LIBRARIES, TUSCALOOSA.

towns in Mississippi received separate consideration, while the entire state of Tennessee, for example, was in some sororities treated as one hometown.

Back in those hometowns certain groups were favored over others. "In Meridian, it's Tri Delt, Chi O, KD," reported an extremely popular Tri Delt. "And there's kind of pressure to do one of those top three. I mean, I had a good rush . . . but there were girls from Meridian who didn't. And I mean, the talk of the town is what happened to so-and-so during rush."[57]

Pity the poor Yankee. "I think it's hard on them, because they're from a completely different culture, and they don't come down here to change the way they are," noted an out-of-state active. "They just want to be involved in a group. So when they get down here and realize, pretty much, if you're not southern, no matter how you talk . . . you have so much less of a chance of getting into anything here."[58] An Alabama active from the East Coast noted her southern sorority sisters were leery of nonsoutherners, for whom they were usually unable to obtain a firsthand reference.[59] In some houses, an unwritten "Mason-Dixon line" rule limited nonsoutherners to two or three pledges per year.[60]

Even without a quota, regional differences informed the practice and outcome of rush. The ability to compete in an exacting southern rush system was a badge of honor and a key to social rewards for years to come. As recruitment elsewhere went informal and inclusive, southern sororities took pride in continuing to stage a full-blown "frilly" rush. Characterized by flawless execution, over-the-top embellishment, and exorbitant expense, formal rush at large southern schools was relentlessly demanding on both sides—and part and parcel of the competition. Deploying drapes and decorations, electronics and major floral budgets, sororities completely revamped their houses from night to night, creating thematic dreamscapes designed to amaze and disorient impressionable rushees. With the clampdown on "dirty rush" practices, the chance to impress rushees was confined largely to formal rush, leveling the playing field but escalating the stakes. Gone were the mash notes, the summer contact, the dinner treating, the mysterious gift deliveries—all the surreptitious expressions of desire that had given old-school sorority rush the steam of an illicit affair. In their place was a charged theater of attraction of visible charms and palpable influence. In this formidable setting success on either side was cause for triumph. Rushees experienced a sense of authenticity—they enacted a ritual and perpetuated a social structure created by their mothers and grandmothers. Actives received validation—group status was reaffirmed along with the entire system of rush.

Actives blamed the elaborate nature of southern rush on regional standards of hospitality and etiquette that place a high value on first impressions. Within a highly structured campus social scene, over-the-top renditions of rush foreshadowed the competitive social entertaining that awaited participants upon graduation and served as venues for proving competency in social graces. Along with dressing up for football games, formal dating, and old-fashioned engagement rituals, a southern frilly rush was part of an entire realm of social interaction dictated by tradition and dedicated to upholding it. "The pageantry doesn't let up," an Alabama Phi Mu wryly noted.[61] For all the talk of diversity, the goal and result of rush was a familiar homogeneity and corresponding privilege in which a sister could find comfort.

"I can look at a pledge sister and know she's been raised by a family like mine just by how she eats or puts on clothes," claimed an Alabama Phi Mu.[62] "Girls in the South dress differently," agreed another. "What's 'in' here is not necessarily 'in' in other places. I had a pledge sister from Maryland . . . and she dressed so cute but just different than the way that we dress."[63] A junior Tri Delta from Texas recalled arriving on the Ole Miss campus accustomed to wearing flashy silver earrings and concho belts, only to discover her Mississippi counterparts given to dainty heirloom trinkets, especially rings and necklaces handed down for several generations. "They also had these big necklaces with their initials carved out in them," she said. "And I remember I thought that was funny. Because they would just really deck themselves out in those."[64]

On Pref Night at Ole Miss and Serious Night at Alabama, fraternity men in luxury convertibles circled Sorority Row, checking out the new women on campus and wondering how the evening had gone at their girlfriends' houses. But they could not hurry love. In candlelight seclusion the actives were still turning up the heat, romancing their prey. The Kappas presented handwritten letters to the rushees. The Delta Gammas pressed their own membership pins into the palms of favored prospects. A rondo rippled across the heavy August air: "It's just me and Tri Delta from now on." "Search your heart," echoed the Chi Os. "In your heart, you'll know."

"Oh! It comes down to how much you cry!" laughed a new active about Pref. "They *all* cry. They're kind of telling you more about them, what it feels like to be a Whatever . . . and they sing really . . . cheesy, sentimental songs, and *everybody* cries!"[65] Laugh she might, but at the conclusion of another recruitment season, the rushee tears were flowing. Lining their verandas and sidewalks, the actives, dressed in full-length damask gowns and cupping burning tapers, gathered to sing farewell and bid a dreamy adieu.

In private sorority members reported conflicted feelings about sorority life. Even enthusiastic members lamented the exclusivity of their social clubs. Others characterized sororities as springboards for leadership rather than sheltering sanctuaries. But one thing seemed clear: the ability to "do" southern lady, to trot her out and put her on at will, remained important to many southern women. And sorority rush provided a ritualistic stage for demonstrating a fairly specific, regional understanding of gender. Through speech, gesture, and adornment; through codes of conduct and choreography, a regional, racialized definition of gender was performed, again and again. Only by first performing this particular rendition of gender—by demonstrating that an anachronistic version of womanhood featured in their repertoire and was readily accessible—were women admitted to a dubious sisterhood.

Over the years southern universities earned their share of headlines. Attention often focused on the campuses as conservative political training grounds—the home turfs where national conservative power brokers learned their craft, where members of Alabama's student government "Machine," for instance, made the alliances they would parlay into lifetimes of business and political dominance. But the cultural landscapes of large southern schools, in addition to serving as proving grounds for masculine political power, also nurtured feminine social power too, with sorority rush at the heart. Even as southern universities subjected regional symbols to cathartic debates and instituted policies aimed at racial healing and inclusion, sorority rush remained largely untouched in the ways that mattered most. Hidden in plain sight, rush reinscribed race and region, year after year. For the southern lady, tomorrow remained another day.[66]

CHAPTER 2

Miss Demeanor

ON AN EVENING IN EARLY DECEMBER, THE TEMPERATURE HAD JUST hit the freezing mark—cold for central Alabama. But inside Morgan Theater at the university, the room was heating up. Striding, gliding, and sashaying across the stage were twenty-six young women with high hopes of becoming Miss University of Alabama 2007. With fewer than twenty-four hours until the pageant, there was tension in the air, and more than a few production kinks to work out. An Elvis medley sounded off-key. A French horn player's accompaniment was too loud. An interpretive dancer veered perilously close to the orchestra pit: Would she leap *off* the stage? Talent was not the only uneven segment. As the contestants bounced across the stage in bikinis in eye-popping hues—electric blue, shocking lime, fluorescent yellow—a well-coifed, middle-aged woman with a clipboard stared intensely at the lineup. "Suck your butts under and tummies in," she called out, distressed. "Y'all are sticking tummies *out*. If it feels uncomfortable, it's right."[1]

At dusk the next evening, a limousine pulled up outside Alston Hall, where judges and pageant officials were gathering for a prepageant dinner. The full-length furs and dramatic hairstyles that emerged were in keeping with neither the institutional venue nor the casual repast but complemented the attitude of the assembled. Sweeping in as if to a grand concert hall rather than a B-school conference room, the leggy former competitors and modish men took themselves and their appearances seriously: their air was one of visiting royalty. There was a certain plastic staginess about the group. Aware of their entrance even as they made it, and glancing about to judge one another's reactions, it was as if they were constantly viewing themselves from a dis-

67

tance. Miss Alabama was on hand to warm things up, and she, too, was not without artifice. Like many a photogenic celebrity, she had an unusually large head, wide eyes, and a wider smile on a tiny, toned body. After a year spent crisscrossing the state to cut ribbons and promote character education, vestiges of small-town life still clung to her. She was exceedingly friendly, and her homespun tales about traveling the state and her sincerity about the personal growth she had experienced as Miss Alabama belied the deceit of her stage makeup and false eyelashes. "Why, before I became Miss Alabama, I'd never even been on an airplane before," she said, and everyone just shook their head and clucked. Like bugs to a light, they could not take their eyes off of her.[2]

Minutes before curtain Morgan Theater had the festive noisiness of a family reunion, as generations of patrons connected by the university stood about, catching up. Current students waved to family members across the way. Sororities and fraternities sat in clumps of partisan support. Children played in the aisles. And, twinkling in the darkness as they caught the spotlights, were dozens of tiny crowns, pint-sized tiaras perched atop the heads of preschool girls with wide eyes and hard-to-hide desire. One of forty-eight preliminaries to the Miss Alabama pageant, Miss U of A possessed a certain cachet, so the packed house was no surprise. Though a "closed" preliminary limited to enrolled students, the pageant had produced a disproportionate number of Miss Alabamas, who had in turn competed exceptionally well at the national level. The university was considered a wellspring of southern beauty.

With the first pulse of "Fame," the opening number, the crowd went quiet. Exhilaration and expectation had replaced the clumsiness of the previous evening. Dressed in flashy "casual wear," the contestants strode across the stage, tossing one brilliant smile after another over their shoulders. The method of scoring was announced along with the judges; most had judged numerous contests across the state and region. Then it was straight into the swimsuit competition, with the contestants springing quickly across the stage as they were introduced. Carrie was a dancer from outside Atlanta; Laura Beth, a military brat from Russellville. Some contestants affected a coltish gait; others did not walk well at all. Only three or four wore the traditional one-piece maillot; everyone else had chosen a neon two-piece. Stephanie sported a hot-pink bikini and consummate pageant look. Ashley appeared conspicuously larger than the rest, and Sarah, noticeably shorter. Unlike at the state level of competition, a variety of shapes and sizes were represented onstage, and a good 20 percent were Black.

The talent competition only heightened the sense of range. Tyra, in a flouncy cream dress, offered a powerful rendition of Alicia Keys's "America." Skye lost her footing dancing *en pointe* to the theme from *Romeo and Juliet*. In red sequined shoes Heather tapped to "Ease on Down the Road." Kari played the piano in a manner resembling calisthenics, but Brittney was an accomplished dancer who electrified the audience with long red gloves and a sexy interpretation of "All That Jazz." Michelle, short, muscular, and African American, caused a moment of uncomfortable silence when, in the midst of all the Americana, she danced a sensuous jazz dance to "Endangered Species," a song-poem about strong women artists, set to rhythmic drumming. This unapologetic display of Black female empowerment was not typical pageant fare, and no one was quite sure what to make of Michelle. Stephanie, in contrast, was pageant-perfect with her billowing white gown and aria from *Phantom of the Opera*. In red halter dress and rhinestone earrings, Laura Beth was both a belter and a bombshell. Whitney performed Irish step dancing with energy and precision but ultimately served as a reminder that this style achieves its effect through group performance.

While the judges tallied the voting, past royalty performed another southern pageant tradition. With beribboned boxes decorating the stage, current and former titleholders sang songs of Christmas—the pageant world was widely, unabashedly Christian. Miss Alabama sang "O Holy Night." Up next were two former Miss U of As who together operated Crowned, a Christian music ministry. With their upbeat demeanors and modest pantsuits, they appeared almost matronly next to the contestants, despite being only in their late twenties. The current Miss University then took the stage to huge applause, performing the Dean Martin classic "Let It Snow" as coy duet with her twin brother.[3]

When the results were announced, enough dark-horse contestants placed to sustain the Cinderella narrative that anyone can be plucked from obscurity and win. Kari, the athletic pianist, was third runner-up, and Laura Beth, the busty belter, first. Brittney, the jazz dancer and swimsuit winner, somehow managed only fourth runner-up, and Meri-Glenn, another accomplished dancer, second. In the end time-honored pageant values prevailed: Stephanie, of the opera aria, bouffant white gown, and practiced pageant look received the winner's tiara. With the requisite tears, outward shock, and genuine pleasure, she accepted her sash and scepter as the other contestants crowded around her, joined by small girls in twinkling crowns who quickly converged from the darkness.

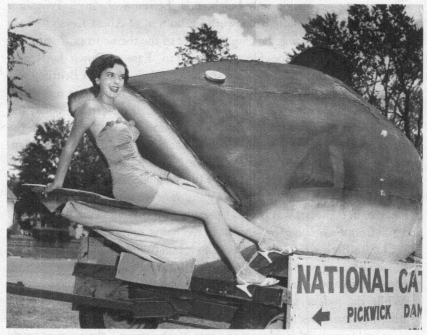

Gail Hooper, 1953 catfish queen, on a parade float at Pickwick Dam.
COURTESY OF THE DEPARTMENT OF CONSERVATION PHOTOGRAPH COLLECTION,
FILE 116, BOX 24, TENNESSEE STATE LIBRARY AND ARCHIVES, NASHVILLE.

Beauty pageants have enjoyed popularity across the country and around the world, but in the modern U.S. South they were performed with such frequency, fanfare, and passion that they constituted a regional pastime. The southern states—among the nation's poorest—spent the most money staging their local and state pageants. In the largely rural and relatively sparsely populated states of Dixie, a disproportionate number of pageant-age young women entered competition. In the states of the former Confederacy, competitive beauty was not just popular but big business: home to the groomers and dressers, coaches and plastic surgeons who not only catered to southern contestants but attracted pageant pilgrims from far-flung states. The region was a beauty power base, home to legendary figures like the late Dr. Briggs Hopson, longtime executive director of the Miss Mississippi Scholarship Pageant, who for many years was known for showing up at the annual Southern States Ball—a private cocktail gathering for the southern contestants and their entourages at the Miss America Pageant—in a tuxedo fashioned from sequined Confederate flags. With its showdowns and celebrities, glitz and glory, southern beauty was a realm of performative femininity akin to a competitive sport.[4]

Historian Charles Reagan Wilson has described this regional obsession with looks as a cult of beauty and counts it among the region's civil religions. Southern culture, notes Wilson, "has accepted the images and rituals of the beauty culture along with strictures for modest behavior for women." Following the lead of antebellum southerners, who posited in White women moral-religious ideas about virtue, purity, and spirituality and offered a revered mythological figure—the southern lady—as proof of a superior southern "way of life," it was only a small leap of faith for modern southerners to shift display of their ideal woman from pedestal to pageantry. Beauty culture functioned as something of a bully pulpit in the modern South, a sacred space that authorized the feminine body to enact regional attitudes about gender, class, and race as they were collectively imagined. Encouraging conservative standards of beauty in service of established hierarchies of race and class, southern pageants were segregating ceremonies that promoted both cultural homogeneity and sectional chauvinism in the guise of entertainment and celebration.[5]

In beauty pageants the expectations associated with White southern womanhood—virtue, purity, deference—were mapped and measured on the body. For contestants the pageant represented a highly visible stage for demonstrating the ability not only to embody a viable likeness of White southern womanhood but to perform a competitive one at that. Over time southern pageant contestants came to enjoy a high profile in national contests, suggesting that this iconic rendition of femininity was broadly accepted and even adopted as a national ideal. Finely honed and widely practiced, the southern-beauty performance accommodated the tensions of multiculturalism, yet allowed a ceremonial celebration of the past. Like other public spectacles of gender performance, the beauty pageant performed crucial negotiations about race and place within southern and U.S. culture.[6]

Practically from the start White southerners exhibited a predisposition for pageantry of every sort. The transplanted Anglicans of eighteenth-century Virginia performed their status in a choreography of social condition played out across the southern landscape. The authority of the ruling class was not so much written in documents as made visible in architecture and patterns of land use and displayed in rituals and everyday movements. Through well-rehearsed patterns of gesture, demeanor, and deference, southerners confirmed the social distinctions and order of authority that gave meaning to their culture. Southerners enacted social place: in the conspicuous oath taking of court days, the gentility suggested by polite dancing, the hierarchical seating in Virginia churches, the exhibition of family standing at quarter races, and the paternalistic treating on election days. In the process they shaped the look and use of southern spaces.[7]

By the nineteenth century southerners were fond of thinking themselves the merely relocated counterparts of European nobility, and they consequently emphasized high forms of pageantry. In May Day celebrations, jousting tournaments, Twelfth Night parties, and Mardi Gras balls, southerners held up White southern womanhood as their emblem of honor. In doing so they took part in a time-honored discourse that equated virtuous womanhood with worthy nationhood. The abstract, masculine "nation" *needed* the embodied morality, "woman," to command the beliefs and practices necessary to hold together a disparate collection of peoples. At the height of the antebellum period, visiting French economist Michel Chevalier credited festivals with invoking civic pride and affirming community values but deemed them incomplete without queens, who provided their real meaning. Without an idolized woman, tournaments and the like "became nothing more than fencing bouts."[8]

Pageantry provided a ritual means for beleaguered southerners to justify their social structure. Through romantic pomp southerners made visual and bodily connections between themselves and the ideals and hierarchies structuring southern society. If in day-to-day life, southern social stratification could prove stifling, pageantry explained the system's benevolence and logic to participants and spectators alike. Like promenading southerners at northern resorts, pageantry demonstrated refinement and hierarchy for all to see. Through pageantry White southerners of every stripe could celebrate themselves as continuous heirs to traditions of noblesse oblige.[9]

In the late nineteenth- and early twentieth-century United States, similar impulses fueled the popularity of historical pageants—grand tableaux featuring large casts of everyday citizens acting out episodes of local or regional history. Women often appeared in cameo roles. Featuring sweeping scenes of settlement, the Civil War, town founding, or industrialization, pageants served to contain stresses on the social order and to instruct new immigrants in the morality, integrity, and work ethic necessary to national cohesion. With their efforts to construct a common culture, historical pageants of the Progressive Era, much like the beauty pageants that followed, endeavored to

Contestants for *The Spirit of the South* pageant, Montgomery, Alabama Homecoming Week, 1926.

PAGEANT PROGRAM, SPECIAL COLLECTIONS, UNIVERSITY OF ALABAMA LIBRARIES, TUSCALOOSA.

obscure race and class differences and to suggest a "level playing field" of liberal U.S. society.[10]

In the segregated South few directors could resist the opportunity presented by historical pageants: the chance to rescript the southern past. White southerners produced pageants that expressed their anxiety over the state of society by acting out "right" versions of the past—grand displays of consensus that reinforced the social order and asserted continuity with a harmonious plantation past. Although some pageants celebrated both the Confederacy and recent economic progress, the backward gaze predominated in southern pageants that dramatized a past of near limitless peace and joy.[11] The stereotypical depiction of slave life was a staple of southern productions, with Blacks depicted as comic simpletons happy under slavery. Enslaved persons in pageants begged to accompany masters off to fight with the Confederacy and ridiculed the notion that they wanted freedom. "Authentic" plantation scenes featured "darkies" in headscarves happily singing spirituals as they picked cotton. Such "antimodernism"—rejecting the present in favor of a preferable, mythical past—dominated southern historical pageantry from the 1920s. Women figured prominently in all the productions, but especially in allegorical *tableaux vivants*, in which they were presented as the embodiment of various virtues. In between historical vignettes women appeared in symbolic dances, as "The Spirit of Progress" or "The Spirit of History."[12] In one typical South Carolina pageant, *The Spirit of the Ante-Bellum South* radiated "all the feeling of the Old Time South, its hospitality, its entertainment, and its feudal protection."[13] Another featured a reenactment of the inauguration of Jefferson Davis as well as *The Spirit of the South* (chosen from among eleven local beauties) sending "Chivalry" off to war.[14]

In an effort to claim gentility and reiterate the nation's Anglo-American identity, southerners wove Elizabethan rituals into pageant scripts and these, too, featured women. Like the actual rites after which they were patterned, onstage maypole dances, May queen pageants, and *tableaux vivants* all featured feminine performances that promoted remembrance of the South as an offshoot of European aristocracy. The custom of casting descendants in the roles of their ancestors made similar legacy claims. In the end the southern historical pageant amounted to an elaborate spectacle of social position that distorted history in favor of an idealized version of the past.[15]

The Miss America Pageant eventually came to represent national ideals too, but it started out as something quite different. The mid-1880s had seen the rise of photographic beauty contests—originated by entertainment promoter P. T. Barnum and quickly imitated by mass-circulation tabloids—but elites considered them an outrage, and actual, live beauty contests remained outside the reaches of respectability. Held in marginal venues—carnivals, fairs, dance halls, and dime museums—beauty contests remained associated with sleaze for many years.[16] But the decades leading up to the first Miss America Pageant in 1921 saw a burgeoning of the middle class, the rise of public amusements and commercial culture, an increase in women working outside the home, and a corresponding shift in public opinion about public displays of the female body. The increasing use of beautiful women in advertising, coupled with the growing acceptance of modeling and chorus-line dancing as (marginally) suitable pursuits for young middle-class women, helped diminish outrage over female exhibitions.[17]

Beauty and morality got within waving distance for the first time in 1921, when the first Miss America "bathing beauty" contest was held on the beaches in September. The event was the brainchild of the Hotelman's Association of Atlantic City, New Jersey, who wished to entice tourists to re-

Neptune Hudson Maxim and Miss America Margaret Gorman
at the Atlantic City Carnival, September 7, 1922.
BAINS NEWS SERVICE, PHOTOGRAPH 91719090, LIBRARY OF CONGRESS, WASHINGTON, D.C.

main in that resort city past Labor Day, the traditional end of summer.[18]
The initial eight contestants, called the "Inter-City Beauty Contestants"
were quite young—fifteen to seventeen—and from randomly chosen East
Coast cities such as Pittsburgh, Philadelphia, and Washington, D.C. Margaret Gorman, Miss Washington, was only fifteen when she was named the
first Miss America, and it didn't bring her fame back in high school, where
her title was largely ignored. But the pageant was an immediate hit, and the
next year saw the creation of preliminary competitions and a dramatic rise in
number of entrants, with fifty-seven contestants competing.[19]

The 1920s saw the Miss America contest grow in both size and scale.
Originally one of a slew of weekend events—including a night carnival, a
"rolling chair" parade, a costume ball, and a "Bather's Revue" featuring
men, women, and children—the Miss America segment gradually emerged
as the dominant event.[20] Along with preliminaries, the evening-gown competition was introduced in 1922. As the number of entrants increased, so
did their age and sophistication. But despite the pageant's growing popularity and profitability (or perhaps because of it), it remained plagued by

charges of sleaze. Though the relaxation of Victorian gender conventions had brought new freedoms in fashion and leisure pursuits, corresponding demands for enfranchisement and better work opportunities sparked renewed anxiety in many quarters about middle-class women's loose moral state. Miss America faltered in the early thirties, condemned by civic and religious groups (especially elite women's clubs) as indecent, exploitative, and corruptive—the last because it encouraged competition among women. At the height of the Great Depression, with few funds, no monetary prizes, and only a handful of wary contestants, the pageant was a financial bust and was abruptly discontinued.[21]

It took the appearance of Lenora Slaughter in 1935 to change Miss America's fortunes—and the pageant's reputation. Having successfully produced a "Parade of States" for the Saint Petersburg Florida Chamber of Commerce the previous year, Slaughter was hired by Miss America officials to resuscitate the program. Specifically, she was charged with making the pageant respectable and legitimate once and for all—and she did not disappoint. During her thirty-two-year reign as "Mother Superior" of the pageant (some contestants called her "the dictator"), Slaughter instituted sweeping changes and specific rules that would forever distinguish the pageant's value system and reputation.[22]

Slaughter started by framing the contestants as in need of surveillance and worthy of protection. She banned contestants from nightclubs and bars, instituting an early version of the rule prohibiting Miss America from appearing in any establishment that serves alcohol. She introduced a nightly curfew and a prohibition against talking to any man—even a contestant's father—during pageant week. In this cocoon of enforced, watchful protection—one echoed by the rules surrounding sorority rush—men remained a hidden, if crucial, ingredient. To enforce these rules, she invented the "hostess" concept: during pageant week each contestant spent every waking moment in the presence of an assigned hostess, a local female volunteer who served as a chaperone. In 1938 Slaughter formalized the rule of state representation, eliminating entrants representing such questionable venues as amusement parks and fairs. The pageant was further limited to young, single, never-married women, age eighteen to twenty-eight. (Rule 7 of the Miss America handbook stated, "Contestants must be of good health and of the White race.") Faced with continued resistance from traditional women's clubs, who still considered the pageant obscene and degrading, Slaughter managed to "out women's club the women's club" by convincing the Junior

Chambers of Commerce (Jaycees) to sponsor the state pageants. With her introduction of college scholarships and scheme of having World War II–era winners crisscross the country selling war bonds, Slaughter put a seal of respectability on Miss America.[23] Slaughter saw to it that Miss America celebrated patriotism and modernity on the modest and virtuous feminine body. Thanks to her, the pageant became a civic ritual of honor and glory. And though thousands of other beauty pageants existed—including those in the Miss USA system, with its looser walk and flashier attitude—Miss America emerged as the gold standard of U.S. pageantry. Other pageants were perhaps more fun, showed more skin, had prettier contestants, or garnered higher television ratings, but when it came to embodying national ideals, Miss America reigned.

In the second quarter of the twentieth century, the race and gender preoccupations of White southerners and the ambition of Lenora Slaughter conspired to create a place atop the hierarchy of beauty pageantry that southern White womanhood could instantly occupy. Indeed, the growth of the Miss America Pageant and the persistent ideal of White southern womanhood share an intertwined history. To understand how southern contestants came to dominate the Miss America Pageant and epitomize the embodiment of U.S. nationalism, it is helpful to consider another nationalism: the White southern nationalism of the Lost Cause. This post–Civil War movement provided White southerners of varying classes and geographic locations a means of finding meaning in defeat and of imagining themselves a coherent community. Drawn together in sorrow, they remained together in Whiteness.[24]

With their dreams for a separate political nation denied, White southerners longed for a separate cultural identity that would dignify the Confederate cause and provide meaning for its loss. The Lost Cause supplied it, effectively linking religion and history in a religious-moral identity positing White southerners as a chosen people. Featuring the Confederate hero as the embodiment of transcendent myths about the redemptive power of southern society, the Lost Cause addressed the profound postwar concerns of White southerners. Organized in religious fashion around a sacred symbol system—the movement boasted its own signs, mythology, organization, and theology—the Lost Cause found its most potent embodiment in ritual, in those occasions designed to garner wide participation in reverent acts. Days of fasting and prayer, Confederate Memorial Day celebrations and reunions, funerals of wartime heroes, and Confederate monument dedications

Members of the William Hughson Burr Chapter of the Children of the Confederacy in front of a Confederate monument erected by the Talladega Ladies Memorial Association, circa 1900–1909.

inspired the mass outpourings of emotion critical to allegiance. As the Lost Cause gained momentum, these ritual celebrations increasingly featured the figure of the White lady, raised up by men's, women's, and veterans' groups alike as the emblem of southern civilization lost. Solemn tableaux and noisy reunion typically climaxed in the presentation of a local maiden clad in virginal white—a living, breathing justification for why the South had gone to war. Along with stirring oration that honored dead heroes and hallowed the southern cause, the Confederate daughter on display—pure, beautiful, and endangered—was the perfect reminder of what Lost Cause faithful considered their utter rape by the North. On the bodies of young White women, defeated southerners sanctified their suffering. Recreating mythical time through ritual, southerners paid tribute to noble ancestors and vowed never to forget.[25]

The denouement of the Lost Cause dates to about 1920, when the Confederate memorial movement erected its last monument, and the remaining Confederate veterans finally passed away. In its wake came a proliferation of public activities that employed feminine performance to reiterate southern Whiteness. Indeed, it was in the very next year—1921—that the Miss America Pageant made its boardwalk debut. In the South in the following decades, a vibrant and influential regional pageant system emerged that gave White southerners a new site for celebrating and consecrating racial dominance, even as segregation grew untenable and increasingly unpopular across the nation.[26]

By 1954, the year that the Miss America Pageant was first televised, the South had a fully developed system of local pageants in place for feeding the national contest. It was also on the brink of perfecting another system—massive resistance to racial equality.[27] The *Brown v. Board of Education* Supreme Court decision that declared segregation unconstitutional the same year fueled both phenomena. Twin responses to the central threat of racial equality, the two systems emerged in parallel—the one fashioned from belligerence and fear, the other from the power of symbolic ritual, from the ability of the southern beauty to repeatedly embody the White southern nation's dreams of distinctiveness and power. If loud and graphic White defiance would come to define massive resistance—with police dogs and fire hoses, bloodied Black bodies and hating White faces appearing nationwide on the nightly news—serene, smiling icons of femininity and composure would come to define the passive resistance of pageants.[28]

For collegiate White southerners the years between World War II and

Tennessee's rhododendron queen contestants of 1955 on Roan Mountain.
COURTESY OF THE DEPARTMENT OF CONSERVATION PHOTOGRAPH COLLECTION,
FILE 134, BOX 53, TENNESSEE STATE LIBRARY AND ARCHIVES, NASHVILLE.

the early 1960s were something of a golden age of abundance and privilege. While the entire country exhibited an optimism associated with the booming economy, the bullish atmosphere down South stemmed from more than rosy financial prospects. White southerners touted the superiority of their segregated "southern way of life" and rationalized their continued racial dominance even as African Americans outmigrated in massive numbers and Black veterans expressed their dissatisfaction with the system. White campus culture supported the justification, providing pleasurable proof that the good life was the southern way of life.[29]

In a profusion of campus pageantry, White southern collegians celebrated traditional gender roles and perfected their public performance. In the southern beauty the medium of resistance was also the central message. Louisiana State University selected a rodeo queen, freshman day queen, Pan American queen, water show queen, engineering queen, agriculture queen, and education queen. These titles were in addition to homecoming queen, beauty court, and, most coveted of all, the "Darling of LSU." "An old southern mansion was the setting for presenting our beauties," noted Louisiana State University's 1956 *Gumbo*. "As each girl appeared in the garden, applause greeted her along with the last strains of 'Moonlight, Magnolias, and You.'" The University of Alabama chose Miss Venus, Miss Corolla Beauty, Miss Bama Day, Miss Crimson Tide, Miss Homecoming, and queen of the Military Ball. None other than Miss America Lynda Lee Mead traveled to Tuscaloosa to interview the top ten finalists (of forty-five contestants) for Miss Homecoming 1962. South Carolina students vied for the title of Miss Venus with bags over their heads; only their legs were evaluated. May queen candidates, though, openly competed for votes, holding numbered cards before them. Students at the University of Mississippi selected Miss Ole Miss, rebelee queen, homecoming queen, and Miss University, in addition to holding a robust annual Parade of Beauties.[30]

A tradition of male judges, whether celebrities or students, accentuated the gender divide. In 1951 entertainer Bob Hope selected five Ole Miss beauties from a Parade of Favorites numbering forty-eight. Pop singer Pat Boone visited Tuscaloosa in 1956 to choose the top Corolla Beauties and Favorites. Actor Fred MacMurray judged the 1957 Parade of Beauties at Ole Miss. At the Louisiana State University *Gumbo* Beauty Ball of 1956, Beauties, Favorites, and "The Darling" were selected in a male-only vote. In 1958, after years of midshipmen from Annapolis and students at Washington and Lee University selecting the Darling and beauty court of Louisiana State University, that responsibility was "placed directly in the hands of the men of LSU."[31]

When campus beauties prevailed in distant pageants, their conquests were trumpeted back at school. When Alice Corr returned to the Alabama Capstone driving a late-model Ford at the conclusion of her reign as 1953 Maid of Cotton, her romantic prospects were the subject of speculation in the *Crimson-White*. When Kay Burns was selected a top Beauty in 1961, the *Ole Miss* wasted no time in touting her far-flung wins: Miss Mississippi River, queen of the American Royal in Kansas City, Missouri State Fair queen, American Legion Fair queen, National Catfish Derby queen, National Cotton Picking queen, and queen of the Naval Relief Carnival in Millington, Tennessee. Tri Delta was pleased to pledge her.[32]

Local and national press promoted perceptions of a southern beauty mystique with coverage that kept score of queens' conquests like a sport and encouraged speculation about their success. The *Crimson-White* crowed that "Southern beauty reigned" after all twenty candidates for Corolla beauties of 1953 hailed "from below the Mason-Dixon line." Calling the Capstone "major-league scouting grounds" for beauties, the paper predicted a "1.000

An Ole Miss beauty atop a
cotton bale with trophies and
Confederate flag, circa 1960.
ED MEEK COLLECTION, SPECIAL
COLLECTIONS, UNIVERSITY OF
MISSISSIPPI LIBRARIES, OXFORD.

season in statewide contests" for 1956, laying odds on Bama coeds to prevail
as Miss Alabama, state maid of cotton, azalea trail queen of Mobile, and Festival of Arts queen of the Beaux Arts Ball in Birmingham. "It's no new thing
for a Bama coed to win such laurels," bragged the *C-W*. "University girls
have long dominated state beauty contests and have been highly recognized
in national contests." After Ole Miss had supplied two Miss Americas in
three years and placed three state winners in the 1961 national contest, a *Life*
magazine photo spread showcased the school as a hothouse of pulchritude,
asking, "What's Ole Miss Got That No Other Place Has? Beauty Queens
to Spare."[33]

When the dean of women at the University of Alabama managed to ban-
ish the Bama Belle pinup from the pages of the *Crimson-White* in 1958, her
decision set off an uproar among male students, who demanded the right
to ogle female classmates in short shorts. They couched their arguments
in terms of campus chauvinism and competition: rival Auburn University's campus paper, the *Plainsman*, had recently scored a public relations
coup with its "Loveliest of the Plains" pinup of a coed posing in shorts,
jumper, and Confederate hat atop a battle flag, on the occasion of Robert
E. Lee's birthday. Picked up by wire services and published nationwide, the
feminine photo feat infuriated the men of Alabama; they would not let Auburn out-Dixie them! With massive resistance brewing at a distance, south-

ern collegians like those at Alabama continually placed the ideal southern beauty front and center of White campus culture. A more persuasive political symbol did not exist: she embodied exactly what was at stake for White southerners resistant to racial equality. At the intersection of romance, regional pride, and embattled entitlement, the political and the popular joined together, harnessing the power of gender to serve the needs of White supremacy. [34]

Massive resistance and passive resistance fed off each other, solidifying southern Whiteness. Stories of southern universities as sites of racial crisis and massive resistance—including the angry mob that greeted Autherine Lucy when she attempted to desegregate the University of Alabama in 1956 and the deadly riot sparked by James Meredith's integration of the University of Mississippi in 1962—would become touchstones of civil rights history. [35] Numerous writers would explore the campuses as incubators of conservative, masculine political power. [36] But acknowledgement of the southern beauty as a significant form of passive resistance and the role of campus culture in reproducing her would take much longer, despite the fact that White southern collegians perhaps most routinely and consistently celebrated the "southern way of life" in prominent, predictable rituals of feminine beauty. [37]

The region's history of absorbing racial trauma perhaps afforded southern pageantry its advantage. Accustomed to rationalizing and downplaying the South's racial arrangements, White southern contestants appeared unfazed by charges of sexism and racism within pageantry. Historian Sarah Banet-Weiser interprets the twentieth-century U.S. beauty pageant as a site for displaying and containing crises—both the crisis of racial pluralism and that of the autonomous woman. For Banet-Weiser, pageants of the era were "important sites for the construction and maintenance of the White, middle-class American 'ideal'" but also "sites for the construction of female liberal subjects." Caught between their problematic history of celebrating a universal Whiteness and demands that they reflect racial and ethnic diversity, pageants turned to classic liberal stories about individual achievement and cultural tolerance as a means of resolution. [38] White southern contestants, reared to believe and defend without question unsupportable racial truths, met the challenge with unique preparation.

The second-wave feminist movement of the 1960s and 1970s charged pageants with objectifying and commodifying women in what amounted to commercial skin shows. In fact, the feminist protest of the 1968 Miss America Pageant is noted as one of the first political actions of the modern women's movement. Planned by New York Radical Women, a small underground group previously active in civil rights and New Left organizations, the protest outside the convention center in Atlantic City featured demonstrators and onlookers tossing (*not* burning) items of "woman garbage"—wigs, curlers, and false eyelashes; copies of *Cosmopolitan, Ladies Home Journal,* and *Playboy*; dish detergent; steno pads; high-heeled shoes; and, yes, brassieres—into the "Freedom Trash Can." The group targeted Miss America after concluding the pageant was "patently degrading" to women (promoting "ludicrous 'beauty' standards that enslaved all women"); racist (no African American woman had ever been a finalist); immoral (the winners were shipped off to Vietnam to entertain troops as "death mascots"); and crassly commercial (the underlying purpose was to sell sponsors' products). Organizer Robin Morgan proclaimed the contest a blatant "commercial shell game" and asked, "Where else could one find such a perfect combination of American values—racism, militarism, capitalism—all packaged in one 'ideal' symbol, a woman?"[39]

Pageants in the Miss America system responded to the criticism with a dazzling move at once self-serving and redemptive. With only a few superficial changes to the program—an increased emphasis on interviews, the introduction of social issue "platforms," a revamping of the swimsuit competition—the Miss America system was suddenly all about choice: about self-actualization, opportunity, and the right to speak. Pageants were suddenly about *scholarships* and the spin was so deft that many viewers (and contestants) actually believed it. Like the rushee looking to sororities for self-development (not a social life), the pageant contestant came to view competition as a healthy form of networking and self-actualization.

Employing the language of feminism but subscribing to none of its tenets, pageants absorbed feminism, became "postfeminist." By positioning those parts of the pageant traditionally targeted by feminists as unimportant—especially the swimsuit competition's objectifying display of an idealized body—pageants reframed themselves in more serious terms (as scholarship *programs*), in part by successfully emphasizing their commonalities with feminism. The bright, savvy, and assertive "delegates" seen onstage were there by choice—thanks to the women's movement. In this free market of beauty, the decision to implant, liposuck, dye, and nip and tuck was evidence of creativity and strategy, not a lack of self-esteem. Incorporating both the objectified body and liberal feminist rhetoric, pageants presented highly disciplined feminine bodies as the success of feminism. The true crisis presented by feminism—the dismantling of hierarchical and gendered structures of power—was managed by the twin performance of femininity and commitment to liberal society.[40]

Pageants likewise became postraced, spaces for celebrating diversity while simultaneously managing the potential crisis lurking within multiculturalism. Faced with resolving the tensions between an increasingly diverse society and the desire to continue representing nationalism through White femininity, pageants enacted crises, but ones comfortably resolved onstage. Like sororities that had been "cosmetically retouched" (but not meaningfully restructured) by token minority members, the onstage presence of women with bodies of various hues served as visible evidence that pageants were serious about diversity. At the same time they threatened to disrupt the White woman-as-nation equation. If those dark bodies onstage signified America, just what did that mean?[41]

Pageants located the solution to this quandary within their own careful construction. Responding to the moral panic over an endangered national identity, pageants demanded the performance of a highly specific femininity. Characterized by their celebration of virtue and morality—values historically coded White—pageants in the end became all about *respectability*, with each segment of competition designed to both measure and reproduce this ideal. Disciplining demeanors and viewpoints as well as physiques, the beauty pageant reproduced hierarchical relations of race and class through pliant pageant contestants.

Within such sharp parameters, minority contestants were only as successful as their ability to *pass*, as their ability to perform a dark facsimile of the White womanhood so widely circulated by lighter competitors. When a minority hopeful did manage to claim the crown, she did so in something of a minstrel moment. Performing in figurative Whiteface, she provided "proof" of pageants' commitment to diversity, yet did little or nothing to challenge the pageant's racial construction of acceptable femininity. The dark winner existed as only a minor, visual aberration in pageantry's central, moral narrative. Successfully managing the mutual construction of national identity, race, and femininity, late twentieth-century pageants reassured the nation, assuaging the threat of fluctuating race and gender codes.[42]

This shift, real or perceived, in pageants—from embarrassing and possibly racist anachronism to proud "post-racial" display of "power femininity"—represented an unusual opportunity for White southern contestants, who stood uniquely poised to benefit. Honed on the one hand in a highly de veloped pageant system accustomed to producing winning feminine forms and on the other in a cultural milieu dead set against gender and racial equality, the White southern contestant emerged unscathed, in pristine condition really, and in highly competitive form. With no radical shift in strategy, the White southern contestant enjoyed a new advantage in the new pageant paradigm. With the advent of the postfeminist and postraced pageant, the once beleaguered White southern contestant—so hokey, so predictable— remained proudly at the forefront of pageantry.

In the late twentieth century, southern pageants and other gender rituals provided ceremonial stages for performing southern Whiteness. With their cyclical, clockwork-like reappearance and reiteration of an innocent, virginal ideal, southern beauty pageants reiterated a time-honored notion of femininity that was White by definition, middle class in nature, and heterosexual in the extreme. The myth of the southern lady owed its longevity to feminine rituals, including pageants. If elite southern women were the keepers of tradition, performances like pageants were surely the keepers of a certain type of femininity.[43] If the media made Dixie, created and perpetuated a romantic, "moonlight and magnolias" South that never really was, it was nostalgic public performances like beauty pageants that kept this racialized gender daydream alive.[44]

Robert Lavenda has written about the small-town U.S. beauty pageant as a site for displaying middle-class, local values. Preparing and rehearsing together (sometimes for as long as three months), entrants came to know their competitors intimately. Parties and receptions were thrown in their honor, which, with group instruction sessions in grooming, cosmetic application, etiquette, and runway modeling, added up to the small-town equivalent of a finishing school. In coaching sessions for the interview segment, adult community leaders encouraged contestants toward responses in line with local mores and values.[45]

A distinguishing feature of the twentieth-century local pageant was the selection of contestants—and a queen—who would best represent the community. This meant that class and race memberships were important factors in the local pageant system; in turn this class and race consciousness influenced the national ideal of beauty. Considering the process of contestant selection practiced in many small towns, the promotion of cultural homogeneity was not surprising. The most common sponsorship scenarios included a local business offering to sponsor a particular girl; the pageant matching sponsors with contestants; and, more rarely, would-be contestants locating

Beauty queens at the 2010 Shrimp and Petroleum Festival, Morgan City, Louisiana.
PHOTO BY DAVID WHARTON.

their own sponsors. Such sponsorship practices meant that contestants represented a selective pool of girls already known by and attractive to local business leaders.[46]

Spectators new to the pageant scene frequently expressed surprise at the quite ordinary appearance of the contestants. Next to the polished beauty "pros" competing at the national level, contestants at the local level could seem plain. Local queen candidates were not necessarily the most gorgeous or the best students or even the most talented. Rather, they were "well-rounded"—outgoing joiners involved in many school and community activities. Ambitious, likable, and attractive, they were literally the "girls next door," and they were deeply embedded in the community. Moreover, they were ready, willing, and able: ready to dance and sing and clog; willing to demonstrate their grace, poise, and physical fitness by appearing in a swimsuit; and able to state their views on societal issues. In short, they were prepared to embody community values.[47]

Yet, though the contestants could at first glance appear to represent a cross-section of the community, with the plumber's daughter and the mechanic's daughter competing on equal footing with the daughters of the local attorney, merchant, and physician, in reality the candidates were a stratified group. The myth of social mobility through pageant competition, the Cinderella narrative, was for the most part an illusion. The community status of the parents remained an influential factor in choosing pageant participants, and usually the girls themselves already belonged to a popular social group. Add to this the fact that local pageants were the almost exclusive domain of civic groups like the Jaycees, Kiwanis, and Lions Clubs—groups which in many southern communities had desegregated in only token fashion—and it is not hard to see why "Miss Southern Small Town" was apt to produce a queen who not only enjoyed the prominent social status of her parents but was also lily White. Given the strong influence of the southern "pageant belt" in national and international contests, this class- and race-conscious standard of beauty at the local level took on greater significance.[48]

In the latter half of the twentieth century, southern pageants desegregated with something resembling "all deliberate speed," that stubbornness born of defeat. The pageant ideal was correspondingly slow to incorporate diverse notions of attractiveness and style. The maxim among African Americans that mainstream professional success required them not only to measure up but to work twice as hard seemed fully operable in the world of pageantry. Black contestants who placed or won in historically White pageants seemed to do so not by forcing the pageant aesthetic to expand but by being twice as good at performing a belle-based southern beauty as any White contestant. Through exacting prescription, the White ideal of southern womanhood wrested precise performances from contestants of every hue.[49]

Since the 1940s, as African Americans sought racial and economic progress and political acceptance, Black women's grooming practices had been governed by a politics of respectability that dictated straightened or pressed hair, modest dress, and controlled decorum. Older debates about the racial politics of natural versus straightened hair had been largely abandoned as Black women put their everyday bodily presentation on the line for civil rights. In a hostile environment grooming and refinement became strategies for asserting dignity and winning respect. Black women didn't straighten their hair or attempt to lighten their skin in a desire to approximate Whiteness but in an effort to claim the economic opportunities White women enjoyed in a society that measured respectability according to hair, dress, and skin color.[50]

This equation continued to prevail in historically White pageants long after a parallel universe of Black pageants—launched as middle-class vehicles for racial pride but plagued by colorism and elitism—had expanded the range of images they celebrated. Even as sixties' social movements for civil rights and Black Power saw Black collegiate pageants, in particular, challenge the aesthetics of respectability with Afrocentric stylings and performances, this shift did not carry over to majority culture pageantry. Black entrants in predominately White contests typically considered their competition a civil rights action: a challenge to the color line and chance to transform the image of Black women in the national imaginary. They also considered White pageants (especially those in the Miss America system) the "real" competitions, offering more visibility and opportunities. But in the end attempts to win "firsts" offered limited victories, as the presence of Black contestants altered the optics of the contest, but not its form or logic. For a Black contestant to win a traditionally White pageant often meant nailing a rendition of beauty characterized by containment, virtue, and deference—values historically coded White. Scholar Gerald Early claims he didn't realize Vanessa Williams was Black until the day after her historic victory in the 1984 Miss America pageant, since he'd watched the contest on a snowy black-and-white television. (He deemed her able to "pass for a fairly pronounced octoroon.") Heralded as the first African American winner but dethroned midway through her reign for having once posed for nude photographs, Williams exited the pageant world in shame, a classic "tragic mulatta" figure whose public redemption would come only after the passage of many years and a successful singing career. Embodying lingering regional anxieties about endangered purity and interracial sex, the southern pageant contestant in the late twentieth century symbolized what Early called "our deep neurotic obsession with chastity," our culture's "sick fantasy of girlhood and innocence."[51]

"Who're your *people*?" This folksy, get-acquainted query may produce laughter, but the southern fixation on lineage and kin is widely acknowledged. In the context of twentieth-century pageantry, it was not without weight. Pageantry had always been as much about *the people* as about the contestants; the successful southern beauty was the one who embodied *her people*.

The notion that local pageants exhibited the values and mores of the host community helped explain why Black winners were sometimes described as having "come out of nowhere." These were the words White teenager Carol McQuary used to describe her predecessor as Miss Houston (Miss.), Tracy McClendon (her African American classmate), when in fact Tracy had grown up in the exact same community as Carol. While both were extremely active in community and high school activities (Tracy was a drum major and thus highly visible), Carol understood herself as more representative of the Houston social structure.[52]

It also provided at least one reason why Leslie Lindsay, a college-age orphan living in a group foster home while attending community college, was frequently runner-up rather than the overall winner in pageant competition.[53] And it explained the fate of one lovely and talented young woman, one of several Black contestants for the title of Miss Lafayette (Miss.) 1996. An exchange student from Barbados attending the historically Black Rust College, she seemed a cinch to win the title. But with her sensual, hip-moving modern dance; her rounder, heavier figure; her numerous braids; and her exotic platform about the need for international communication, she was out of touch with the prevailing local ethos. In the end these problematic contestants were unable to answer that question so important to placing people in the South: "Who're your people?" Performing an unfamiliar, unmistakably Black femininity (and with no people in sight), the Rust College student's place was ultimately no place, and she did not place in that particular pageant.

Few "pageant people" cared to claim that label. It was a little like admitting a soft spot for what historian Catherine Clinton dubbed "Confederate porn," the racist, caricatured Old South memorabilia, vintage or contemporary—the Mammy salt and pepper shakers and the Sambo figurines—capable of commanding fascination, disgust, and shame all at once.[54] After the 1996 murder of six-year-old pageant veteran JonBenet Ramsey, pageantry of every sort experienced scrutiny by the U.S. public.[55] So pageant people already considered themselves misunderstood, at best, like a member of an exclusive club. At worst, they felt a bit ashamed, because it was too narcissistic, wasn't it, to spend so much time, money, and effort on beauty; to be so obsessed by looks? It was much better by far to have just entered on a lark, at the last minute, and to have beauty come naturally, with no effort, or at least to make it appear so. Like Florence King's "self-rejuvenating virgin," who just wanted to keep getting carried away by passion—again and again!—the southern pageant contestant wanted her beauty to keep appearing (as if by magic) a natural, wonderful surprise, even (especially!) to her. Anything else was calculating and therefore shameful.[56]

And so the contestants showed up on the first night of pageant rehearsal in their raggedy jeans, flannel shirts, and expensive running shoes; in full makeup, yes, but with an attitude of studied casualness and with the bored expression of someone who had been talked into this, not someone who had just driven a good 350 miles, clear from one end of Mississippi to the other, to compete to be the next Miss Magnolia. They had the look of someone who was thinking, "Well, this is something we're all gonna do, okay, but I'm not really interested." Yet all the while they glanced around, sneaking sideways looks at one another, at the competition.[57] No, the beauty innocent of her good looks was surely the most beautiful of all. And so there were the surprised, hopeful looks they gave the audience (and the judges) as they first strutted out onstage, the looks that seemed to say, "Oh, gosh! I'm really here! Wow! I hope you like me!" Performing innocence was the first lesson in performing femininity in the South.

Yet the beauty infrastructure surrounding the southern contestant belied and denied any such innocence. As an advertisement for one plastic surgeon noted, "Sometimes Southern Beauties Aren't Born, They're Made."[58] Little Rock plastic surgeon Dr. James Billie claimed to have operated on contestants from all but three of the fifty states.[59] One Miss Maine, Mary Nightingale, noted of her experience at the national level, "The girls from the southern and western states were like another species of female—very cosmetically sophisticated."[60] Another contestant complained that there should be a separate pageant for the southerners.[61]

Framing the southern pageant landscape were not only creeping kudzu and hanging moss but less picturesque parasites as well. Also thriving and clinging in this fertile clime were professional groomers and wardrobe planners, voice coaches and strength trainers, pageant directors who knew their onions and tailors who knew their sequins. Dotting the southern landscape, far off the interstates in out-of-the-way towns, were the cottage industries that formed the backbone of southern pageantry. Located in private homes or in the back rooms of other businesses, and typically available only by referral, were the experts who shaped and perpetuated the system. Isolated geographically but tightly connected by the business, these experts formed a sophisticated network of beauty knowledge. Hidden in plain sight was a subterranean beauty economy, the understated, private twin to southern beauty's outsized public face.

Contestants initially admitted their knowledge of this insider's world only in roundabout ways. Often they whispered, blushing, "Last year's winner told us about this lady in this little town in Alabama." "There's this seamstress near my hometown who makes a lot of the girls' gowns." "There's this lady who used to direct pageants who will rent you the right swimsuit." Only with gentle pressing would details come out. But when they did, they revealed a force field of expertise directly at odds with contestants' purported innocence. Southern winners knew: private knowledge was the key to performing public innocence.

For Miss University of Mississippi 2000, Megan Flowers, it was a friend's tip that led her to a small Alabama town three hours' drive away. There she was ushered into the back-bedroom workshop of a dressmaker regionally renowned for having dressed Heather Whitestone, Miss America 1995. (Later she would dress Deidre Downs, Miss America 2005.) "It was the most amazing thing I've ever seen," recalled Flowers. "We walk in—and you have to make an appointment; it's real kind of secretive; it's funny—and I mean you don't just look through their dresses. They look at you and say, 'I think you need to wear a White dress.' And you're like, 'O . . . kay . . .' Then they just start pulling dresses, and they put them on you, and they *know* what they're talking about, so you just kind of go with what they pick."[62]

Flowers's visit to Ann Northington's North Oaks Pageantwear in Vernon, Alabama, traced the steps of many a pageant pilgrim. The frame house on the old highway through town offered no outward clue of the glamour inside. But one glance at the full-length runway occupying the living room and five minutes with Northington, official formal-wear designer for the Miss Alabama Pageant since 1989, and contestants knew they were in the presence of one of the South's fabled queen-makers.[63] Contestants from across the country had long navigated their way to remote towns like Vernon and like Russellville, Arkansas (pop: 27,920), where for many years the late, legendary Randy Dimmitt granted audiences to pageant hopefuls. Wedged between a foot-care clinic and a convenience store, in a small, red brick house with white shutters, was Dimmitt's dress shop, Randy's Another World. To those outside the pageant world, this unassuming structure was all but unnoticeable. But to insiders Randy's ranked among the uppermost of the innermost—a critical way station on the holy road to beauty mecca, Atlantic City. Written up in *Women's Wear Daily*, *Good Housekeeping*, and *Cosmopolitan*, Dimmitt in some years dressed nineteen out of fifty-one Miss America contestants.[64]

Inside was truly otherworldly. The beauty faithful, having made their Ozark pilgrimage via plane, rental car, or cab, stepped through a series of small rooms to sort through racks of shimmering, glimmering gowns. Armloads of debutante gowns hung from a shower rod in the bathroom, while billowing pageant gowns (nearly all size six or eight) overwhelmed the living room. Though the surroundings were simple, the atmosphere was one of secret pleasures. Within this inner sanctum pageant postulants surrendered themselves to pure indulgence, luxuriating in an almost enveloping realm of feminine intimacies. Dimmitt and his small army of assistants (some days numbering as many as nine) knew that pleasing their particular clientele was as much about feeding egos as fashioning winners. Flattering as they fit and pampering as they pinned, Dimmitt and company indulged whims and fulfilled finicky requests with pleasure. Waistlines were cinched infinitesimally, hems let out a quarter inch, shoes dyed a half-shade darker, bodices hand-beaded overnight. Coddled and catered to, the hopeful contestants felt special. Basking in all the attention, they *were* queens—at least for a day. Contenders for national titles, accompanied by their pageant directors, "shopped till they dropped" a bundle of money.[65]

At the state and national levels of pageantry, outfitting contestants was never cheap, and the wardrobe for the formal competition segments was only the half of it. Besides outfits for the evening-wear, swimsuit, talent, and interview contests—the clothes the judges saw—there were those occasions of informal competition to think about. Contestants learned quickly that from the moment they set pump to platform for the week of prepageant rehearsals, they were constantly being judged. Arriving at the airport and signing in at formal registration, at map signings and parades, and at preliminary competitions and cocktail parties, contestants dressed to psyche themselves up—and the competition out. Miss Alabama 2011 Ashley Davis arrived at the Miss America pageant packing attire for seventeen separate appearances. "Everyone looks up to Miss Alabama," claimed Nan Teninbaum, the pageant's executive director. "She always is one of the best dressed contestants." Maintaining such a reputation was expensive. By the time Dimmitt gingerly wrapped a contestant's last garment in tissue paper, her pageant director's purse was between $3,000 and $40,000 lighter. Although pageant people were fond of pointing out that competition needn't be costly—recalling the winner in the borrowed dress and the swimsuit purchased on sale—frugality never featured at pageant boutiques. Rather, opulence did, or at least a flashy imitation of it. By the time a contestant competed at the national level, she and her sponsors were heavily invested in finery and in the vanity it supported in the name of sport. Far from a moral flaw, personal

Pageant director Mary West gives backstage instruction to contestants in
the 1998 Miss New Orleans pageant.
PHOTO BY KATHY ANDERSON, COURTESY OF *TIMES-PICAYUNE*.

vanity—backed by regional pride, encouraged by calculating coaches, and
embraced by contestants smart enough to conceal it—was a tactical advantage for southern contestants.[66]

At hundreds of other spots on the southern pageant landscape, the scene
was replicated, one dream at a time. In downtown Vicksburg, Mississippi,
the inner sanctum was Crown to Heels. Aspiring queens from across the
South made pilgrimages to J. S. Fields and Company, outside Nashville. In
the hinterlands of western Kentucky, Debbrah's, in Paducah, was the destination. For the makeup artists, photographers, strength trainers, and other
service professionals associated with pageants, the story was much the same.
In secluded salons and isolated ateliers, large sums of cash changed hands as
contestants chased crowns.

If only appearances were enough. But though plenty of contestants managed to achieve a competitive pageant look, few emerged to compete at the
national level. An inevitable fallout occurred as contestants moved up the
competitive ladder of pageants. In the big leagues of beauty, only seasoned

veterans made it to the playoffs. The difference came down to training—training of the body, yes, but also training of the heart, mind, and soul. More than anything else, it was the southern contestant's access to, belief in, and dedication to training that placed her time and again in the national winner's circle.

Training of the sort that produced national beauty queens was the almost exclusive domain of coaches. And the southern beauty economy boasted some of the most legendary coaches of all. Hidden in plain sight were the modern-day Pygmalions who shaped bodies and molded minds to pageant perfection. Like their retail counterparts in the southern beauty economy, advertising was not necessary; word of mouth kept them solidly booked, and with waiting lists to boot. The sufficiently renowned among them were justifiably picky about potential clients; nothing increased status among pageant people like repeat success.

Television viewers got a belated peek at a successful southern pageant coach with the 2009 reality television series *King of the Crown*. Featuring Cyrus Frakes, proprietor of Gowns and Crowns Complete Pageant Preparation in Columbia, South Carolina, the series capitalized on garden-variety voyeurism—the desire to sneak behind pageant scenes—but also on a widespread desire to consume a caricatured South. The program joined a rash of reality television shows catering to a fetish for southern weird—and Frakes did not disappoint.[67] With flamboyance and deep expertise, Frakes played the parts of glitzy ringmaster and knowledgeable guide. There was no shortage of spice: ambitious pageant moms and controlling dads; sibling and class-based rivalries; bombshells, belles, and beauties who endangered their chances with tattoos and racy photos; and unsavory behavior all made appearances. Pageant mechanics got full close-ups: scenes of wardrobe anxiety, cosmetic enhancement, interview incompetence, and corporal education were sufficient for even the most prurient of viewers. But some of the most intriguing scenes dealt not with the art of packaging appearances but with the skill of shaping motivation and inspiring obedience. Commanding meekness and restraint from strong-willed competitors, Frakes sculpted submission from keen desire.

King of the Crown must have been a revelation to the curious and uninitiated, but not to those familiar with legendary southern coaches like Mary Francis Flood, who, with a handful of late twentieth-century peers, created and perfected the method of immersion preparation. For more than half a century, Flood ran a busy pageant-consulting business in the heart of the Mississippi Delta, advising clients from the age of twelve.[68] In Memphis Rick Caccamisi and Dinnie Bright ran a combination photography-studio and coaching business dedicated to pageantry, organizing pageants for the Miss America and Miss USA systems. In Fort Worth B. Don Magness micromanaged the Miss Texas franchise for twenty years, seeing eighteen Miss Texases make it into the Top Ten and two become Miss America before he was forced to resign in 1990 amid allegations of improprieties. A larger-than-life character who directed with a cigar in his hand, "Mr. Miss Texas" was known for his off-color jokes and self-promoting T-shirts, including one that read, "Matthew, Mark, Luke and B. Don."[69] In El Paso, Texas, Richard Guy and Rex Holt made up GuyRex Associates, directors of the Miss Texas–USA and Miss California–USA franchises and the coaches responsible for five consecutive Texas wins at Miss USA. Sequestering protégés within their hacienda-style home-office complex, the duo put contestants through a yearlong beauty boot camp designed for victory at the national pageant. With speech coaches tweaking accents, dieticians plying healthful concoctions, trainers overseeing workouts, and tailors stitching outfits in a taffeta-strewn workshop, GuyRex left nothing to chance. As Guy told *Time* magazine, "There are no more queens. Momma doesn't make apple pie anymore. It's all frozen, all corporate-owned." In a similar vein the late Dr. Briggs Hopson, longtime chair and CEO of the Miss Mississippi Corporation, and his wife, Pat, took many a Miss Mississippi into their own home to prepare her for Atlantic City.[70]

The southern "coach approach" only picked up steam in the twenty-first century, as social media shout-outs replaced word-of-mouth referrals, and pageant gurus hyped the cachet of boutique preparation across digital channels. Clients of attorney Bill Alverson, dubbed "The Pageant King of Alabama" by the *New York Times Magazine* in 2014, willingly reached him by text, video calls, or drives to his home in tiny Andalusia (pop: nine thousand), where he specialized in interview preparation. His success in coaxing convincing storytelling from contestants—including a streak of four Miss America titleholders—led to a TLC reality show, *Coach Charming*. His counterpart in Houston was J. J. Smith, equally known for his waist-length blond hair, flamboyant demeanor, and interview-preparation success. The names occasionally changed, but the strategy remained the same: regional tastemakers oversaw small fiefdoms of pageantry, ruling over those who would reign.[71]

The central tenets of successful pageant coaching had not really changed since Mary Francis Flood and her peers set the benchmark some thirty years prior. For a flat or hourly fee, clients were ushered into a studio, where they wasted no time moving past dreams and hopes to work on skills and technique. Desire was important, but determination and knowledge of detail, better. Makeup and hairstyling were studied. Bodies were evaluated, sculpted, and sometimes surgically enhanced. Videos of pageants past were scrutinized like Super Bowl game–day tapes. Knowledge once taken for granted—how to walk and talk, how to dress and accessorize and shop— was reconsidered in light of the prevailing pageant aesthetic. Those willing to strip themselves of prior know-how and submit themselves—tabula rasa—to a total makeover were most likely to succeed. Contestants learned to walk and smile and execute a full turn, how to hold their feet in a ten-and-twelve position, and how to make eye contact with the judges. Back in her day Flood took those in her tutelage shopping, then put them through their runway paces in a local auditorium. If a girl lived too far away to go home at night, she put her up in her own home.[72]

Just as the successful sorority rushee knew how to perform the lady and the belle in turn, the successful pageant contestant embodied two halves of a whole—knowledgeable contender and innocent contestant. One of the chief lessons pageant coaches taught contestants was how to make artifice and natural beauty appear to run together. Successful illusion was the prevailing aesthetic; "Don't ask, don't tell" could have been inspired by pageantry.[73] In fact, the very rules of competition, while appearing to emphasize the natural, maintained a distinct appreciation for artifice. Updated guidelines meant contestants could go barefoot or wear high heels, and they could choose two-piece, off-the-rack suits in addition to so-called competition suits—sturdy, ribbed, almost rigid one-piece suits that molded and held the body. In a nod toward realism, contestants were required to do their own hair. But silicone breast enhancers and surgical implants, cleavage created with electrical tape, teeth smeared with Vaseline, and buttocks sprayed with baseball adhesive were all okay. Puffy eyes on pageant day? Contenders knew that a dab of Preparation H would shrink those blood vessels right down. Wrapping the torso in cellophane made for a lightweight, undetectable girdle. "Make us believe it because we are ready to believe," was the unspoken credo of pageants. Authenticity was the aim, but artifice was the mode.

Supple surfaces alone, though, were no guarantee of a tiara. Beauty pageants placed great stock in the interview segment, and then even the D's

were not enough. Dreams, desire, determination—even mastery of details
and memorization of data—paled next to the qualities coaches and pageant
judges looked for in potential winners. Once asked what she looked for in a
girl, Flood had been quick to reply, "Humility. Humility and sincerity. I look
for qualities that make a girl a good person."[74]

Flood knew that the interview was where humility and other signs of
"inner beauty" were measured. Inner beauty was pageantry's most difficult
trick of the trade—and the most crucial. It was in the interview—whether
onstage questions or the three-minute prepageant meeting with judges—
that the successful contestant performed a particular constellation of attitudes, opinions, and beliefs. Humility was central to this performance. The
interview was the time to mention God or, better yet, Jesus. Contestants
professed devotion to their faith and to self-maximization and body stewardship as a means of serving divine purposes. The interview was also the occasion for "platforming"—expressing commitment to action on behalf of a social cause. Actual career goals were best mentioned in the same breath with
plans for motherhood and family. Participation in pageantry was explained
in terms of opportunities—the chance to "give something back" or to "experience personal growth." Most of all, the contestants did their best to display humbleness and virtue, proof that persistence and meekness could co-
incide in one beautiful, spiritually disciplined body. They tried to reveal an
"inner beauty," the source of their "outer charms." Like the successful sorority rushees, the successful pageant contestants could turn on a dime, balancing determination with obedience and success with righteousness.[75]

Even as pageants became more accepting of forthright ambition and left-
leaning platforms, the interview remained the venue where crowns were
won (and lost). In the twenty-first century *what* contestants espoused became less important than *how* they said it; demeanor and delivery trumped
content. Bill Alverson tapped his legal expertise to train contestants in telling consistent, compelling stories—narratives crafted to showcase their
most appealing traits and heartfelt convictions. Like the criminal defendants
he taught to appeal to juries by editing their life stories, Alverson trained
pageant contestants to shape and connect compelling elements of their lives
to optimize their chances with judges. Brainy and progressive answers were
okay, but, even paired with remarkable beauty, were almost guaranteed to
go nowhere unless delivered with panache, humor, and, yes, humility. In
the end the worldview and voting habits of individual judges—painstak-

ingly researched by Alverson—schooled contestants like no other. As in the past, twenty-first-century winners delivered seamless nonthreatening performances that deftly balanced innocence and knowledge. In the end deference—especially gender deference—was the biggest D of all.[76]

By the time a young woman was chosen Miss Mississippi, she was no stranger to training. The final regimen to which she willingly submitted was typical of those used in the "strong" states of "America," as pageant people called the Miss America system. (The strong states were those most serious about beauty pageants, and, with four Miss Americas to its credit, Mississippi was acknowledged as among the strongest states.) Miss Mississippi was likewise physically strong—or capable of becoming so quickly. Cut off from family and friends, she was literally sequestered—a latter-day Rapunzel—the better for focusing on her goal. For many years this meant moving into the Hopsons's Vicksburg home, often on the very night she was crowned, to begin a preparation crash course marked by rigor and almost religious devotion. With a scant seven weeks left to prepare for the pageant, Miss Mississippi experienced a whirlwind, revved-up finishing school. (Mississippi traditionally held the last of the state pageants, perhaps to accommodate the state's numerous preliminary contests or maybe because this provided knowledge of the competition.) Personal trainers tailored a program of strength training and exercises specific to the swimsuit competition. A low-calorie diet was followed. Water was drunk at every turn. A professional in the contestant's talent area assisted in repeated rounds of rehearsal and critique. Community volunteers took turns grilling her on current events. From the time she arose for her early morning workout until she retired after soaking up the evening news, Miss Mississippi ate, thought, and breathed pageant.[77]

The subterranean economy of beauty expertise was big business in itself, but it supported something even bigger—the southern pageant world. "More is more" might have been pageantry's southern slogan. From Tiny Miss Mosquito to Mrs. Georgia, there were simply more pageants of every persuasion on southern terrain, more independent mom-and-pop operations, more kiddie pageants, more grandma titles, more agricultural contests, and more local prelims to state pageants. There was more participation at ev-

Victoria Carriere (*second from right*) and other seven-year-old contestants
demonstrate their stage projection in a 1998 Queens and Kings of America Pageant
preliminary in Baton Rouge.
PHOTO BY KATHY ANDERSON, COURTESY OF *TIMES-PICAYUNE*.

ery level of pageantry too. More girls entered more preliminaries, and more
of them were willing to enter more than one pageant in pursuit of the state
crown. There was simply more pageantry.[78]

Within this hothouse of competitive beauty, an inevitable cross-
pollination occurred. The same contestants, judges, directors, and beauty
experts encountered one another in endless combinations and venues. For
all its long reach, southern beauty was a small world. The director of one
pageant served as the judge of another; a contestant in one pageant emceed
it the following year; a former pageant director approached a girl as a potential client for her new coaching business; the field director to a state's national preliminary was a frequent local judge. Elsewhere such cozy familiarity might have been branded incestuous, bad beauty business. But within
southern pageantry it was considered smart science, a healthy breeding practice that led to national success. But these were no ordinary hothouse flowers. The same unique microclimate that encouraged beauties to thrive also
forced them to compete; delicate specimens were quickly trampled. If southern beauty was a hotbed, it was one of politics and competition. With its
powerful precinct bosses and grassroots organizers, its practice of patronage,

its long-term strategic planning and last-minute maneuvers, it all added up to a southern beauty machine as formidable as any political counterpart.

The southern beauty machine was most visible at the state level of competition. Contestants in the Miss Mississippi Pageant, for example, quickly came to understand the necessity of repeat competition. Anyone naive enough to think first-time entrants stood a chance of winning was not looking at the total institution of southern pageantry. In "strong" pageant states like Mississippi, pageant directors and judges got national results because they sent only seasoned veterans to Atlantic City. And they meant seasoned veterans *of their state pageant.* "The judges don't even look at you your first year down there," said a Miss Mississippi contestant headed back for her second try.[79] In effect considering each girl's cumulative pageant record, judges pitted contestants not only against one another but against their own previous performances. Should we send her this year? Or send her back for another year of finishing? Did last year's runners-up decide to try again, to risk another year of rejection? Which rookies are back? Demanding that contestants return year after year before they might be selected queen, judges winnowed out those unable or unwilling to sublimate their desires, beliefs, and techniques to those of the system. Rewarding tenacity, competency, and desire but also patience, obedience, and humility, the southern beauty machine fine-tuned pliant contenders and churned up and spat out those unwilling to acquiesce. This explains why, even in those years when a nonsoutherner was chosen Miss America, southern contestants often surrounded her in the Top Ten.

Although some pageant goers disdained "crown chasers"—contestants who entered more than one state pageant in hopes of reaching "Miss A"— contestants trained within the southern beauty machine regarded them merely as professionals. When Tara Dawn Holland, Miss Kansas 1996, was crowned Miss America, news reports noted that she had won the Kansas state title only after three failed attempts down South to win the title of Miss Florida.[80] To southern pageant goers, this maneuver wasn't anything sneaky but simply good strategy; many a southern beauty queen had decamped to where the competition was easier before claiming a coveted title.

It was hard not to love a southern winner. After all, she represented such an investment. Backing the southern beauty machine—that total network of people and pageants responsible for building the better beauty—were more material goods, more sponsors and prizes, bigger budgets, better wardrobes, and higher wattage publicity. In return contestants were more than willing to transform themselves into a neat bundle of boosterism. If the southern beauty machine, with its enviable track record, was willing to back them, they were willing to transform themselves into a saleable product and in turn to promote just about any legitimate saleable goods.

This highly developed system of pageantry was not universally appreciated, however. Outsiders encountering the southern beauty machine in competition for the first time occasionally balked. When Tennessean Kellye Cash, niece of country-and-western singer Johnny, was crowned Miss America 1986, she won in a field of ten finalists, eight of whom hailed from southern states. Veteran pageant watchers were not surprised at this scenario, as southern states had traditionally and consistently dominated national beauty pageants. But to some disgruntled outsiders, this southern success smacked not of the region's mythic grace and charm but of a beauty monopoly. One nonfinalist told reporters that the judges obviously wanted a "sweet kind of non-aggressive Southern belle."[81] Another contestant reportedly remarked, "There ought to be a different category for southern girls. They've been doing this since they were born. They're *professionals*."[82] Some audience members expressed their displeasure more dramatically. When the finalists' names were called, a group of spectators exited the auditorium shouting, "Confederate pageant! Confederate pageant!"[83]

The contestant who could perform it all—the looks, the talent, the deference, the answers, the sparkle, the stamina, the know-how, and the innocence—was said to have "the package." Pageant directors and judges were constantly on the lookout for contestants who possessed the package, and in 1996 Kari Ann Litton was said to have it. Kari Ann was crowned Miss Mississippi in her fifth year of state pageant competition. The word on the street throughout pageant week was that this time she would win it. She deserved to win. "She's really worked for it," people agreed as they discussed her devotion to the contest. It was as if the pageant faithful were saying, "If she loves us this much, enough to come back so many years, we are willing to love her too."

As the week progressed, she became the crowd favorite. Local and statewide newspapers wrote of her persistence and desire. Feature stories detailed her training regimen. In her gingham one-piece, she triumphed in the swimsuit competition. Then, as if to dare the judges to deny her one more time, she sang a torchy nightclub version of "Don't Rain on My Parade." On the final night of the pageant, Kari Ann was victorious, and she clutched her crown, scepter, and roses with the sort of emotion expected of American royalty. With her singular devotion to her goal, her self-denial, her rock-steady faith, and her repeated rebirth, Kari Ann's was a spiritual journey, a beauty vision quest. Throughout it all she had executed with precision the sort of beauty competency southern culture demanded of its women, and many southern women demanded of themselves.

This competency was essentially a repertoire of beauty gestures, attitudes, techniques, and strategies that the woman could perform at will. "A tradition of behaviour," notes memory scholar Paul Connerton, "is unavoidably knowledge of detail."[84] Pageant contestants spoke of having "totally different" wardrobes in "real life." "This is not the real me," many claimed, describing a typical wardrobe of T-shirts, jeans, and baseball caps.[85] Yet the ability to "do pageant," to perform a fairly specific version of femininity, was clearly important to them. As one teenaged pageant veteran explained, "If you don't do Beauty Revue, well, you're just not accepted."[86] Patti Dunham, a Miss Magnolia contender who didn't make it to the state level, vowed to persist in her quest, telling reporters, "There is nothing you cannot improve on."[87] Feminine beauty as an attainable goal was a common tenet among contestants. Miss Mississippi Susan Akin became Miss America in her one hundredth pageant.[88] As the *Pontotoc (Miss.) Progress* noted of the four contestants (a record number) the town had sent to the state pageant in Kari Ann Litton's victorious year, "We send them to win."[89]

For many years the Miss America program successfully deflected criticism about the objectification of women's bodies by pointing to large kitties of cash. After changing its name in 1993 to the Miss America Scholarship Organization, the corporation routinely claimed it was the largest women's scholarship program in the country—ostensible proof its concern lay not with young bodies but with young minds.[90] (Never mind that the winner of each state pageant—not to mention Miss America—typically dropped out of school for a year to fulfill her "reign.") Like Lenora Slaughter's respectability campaign, the scholarship narrative lent the pageant a Teflon quality: in the face of sizeable funding for women's education, criticism that the pageant was an out-of-date skin show simply refused to stick. If the stated total of scholarships on offer—$45 million!—seemed improbable, it was but a minor distraction to pageant faithful, who appeared to view the subject from the general standpoint of pageantry: "Let us believe it because we are ready to believe." It would take comedian John Oliver, host of HBO's *Last Week Tonight* to expose the organization's misleading financial claims. In the space of a single week in 2014, Oliver (as a Brit, unencumbered by any nationalist sentimentality for Miss America) used tax returns to determine that the organization routinely awarded only a tiny fraction of the scholarship monies it implied offering. The discrepancy was traced to creative math on the part of the pageant that included every in-kind and monetary gift "made available" to contestants, a number that dwarfed those actually disbursed. After a flurry of media attention, the pageant world responded with something of a collective shrug: it had never been about the money anyway.[91]

Given the cost of the kind of continuous competition for which southern contestants were known, the scholarship argument had always been a wash. "They give you $1,500 just for going to Miss Mississippi," noted Megan Flowers in 2000. "By the time you purchase all the things that you do, by the time you pay for your pictures and your coaches and all the other things, I feel like I just kind of broke even."[92]

The scholarship argument also failed to explain the presence of wealthy contestants. It did not explain, for example, why Miss Mississippi 1995, Monica Louwerens, a surgeon's daughter and graduate of Wesleyan University, would want to come home to compete to be Miss Mississippi; or why Honey East, the daughter of a prominent car dealer in Jackson, Mississippi, would choose to come home from Harvard the spring semester of her senior year to compete for the same title.[93] Rather, the pursuit of feminine beauty was prized by the culture for accomplishing important work. Although pageant sponsors and officials were perhaps in it for the money, when all was said and done, contestants and spectators talked about the glory, not the goods.

There was glory in a crown. True, the southern beauty machine ran on money—on entrance fees and sponsorships and prizes and advertising sales—but that was not what brought new queens to tears. Rather, it was the realization of a dogged dream, and pageant contenders did not dream alone. With participation in southern pageantry's higher levels of competition came more community support, more recognition at the local level, more booster clubs of family and friends. Queens could count on headlines and feature stories in the weekly hometown paper, maybe even a parade. Because in the small towns where pageantry meant the most, a local queen was still a celebrity; she was still news. After Mikka Lynn Darby was crowned Miss Kentucky 1988, a local company posted signs at the county crossroads to inform motorists they were entering her home county. Magoffin County schools then made plans to dismiss classes for four days (longer than the scheduled winter break) to allow Darby's fans to follow her to Atlantic City for the Miss America pageant.[94] Prior to Melyn Prewett's third trip to compete at Miss Mississippi, she modeled her entire pageant wardrobe in a trunk show held in the Family Life Center of Kosciusko's First Baptist Church. The event, which featured two pageant-connected emcees, warranted a full-page photo spread in the local paper.[95] In small southern towns a queen's reign still commanded attention, and this local meaning was the source of her glory. It all translated into a positive passion for pageants.

"It goes back to the validation from the community," said Leila Holley, Miss University of Alabama 2000, who went on to serve on the pageant committee. "Being raised in a small town, the women I aspired to be like were the garden party women . . . [laughs] a white-glove lady that has tea in the afternoon and that everybody calls about flower arrangements. To a certain extent, these programs help you to prepare to be the woman that you aspire to be. . . . And if you can walk across a stage in an elegant evening gown and answer a question . . . and sing, whether it is beautiful opera or mediocre Broadway, then you can probably handle yourself later in life, whether it's a Junior League committee or hosting a cocktail party in your home." Recalling her participation in a garden club–sponsored children's club, Holley continued, "I remember being four or five years old. . . . I learned what a woman is supposed to do. I think that has changed in most of the country. Here, women still aspire to be southern ladies."[96]

CHAPTER 3

Hoop Dreams

FIFTEEN MINUTES BEFORE CURTAIN THE SCENE INSIDE THE CITY AU-
ditorium in Natchez, Mississippi, was nothing if not familiar. Teenage girls in
hoopskirts glided about. Small boys in knee breeches rolled wooden hoops.
A young man unfurled a Confederate flag. Tourists milled about, smiling
with uncertainty and expectation. At the dawn of the twenty-first century,
it was almost time for another Confederate Pageant, the city's venerated
tourist production. Although some details had been altered over the years,
the spirit and the substance of the performance, known to locals as simply
"the pageant," had not changed in generations. In Natchez continuity was
paramount.[1]

The lights dimmed, and the crowd grew silent. An emcee welcomed visitors to the city, presented the president of the Natchez Garden Club and
her escort, and pointed out that the pageant's "entire cast is local." Then he
leaped backward into a land that time forgot. "Step into the past with Natchez," he implored, and with each phrase the prospect grew more enchanting
if not more plausible. "Romance, grandeur, chivalry, wealth . . . adventure,
action, boldness, strength—all these are Natchez." He then depicted an antebellum wonderland peopled by the likes of Aaron Burr, Jefferson Davis,
and Andrew Jackson. The so-called five flags of Natchez were mentioned,
evidence of the city's cosmopolitan history. Not only the "oldest settlement
on the Mississippi River" but one with "more millionaires for its population
than any other city in America," Natchez, the emcee emphasized, was an
"early magnet for men with a lust for life . . . a bustling river town full of passion, power, and paradise."[2]

But mostly, it seemed, Natchez was a place of refinement. At house parties and garden parties, dances and weddings, even the hunt, early Natchezians "enjoyed life," and what a charmed life it seemed. "Before the War between the States, times were different," the emcee reminded the audience; Natchez was a place of "rustling silks, fluttering fans, and the perfume of lovely gardens. . . . Come tonight and visit this world," he urged, adding, "Before the war it was a world unto itself."[3]

Antebellum Natchez may or may not have been a world apart, but one thing is certain: the version Natchezians performed for tourists for more than eighty years represented a past apart. In tableaux presented between 1932 and 2014, the elite of Natchez enacted a ritual of remembrance, a heritage of their own persuasion. In this romantic fantasy the city was a place of gentility, festivity, and harmonious social relations. Commitment to this portrayal presented representational challenges over the years (African Americans were conspicuously absent by the 1960s, having rejected earlier roles as happy cotton pickers) but none were deemed insurmountable. To wit: a full decade into the twenty-first century, imaginative resourcefulness yet prevailed. An overdue reworking of the script in 2007 had reinstated African American Natchezians to the story beside their White counterparts, but the production still depicted only the most cherished moments and notable personages in the city's history—and not all the Blacks mentioned in the script were represented onstage. In this dreamy rendition of the southern past, all the women were ladies, all the men were gentry, and all the Blacks were exceptional. William Johnson, the free Black "Barber of Natchez," at last shared the narrative (if not the boards) with early explorers like Hernando de Soto and Robert de La Salle, and the unusual tale of Abdul Rahman Ibrahima, the African prince enslaved in Natchez for forty years, was told in turn with the stories of visiting luminaries like naturalist John James Audubon and opera's "Swedish nightingale," Jenny Lind. These were welcome changes to a production that had long featured a cast improbably White and a story simply improbable. But in the end loyalty to a "best and brightest" formula failed to truly integrate the Natchez story, neglected to recount the ways that the region's social hierarchies and central institution—slavery—had wrought tragedies as well as glories. The diversity on display remained skin-deep, a superficial show that concealed as much about the city as it revealed.[4]

But who had time to ponder such details when there was such spectacle to behold? As in earlier productions, all the children were dancers, and be-

tween the cancan, the Virginia reel, and the sweetheart waltz there was little room for realism. Rather, romance remained the watchword, and connection with a fabled past the imaginative goal. Everyone did their part: from
preschoolers wrapping the maypole in spring colors, to teenagers performing
the Virginia reel, to middle-aged men toasting the hunt to the strains of "My
Old Kentucky Home," the pageant evoked enchantment and proclaimed
gentility. In this context a vignette added in 2007 to diversify the production—an African American soloist's "Ole Man River"—fit seamlessly into
the show. For participants and spectators intent on reverie, the historical record had never presented a serious obstacle. Given Confederate-themed tableaux including "A Natchez Bride for Jefferson Davis" (Varina Howell was
a local belle) and waltzing cadets on the eve of war, one would never have
guessed, for instance, that Natchez had largely opposed secession. From a
central civic space, Natchezians had long ago fashioned a sacred space: a site
for simultaneously constructing regional identity and reiterating local status
through the gendered performance of nostalgia.[5]

The approach had eventually placed the production out of step with
trends in public history. Whereas at many historical sites, the stories told
about the southern past had undergone revision to give voice to enslaved
persons as well as slaveholders, the Natchez pageant in the early twenty-first
century still delivered something less—something too little, too late—to
make representational amends.[6] While no longer the unapologetic holdout
that had continued presenting the Old South as a full-blown "moonlight and
magnolias" myth for decades beyond credibility and public acceptance, the
reworked pageant was no revisionist production either. Black Natchezians
no longer appeared onstage picking cotton and eating watermelon, as they
had in early years of the production, and they were no longer completely absent, as they had been since the 1960s. But in something of a dramatic sleight
of hand, the revised pageant managed to include a few African Americans in
the cast while maintaining a characterization of the southern past that was
alternately dreamy and upbeat. By slotting African American cameos into
the existing narrative of romance and exceptionalism, the pageant managed
an onstage color adjustment without a corresponding shift in interpretation.
The radical rewrite that would have infused the production with emotion
and complexity by incorporating slavery into the script was nowhere to be
found. Granted, the pageant was no historical site (the garden clubs called
it simply "an entertainment"), but it was a tourist display, and by virtue of
its very name claimed legitimacy for the story it told.[7] Presenting one imag-

inative version of the past—the happy, benevolent South—while eschewing others, the pageant endeavored to determine public memory. But, given the shifting landscape of heritage tourism, such static representation produced as much unease as comfort. It was one thing for the pageant to have celebrated the Confederacy and sentimentalized slavery back in the early 1930s, when such Lost Cause celebrations were popular and undisputed even by most historians, but quite another for the production in the early years of the twenty-first century to so eerily resemble the original.

Perhaps recognition of this on some level was responsible for the hint of decline that hovered over the festivities. For all the theatrics, the exuberance seemed a bit contrived, the fanfare a little fake. A glance about the in-the-round auditorium confirmed there were as many seats empty as filled, even among the prominent box seats reserved for pilgrimage "royalty" and their guests. What's more, the sense of waning enthusiasm seemed to emanate as much from the participants as the audience. For every beaming septuagenarian, there was a teenager looking a little bored. For every garden club member basking in her finery, there was a spectator looking apprehensive. But in the end form prevailed: the clock struck eight, the actors rallied, and the Old South came alive once more.[8]

For those invested in the performance—audience and actors alike—imaginative dividends abounded. Through consumption of this ordered world, spectators could reaffirm ideas about the southern past they had long held dear; for some Whites in the audience, it was a chance to reaffirm their southernness. Performers did this and more, reminding spectators of Natchez's place in southern legend and themselves and other locals of their place in Natchez society. This was as it had been since 1932, the year two local, private women's clubs started the pageant as part of Natchez's "Spring Home and Garden Pilgrimage." A site for the construction of regional identity, the pageant over the years maintained a remarkably consistent enactment. This was no mistake. With continuity of performance comes continuity of memory, and with continuity of memory comes connection with the past. So, upon conclusion of the emcee's prologue, the Confederate Pageant opened once more in much the same manner that it had for decades.[9]

A pair of adolescent girls in elaborate petticoats introduced the audience to the evening's production and its amateur nature. To tinkling recorded music the girls teetered and turned, silently "announcing" the first of numerous tableaux through enormous title cards. Locals knew that their selection as "placard bearers" indicated hard work and high status on the part of their mothers.[10] Suddenly—Indians! Or at least the ominous sound of tom-toms seemed so to threaten. But Great Sun, chief of the Natchez Indians, was but a lanky, shuffling youth, quickly dispatched. In a kaleidoscope of music, color, and motions, he was supplanted by a host of stock characters representing Natchez's five dominions before landing spectators safely back on U.S. soil to the strains of "Yankee Doodle Dandy."

Civics lesson safely dispensed with, the pageant turned to the performers' preferred topic: themselves. This festive ritual was as much about the contemporary South as the Old and about Natchez in particular. In truth the pageant was a performance on two levels—one for the tourists, the other for the citizenry of Natchez. On the surface was the happy plantation South of legend, the unabashedly dreamy one of belles and beaux, parties and dances, the one that kept the tour buses coming and the pageant tickets selling. But hidden in plain sight was a simultaneous performance of local knowledge, a coded ritual of social status that any insider could read at a glance. With participation structured by a ranking system that combined honor of lineage with reward for club work, and roles and costumes signifying a cachet apparent only to participants, the pageant was as much choreography of the local social structure as Old South display. Key to both productions was the stylized rendition of regional gender icons. While, unlike in sorority rush and beauty pageants, physical beauty was not especially important to participation, the Confederate Pageant most explicitly tied region and remembrance to gender performance, especially feminine performance. Women controlled both the social and touristic structures of the city, and it was renditions of the lady and the belle—receiving at tour homes, appearing in the pageant, featured in advertising campaigns—that pervaded the Natchez imaginary. Through credible performances of the gracious southern lady, the flirtatious belle, and their masculine counterpart, the courtly southern gentleman, Natchezians not only produced the pageant fiction that served as imaginative mechanism but also drove the financial success of the pilgrimage while reinforcing their own real-life privilege. Only Natchezians of a certain standing might promenade in silks and hoops; in turn nothing quite so well demonstrated continuity with the past social order as ritual performance of antebellum gender figures. On the Natchez stage caste determined cast, and cast reiterated caste. As a result, Natchezians of a certain ilk performed *belle* and *lady* and *gentleman* as if their lives depended on it. In social and financial senses, it did.

The atmosphere turned expectant at the start of the final tableau: the

Natchez Garden Club queen
Diague Gadbois and king
Hugh Stahlman, 1962.
MABEL LANE COLLECTION,
HISTORIC NATCHEZ FOUNDATION.

lights dimmed to near blackness, the floor emptied, and the crowd grew silent. Quietly at first, then louder, came the slow strains of "Dixie." Swelling, the tune segued into the theme from "Gone with the Wind." Then—suddenly!—an adolescent boy, lit only by a spotlight, tore across the floor, waving an enormous Confederate battle flag so vigorously it crackled and snapped. The lights went up, "Dixie" filled the hall, and the king of the pilgrimage entered the room.

At the opposite end of the auditorium, the stage curtain rose to reveal the queen of the pilgrimage and her court, arrayed and waiting. Except for her sparkling tiara and glittering wand, the queen looked like nothing if not a bride. In a white, rhinestone-encrusted gown and train, the queen slowly circled the floor with her king, periodically pausing to wave a wand over willing subjects. The evening concluded with a formal presentation: "Ladies and Gentleman: The Queen of the Natchez Pilgrimage."[11]

Rivaling the production in artifice and romance is the often-told history of the Natchez Pilgrimage. Just as the pageant emphasized plantation legend over plantation details, the garden clubs of Natchez perpetuated a myth of origins worthy of one of their own pageant narratives. According to local lore, in the spring of 1931, the fledgling Natchez Garden Club offered to host the annual convention of the Mississippi Federation of Garden Clubs. A tour of old-fashioned gardens was promised, but an unexpected late freeze spoiled those plans. With little else on hand to amuse their guests, the club hastily arranged a tour of old houses instead.[12]

Or so the story goes. But historians have suggested there was no freeze that weekend in 1931, and that club members had planned all along to showcase their town's remarkable collection of homes.[13] "The first regular state convention of the Mississippi Garden Club was to be held in Natchez that year (1931) and we had been asked to arrange four garden tours for the visitors," recalled pilgrimage founder Katherine Grafton Miller in an interview thirty years later. "Realizing that Natchez at that time really had no well-kept gardens to show, I impulsively sat down and wrote to the state secretary of the club and said that we wanted to show our houses instead."[14] By making their start sound like luck rather than pluck, like serendipity rather than strategy, the Natchez Garden Club employed an image of feminine passivity as the cover story for their "masculine" public success.[15] It was a gendered tactic the club would perfect as the pilgrimage grew to dominate the financial and public life of Natchez.

In fact, the background of the Natchez Garden Club is fairly straightforward. The club was chartered in 1927 as a civic improvement organization concerned with the beautification, preservation, and perpetuation of the "memory of the lives, traditions and accomplishments of the people" of the Natchez territory.[16] Over the years it proved influential, responsible for reviving the city's flagging economy through tourism.[17] If the living in pre–Civil War Natchez was lush—a robust cotton economy based on land and slaves saw eleven of the country's seventy-five millionaires making their homes there in 1850—the postbellum scene was equally dire, with soldiers returning to find their homes intact but their wealth depleted. Natchez remained in economic and architectural decay until 1931, when the fledgling Natchez Garden Club got the idea—initially pooh-poohed by local businessmen—of showing the homes.

"People lived surrounded by rare furniture and tax collector's bills," wrote David L. Cohn in *Atlantic Monthly*. "Their cupboards were filled with old silver and little to eat. But the town had a Past—a Past that was, if you will, romantic."[18] It was an inspiration that would ultimately resuscitate the city, as tour proceeds enabled homeowners to gradually repair and maintain the homes around which a multimillion-dollar tourism industry would evolve. Indeed, from its inception the club took the lead in local preserva-

Early Natchez Garden Club members at Green Leaves, circa 1932.
HISTORIC NATCHEZ FOUNDATION.

tion efforts, purchasing endangered landmarks and dilapidated structures of architectural or historical significance. With more extant antebellum homes than any U.S. city except Williamsburg, Virginia, Natchez is an architectural treasure, a densely packed site of urban prewar structures. Although the garden clubs maintained nominal programs dedicated to beautification and horticulture, it was antebellum homes that distinguished Natchez, and thus they that received the lion's share of members' money and attention.

Practically from the start the annual spring pilgrimage emerged as the Natchez Garden Club's major project and central organizing principle: a means of preserving both the city's unrivaled collection of homes and the local social structure. The first pilgrimage of 1932 saw the club go all out to attract tourists at the height of the Depression. The club's fifty-seven members wrote feature stories for garden club publications, newspapers, trade magazines, travel bureaus, and automobile associations—anyplace they might get free publicity. They organized tours, sold tickets, fashioned decorations, and made costumes. They planned historical tableaux and a parade, a barbecue and cotillion, a pageant and "Confederate Ball."[19] With business acumen and ambition safely cloaked in the feminine guise of hospitality, the garden club members of Natchez fairly leaped off their pedestals—while giving the appearance of having done nothing of the sort.

When the garden club tallied its receipts, members realized they had entertained some 1,500 visitors from thirty-seven states—an overwhelming success.[20] Plans for an encore were quickly made. But a dispute over how to divide revenues led a disgruntled faction to form the rival Pilgrimage Garden Club. Putting on their first solo pilgrimage in 1937, the club touched off a head-to-head competition with the Natchez Garden Club, which would not officially end until 1946 and would continue to resonate long afterward. Dubbed "The Battle of the Hoopskirts," the rivalry over attracting tourists to separate, back-to-back pilgrimages resulted in brainstorming for publicity, barnstorming for ticket sales, and meeting more than a few times in court before it was all over.[21] Competition may not be ladylike, but the southern lady image again provided the perfect foil. Competing hoop to hoop, the two groups entered into a fierce fray in which each attempted to outbelle the other. In the end the real winner of the extended skirmish was the city itself, as Natchezians of all sorts realized the profit potential in selling the Old South.

In Natchez only the past could be the future. Profit, pride, and social place all depended on the ability of Natchezians to transport visitors to an imaginative space of regional identification, one based on collective memories of race and class privilege. At a time when a popular guidebook series urged Americans to "See America First"—to deepen their sense of national unity by viewing the sites of revolution and westward expansion (an itinerary that by necessity skipped the southern settings of slavery altogether)— Natchez and other southern cities instead lured tourists with quite different assurances. The promise of experiencing White privilege lost was enough to attract nostalgic pilgrims who wished to "See Dixie First."[22]

Travel writers wrote sweeping stories about springtime celebrations from Virginia to Texas, while society-page editors published detailed accounts of the women who embarked on garden tours of the Deep South to see the azaleas in Mobile, the camellias in New Orleans, the magnolias in Natchez, and the bluebonnets in Austin.[23] "Step into the past and re-live the romantic pleasure-filled days 'befo de Wah,' urged advertisements for the Gordon C. Greene packet ship to Natchez.[24] "Enjoy the South This Spring," suggested the Standard Fruit and Steamship Company of New Orleans in an advertisement linking the New Orleans Spring Fiesta with home and garden tours in

Pop culture imagery sold a
romanticized Old South.
HISTORIC AMERICAN SHEET MUSIC
COLLECTION, RUBENSTEIN LIBRARY,
DUKE UNIVERSITY, DURHAM.

Natchez and Vicksburg and azalea trails in Mobile and Lafayette.[25] Visitors
would "thrill to the enchantment of many Southern scenes . . . rooted in tradition and immortalized in fiction," promised the Alabama State Planning
Commission.[26]

A growing pilgrimage movement provided an organizational framework
for selling and seeing southern sites. The term "pilgrimage" refers to a con-
templative journey to a sacred destination, and the South had no shortage
of those.[27] With its abundance of antebellum homes, Confederate relics, and
Civil War battle sites, the South welcomed wistful travelers set on transformation in the presence of holy shrines. Buoyed by the success of the Garden
Club of Virginia's inaugural Historic Garden Week of 1929, which raised
funds for the restoration of Gen. Robert E. Lee's birthplace, Stratford Hall,
by opening notable gardens to the fee-paying public, garden clubs across the
region tried their hand at similar ventures. One of the first to adopt the concept was the Natchez Garden Club.[28]

The Old South experience on offer in Natchez was particularly intense—
saturated with visual symbols and concentrated geographically—but was
otherwise just an exceptionally successful memory project of the sort White
southerners had undertaken for decades. In the touristic marketplace of seg-

regated "Dixie," New South success meant enacting Old South myths, and
so Natchez presented an unparalleled performance of the same. Employing
the city's unrivaled collection of antebellum homes as its stage set, the elite
of Natchez mounted a production of Whiteness worthy of consumption, circulation, and remembrance. As home and garden pilgrimages and historical
pageants grew in popularity across the nation alongside White Americans'
increasing unease over shifting social relations, Natchez staged these productions and more. Presenting visitors with the sights, sounds, smells, ambiance, and tastes of the Old South, Natchez was a sensory oasis of the remembered past, a place of gracious hospitality and arrested social relations,
where travelers could step back in time and indulge themselves in "feeling
southern." "Natchez," noted David L. Cohn, "promised old gardens, mag-
nificent ante-bellum homes, spiritual-singing Negroes, the Mississippi River,
mint juleps, magnolias, moonlight on the levee, fried chicken, and the Quality receiving their paying guests clad in hoopskirts, with Cape jessamines
in their hair. All this spelled Romance to the people of the corn and wheat
states, and the grimy industrial Northeast; it was the stuff of which Hollywood dreams are made."[29]

Local leaders set the tone. In *The Pink Edition*, an annual pilgrimage
guide published by the *Natchez Democrat*, club historian Edith Wyatt Moore
described tour homes in ornate prose, emphasizing the distinguished Confederate service of the original occupants and the miraculous recovery of
items thought lost to the Civil War. The genealogy of homeowners received
lengthy treatment—particularly as it demonstrated, however tenuously, Natchez links to European aristocracy.

A chief feature of the Wyatt Moore article was the depiction of women
and slaves within the homes. Stylized representations of gender and race
were central to constructing a resplendent past and promoting an imaginative connection to it. The Natchez matron was typically depicted as a "great"
or even "renowned" beauty, a member of the Daughters of the American
Revolution or United Daughters of the Confederacy (or both)—every bit
the southern lady but also a creature of special fortitude and ingenuity. In
Wyatt Moore articles (as in local lore), the Natchez lady, left alone during
"the War," outsmarted the Yankees and then defied them during the "dark
days of Reconstruction." A story on the tour home Monteigne suggests the
Wyatt Moore style: "Due to Mrs. Martin's quick wit and fine spirit one of
the huge mirrors remains intact today. As this mirror was being carried from
her home it is said that she seized a stone and faced the vandals with defiance

Pilgrimage founder Katherine Grafton Miller, circa 1940. CALLON COLLECTION, HISTORIC NATCHEZ FOUNDATION.

saying as she did so that they might take the mirror, but if they moved another step she'd shatter it to bits. They evidently realized her seriousness."[30]

Nearly every story highlighted the presence of the loyal Black servant. As important to the construction of Whiteness as the refined southern lady in her antebellum home was the presence in that same home of subservient Blackness. Pilgrimage stories of the era put Black people in their place. An article on Elgin Place took readers on a guided tour of the home, then lingered in the dining room, "the oldest part of the house," where "a main feature of interest in the dining room is the punkah—a hand-hewn oaken fan suspended above the table. It was the duty of a small negro child to pull the punkah cord and keep the flies away in those days before the use of screens."[31] Wyatt Moore represented a modern visit to Natchez as a "return to the garden," a theme generally adopted by travel writers. Describing the "lushness of the foliage" and the "enveloping fragrance," she suggested a visit to Natchez as a means of stepping back into another world.[32]

Pilgrimage founder Katherine Grafton Miller took the Natchez story on the road, traveling to more than seventy-five U.S. cities to deliver her "illustrated talk" to garden clubs, civic groups, and church meetings. Dressed in antebellum costume and armed with tinted slides, Miller transfixed audiences with her depiction of "Natchez, Where the Old South Still Lives."[33] Garnering free publicity was a key tactic in Miller's strategy to grow the pilgrimage, one in which she was extraordinarily successful. If no representative of the press attended her lecture, Miller visited the local newspaper office and invited the journalists on hand to visit Natchez, an invitation many ultimately accepted. Radio programmers received similar advances from Miller, who in a 1934 letter asked announcers from Oklahoma City to Boston and Chicago to Galveston whether they might publicize a "unique entertainment . . . called 'Pilgrimage Week'"—at no cost to the club? With her romantic presentation, persistence, and personal touch, Miller trained the national spotlight on Natchez, and tourism increased apace.[34]

Back home club members maintained a lower profile but matched Miller in assertiveness and aspiration. Given a growing tourism base and the popularity of Old South imagery, the Natchez Garden Club began to think ever bigger. Publicity in those days stemmed from personal correspondence, and garden club members knew nothing if not the art of exchanging letters, notes, and calls. Building on their highly developed understanding of etiquette and the region's reputation for hospitality, the Natchez Garden Club undertook a letter-writing campaign that might best be termed a charm offensive, so powerless did the media appear before it. Club members aimed high and soon had celebrities, editors, reporters, and filmmakers flocking to Natchez, and all things Natchez circulating out across the nation.

National radio programs were among the club's first conquests, beginning with the *Maxwell House Show Boat*, an NBC Radio variety show that broadcast coast to coast in the early thirties. With its sentimentality for the "simpler times" of the Old South and its cast pairing fictional Blackface characters like deckhands "Molasses" and "January" with real-life radio personalities, *Show Boat* was the perfect venue for marketing the pilgrimage. Garden club members convinced the *Wrigley Program, Garden Club of the Air*, the *Esso Reporter*, and other syndicated shows to feature the pilgrimage, and the major networks to run announcements. Buoyed by success, the club approached motion picture producers about filming short features in the city. In 1939 Natchez took to the big screen in *The March of Time* newsreels and in nostalgia-drenched travelogues like *Going Places with Graham McNamee*. After Metro-Goldwyn Mayer filmed a full-length, Technicolor episode of *James A. FitzPatrick's Traveltalks* the same year, it was recorded in five languages and shown in theaters around the globe. The Natchez scenes in Fitz-

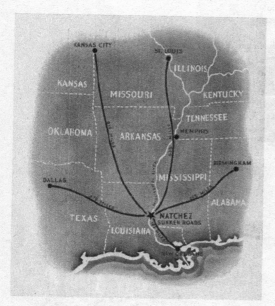

Pilgrimage organizers across the South beckoned automobile tourists with maps emphasizing the ease of travel and proximity. Map to Natchez, Mississippi.
COURTESY OF MEREDITH CORPORATION, *BETTER HOMES AND GARDENS*, © 1938.

Patrick's film attracted major directors, who visited the city to shoot exterior scenes for *Gone with the Wind*, *Suwanee*, and *Show Boat*.[35]

Publications and programs aimed at motorists routinely waxed nostalgic on the subject of Natchez. "Turn Back the Clock," urged the *Pittsburgh Automobilist*, while *Ford News* extolled the "dreamlike quality" of Natchez, and *Buick Magazine* recommended a trip to Natchez down the "Road to Yesteryear." After viewing the "rich gleam of old polished woods, the sheen of fine silver, the luster of handsome china, all reflected in the mahogany and white woodwork of these private residences . . . you will feel yourself in another age," testified *Pure Oil News*. In 1940, the year proclaimed "Travel America Year" by President Franklin D. Roosevelt, the Automobile Association of America's *Touring Reporter* radio show likened the "relics and furnishings" of Natchez to those in *Gone with the Wind*. At a time when long-distance automobile touring was no longer limited to the elite and upper-middle classes, tour companies published maps showing how simple it was to get from, say, New York to Natchez. *Better Homes and Gardens* published a map of *Southern Azalea Trails*, while tour companies employed silhouettes of Blackface field hands and carriage-riding gentry to promote their "Land Cruises to the Deep South."[36]

Mary Regina Prothero and
Tommie Piazza at Devereux,
circa 1940.
CALLON COLLECTION, HISTORIC
NATCHEZ FOUNDATION.

National feature stories followed the local lead, depicting the city as a place suspended in time and peopled by benevolent homeowners and contented Black servants. A Baton Rouge writer assured potential tourists that they "will be greeted by hostesses clad in the billowing skirts, laces and jewels of another era, carefully preserved in lavender-scented chests and taken out only for this occasion. Assisting the mistress of the house will be perhaps a shrunken little Negro mammy who vaguely remembers slave days and who will tell you proudly that she reared two or three generations of the children in the 'big house.'"[37]

Especially after the release of David O. Selznick's 1939 film, feature stories on Natchez baldly appealed to the international craze for *Gone with the Wind*: "Here, say the hostesses of Natchez, is where the Old South still lives, where Melanie and Ashley and Miss Pitty Pat are not anachronisms, where the amber sunlight of Mississippi has caught and preserved in minute detail a way of life which elsewhere has gone with the wind."[38]

Riding the crest of Hollywood success, the Natchez Garden Club convinced an illustrious lineup of publications to feature Natchez—and often to publicize the pilgrimage for free. When club members wrote to the *Satur-*

Old South Perfumers' advertisement for Old South Toiletries,
in *Ladies' Home Journal*, 1947.

day Evening Post, the magazine responded by sending celebrated photographer Ivan Dmitri to shoot a color spread. Stories in *Vogue, Antiques, House and Garden, Mademoiselle, Better Homes and Gardens*, and *Nature* followed. Gordon Lloyd, official photographer for Cypress Gardens in Florida, visited Natchez to shoot a feature for *Holiday* magazine, and photographer W. R. Culver materialized on behalf of *National Geographic*. Actors Mary Pickford, Gale Gordon, and Buddy Rogers; war correspondent Ernie Pyle; auto maker Henry Ford; industrialist John D. Rockefeller; and Gen. Douglas MacArthur all visited the city, attracting celebrities, politicos, and other notables eager to bask in the glamour of antebellum romance. When humorist and Random House publisher Bennett Cerf visited Natchez, he enjoyed a moveable feast, visiting Ravenna, Green Leaves, and Dunleith in a steady round of hospitality.[39]

Licensing agreements meant that Natchez—rather difficult to get to in real life—needed never be far away. Old South Toiletries included a "Natchez Rose Jar" in the boxed collections of powders and colognes it produced in New York and promoted to wistful consumers across the nation in magazines like *Vogue* and *Mademoiselle*. The Natchez Garden Club even convinced Gorham, the silver manufacturer, to design a flatware pattern in honor of Natchez. In a massive national advertising campaign that featured lavish illustrations and a three-dimensional point-of-sale display of the tour home by the same name, Gorham introduced "Melrose" to U.S. consumers. Spode quickly followed suit with Melrose china. Pennsylvania-based Westmoreland Glass Company reproduced pressed-glass plates using Melrose and Mount Repose in their designs. Tomlinson introduced a Natchez furniture line, *House and Garden* sponsored the design of a Natchez bedspread, and Nelly Don brought out a line of spring dresses inspired by the city's native flowers. Mobil Oil distributed calendars picturing Natchez scenes, while Pure Oil service stations offered travelers complete information about the pilgrimage. Congress-brand playing cards featured Natchez belles in front of antebellum homes.[40]

Upon arrival in Natchez, travelers encountered local people and a landscape prepared to deliver on the White promise. With some three dozen grand homes providing the architectural backdrop, lush vegetation engulfing the senses, and costumed residents punctuating the scene, travelers found it easy to step back in time. The city's antebellum mansions, with their antique furniture, china, and silver; verdant gardens; and intriguing storylines, provided curious tourists a rare peek at vanished times. But as much as the stuff of the past, Natchezians' routine performance of unaltered race and gender conventions immersed visitors in a strange, dreamlike place as fantastic as it was alluring. Women in hoopskirts received guests in stately homes, assisted by deferential Black servants, while Black women in bright head rags sold homemade candies nearby. Beginning in 1940 visitors could lunch at Mammy's Cupboard, a twenty-eight-foot-tall concrete structure containing a diner inside wide skirts. Local merchants peddled mementos—photographic booklets, souvenir plates—and urged visitors to "Have Your Photograph Taken While You Are in Costume." Katherine Grafton Miller herself assured travelers that they would experience "special entertainments . . . period balls illuminated by the soft light of candles, sorties and musicales, Negro spirituals, chicken barbecue suppers amid plantation songs and dances. . . . Everywhere you will find the costumes and customs of antebellum days." For travelers so inclined, it was a seductive milieu, the perfect environment for going southern. Wistful sojourners could act out the old ways of old days, luxuriating in the accentuated gender and race differences suggested by genteel tableaux on the one hand and Blackface iconography on the other. Romancing the old order on the stage and in the street, Natchezians and their guests scrambled time, performing and consuming an Old South perfected by remembrance.[41]

The environment was so complete and the ambiance so convincing that, as opposition to Jim Crow gathered steam across the nation, Natchez quickly emerged as a symbol and a platform for White southerners dead set against social and political equality for Black people. In 1948, as the Dixiecrat Party coalesced around opposition to President Harry S. Truman's support of civil rights, Natchez made easy shifts: from site of passive resistance to one of massive resistance and from static tableaux to active performance. Mississippi governor Fielding Wright chose a mass meeting of "Jeffersonian Democrats" at the Adams County Courthouse for broadcasting his "States' Rights" address—and southern belle appearances for validating White supremacy. Denouncing Truman's civil rights proposals by day and inserting daughter Elaine in the Confederate Pageant by night, Wright paired White femininity with White fury. Other politicians followed suit. Natchez native Mary Louise Kendall, chair of the women's division of the state Democratic Party and its States' Rights Campaign, noted, "Women of Mississippi are well aware of the stake they have in this fight for the preservation of ideals and traditions dear to the South." But the most persuasive act of all came from the belles of Natchez themselves. Arriving at the state capitol to extend pilgrimage invitations to Governor Wright and members of the legislature, three teenaged beauties in antebellum garb brought the business of government to a standstill as secretaries, legislators, and visitors crowded the corridors to get a glimpse of the Confederate emissaries. As a bit of political theater, it was powerful play. Governor Wright smiled broadly, accepting their invitation to wild applause. He could not have asked for better figureheads for segregation than three living, breathing southern belles from "Natchez, Where the Old South Still Lives."[42]

Visitors were sometimes unprepared for Natchez. They would pile off their tour buses ready to take in the sights—to marvel at sumptuous decor, indulge in regional repast, and pick up a trinket or two. But they often arrived ill-equipped for the single-minded re-creation of a bygone age they encountered. In one mansion after another, hoopskirted tour guides received them with a seriousness they had not expected. Neither hurried nor hustled as they moved from room to room, tourists ("our guests") were treated as if visiting by special invitation. Pointing out the furniture, draperies, paintings, and woodwork with thoroughness and precision, hosts approached their task with an air of quiet stewardship. Considering their close ties to the homes, this was not surprising. The treasures of Natchez may have encapsulated a particular era and an entire region's way of life, but they were also intensely personal, familial keepsakes that linked local generations and anchored them in place. Through preservation and narration Natchez tour guides took simultaneous care of personal and regional pasts.

Objects and images are conduits of memory, devices through which memories are shared, produced, and circulated. In the process they become imbued with cultural meaning. Memory attaches itself to specific objects, images, and places, and in turn these things become central to calling up cultural memory. Collectors, meanwhile, make meaning by possessing and controlling objects, by securing, sorting, selecting, grouping, and displaying stuff with deliberation. Collections promise totality, the defeat of time, the possibility of representing lost worlds. The curated display captures particular times, places, identities, and entire ways of life. In modern Natchez the confluence of preservation, performance, narration, and display created a perfect spell of remembrance, a conspiracy of referents and reverence that amounted to a sacred space.[43]

In the resurrection season, against a background of spring air, fresh blooms, and homesteads consecrated by considerable living, Natchez pilgrimage tours could take on a spiritual quality associated with sacred journeys. Preserved like sacraments in china cabinets, basements, attics, and steamer trunks were remnants of particular lives and a regional past that assumed iconic status among pilgrims. For if "pilgrimage" is a religious term, the almost daily recitation of local finery and finishes was a litany of privilege, an incantation that with each repetition recalled the southern past as fabled golden age. To hosts and guests alike, the ritual of receiving, with its predictable pattern of query and response, was a catechism of sorts, a chance to recall and reconnect with the past by dwelling on relics. To supplicants prepared to receive them, the domestic objects of Natchez were sacraments of a revered southern past and, as such, central instruments of memory.[44]

Tourists often joked that Natchezians were "living in the past," but one thing is certain: those associated with the pilgrimage lived *with* the past to an extent unimaginable to most. If Natchezians were possessed by the past, perhaps this was in part because they possessed the stuff of it in profusion. "We don't part with anything," is the way Virginia Beltzhoover Morrison, the third generation in her family to own Green Leaves, once put it. Inside tour homes museum-quality collections of empire, rococo, and federal furniture cohabited with hand-painted china attributed to John James Audubon, the celebrated naturalist. An oil portrait of Confederate vice president Alexander Stephens was set off by Baccarat crystal and Sevres sconces. Scrapbooks of southern generals lay open, framed letters signed by Sam Houston and Jefferson Davis lined the walls, and ancestors' Confederate uniforms hid behind the door. For pilgrims keen to commune with the southern past, these were the belongings that conjured belonging.[45]

But just out of sight of the official tours were mementos that meant as much or more to homeowners. Behind the velvet ropes were private remnants that too served as conduits of memory. In addition to the family portraits, silver collections, period textiles, and finely carved cornices were abundant assortments of stuff both less notable and more precious, the odds and ends of a past at once familial and regional—and so too meaningful to toss. In rooms off-limits to tourists, the ordinary trappings of contemporary life shared space with keepsakes both personal and specific to Natchez. Bookcases burst with dolls. Pieces of dainty French porcelain covered every flat surface. A hundred teddy bears, antique and modern, held court. Roof finials and dolls' limbs lined basement shelves. The past piled up in Natchez, in ways unfathomable to most. Whereas in some places heritage homes were essentially museums, many Natchez homes had been owned and inhabited by the same family continuously for upward of 150 years. Tour homeowners sat on the same furniture and ate off the same china as their great-great-grandparents. "Most of these things would lose their meaning if they were taken out of the house," noted Morrison. "They don't really belong to us." With stewardship came responsibility. As Alma Carpenter, of the Elms, liked to put it, "I don't know if I own this house or it owns me." New Orleans antiques dealer Peter Patout called owners of historical homes, "the caretakers of the history of their own families and of the South itself."[46]

To confuse matters further the authentic and the fake coexisted, with the visual and material cues of antebellum Natchez and those of its long-running commemorative production, pilgrimage, converging. In the attic of the Elms, aged hoopskirts lined the walls, but what at first glance appeared to be antebellum relics turned out to date back only to early pilgrimages of the Depression era. A Scarlett O'Hara doll perched on a genuine Parisian parlor suite from the 1830s. Natchezians could be egalitarian in their fondness for southern mementos, as pleased with commercial keepsakes as with authentic heirlooms. Perhaps after a time the facts and fantasies of the southern past ran together, each as useful as the other in responding to tourists. Scholar Michael Bowman found that many tour guides at southern plantation museums treated the facts of southern history as mere suggested starting points for bringing a tour home to life. Posing teasing questions about the homes to tourists and then answering their own riddles by stringing together anecdotes about architectural design, construction, and furnishings, the tour guides he observed encouraged a sense of wonder about the Old South. When the recitation of factual details got stale, guides sometimes amused themselves and one another by improvising and embellishing the stories they told, spinning patently ludicrous yarns about the rarified provenance of quite ordinary objects or delivering spiels laced with contempt for certain audiences, like, say, Yankees. In narration the past and present, familial and regional, authentic and fake mingled in pleasurable temporal confusion. As Robert Penn Warren noted, "When one is happy in forgetfulness, facts get forgotten."[47]

Visitors seeking a complete suspension of time inevitably found their way to Longwood, Dr. Haller Nutt's never-finished tribute to the Middle East. Construction of this six-story, onion-domed, octagonal house was interrupted by the Civil War. Nutt was a Union sympathizer, and after Confederate troops fired on Fort Sumter, the Philadelphia artisans he'd hired fled for the North, leaving the Byzantine fantasia of a house half built. Nutt moved his wife, children, and servants into Longwood's ground floor, the only completed level, to wait out the war, but he ultimately caught pneumonia and died, penniless, before its conclusion. The next owners left Longwood intact and untouched, a poignant commemoration of a way of life, interrupted. The pristine, completed exterior of Longwood was always of architectural interest, but it was the never-finished, abandoned interior that drew the most fascination from tourists, who gazed wide-eyed at the original construction tools left right where they had been dropped, the dry, hard paint in buckets, the lonely scaffolding and kegs of rusty nails, and the disintegrating, empty steamer trunks covered in fine white dust. In the empty shell of the house, the naked brick walls, the bare beams, the vacant alcoves, and the skeletal dome, time stood still for a moment, assisting ardent pilgrims in their contemplation and imagination of a lost civilization.[48]

But most visitors seemed content to switch rapidly back and forth between the present and the past, just like the pageant children in pantalets playing backstage on their electronic devices or the garden club member driving across town, her hoopskirt engulfing her small hybrid car. Still, some visitors appeared intent on warping time. For them the hoopskirt— that quintessential shape of the Old South—was the imaginative mechanism of choice. One customer of a local dressmaker, stranded in Natchez by the eruption of Mount Saint Helens after attending Atlanta's fiftieth anniversary celebration of *Gone with the Wind*, turned unexpected detour into antebellum reverie by wearing her hoops around the clock. "She was here for nine days longer than she had planned," recalled Sandra Stokes. "And, honey, she wore that hoopskirt to the bank; she wore it to the grocery store; she wore it everywhere she went." A California woman surprised her husband once a month by greeting him in the evening with her young daughter, both dressed in their Natchez hoopskirts. The hoopskirt held fascination even among local women. "When you have a new person who moves in and they get to join the garden club, they're a little more excited," said Stokes. "Because they've just never worn a hoopskirt." Dressmaker Cynthia Whittington agreed. "Once they put that hoop on, that's it," said Whittington. When an adult relative put on her first hoopskirt, said Whittington, "She shimmied that hoop, and she preened and she posed. Turned this way and that. She didn't want to take it off. She was Scarlett."[49]

Elite local children learned early the power of performance. Garden club children typically began taking part at the age of three, many never to quit. Within a public production downplayed as "just something fun for the tourists" was a private ritual of social status that was no laughing matter to lo-

May Festival Tableau, 1962.
MABEL LANE COLLECTION, HISTORIC NATCHEZ FOUNDATION.

cals. What to the tourist appeared only a festive display of music and dance
to the educated eye spelled a nuanced story of social place. Lineage dictated
in part the assignment of pageant roles. All young participants (save the
dancers provided by local studios for certain tableaux) were the children or
grandchildren of garden club members. But beyond this key requirement, an
imperfect meritocracy prevailed regarding nearly every facet of the pageant.
Key roles were awarded on the basis of the mother's length of club membership and record of work. Children with active mothers typically grew up
dancing up the ranks of the pageant, then playing feature roles in the wedding party and possibly the court. But certain status roles (or "spots") went
only to those whose mothers had worked especially hard for their club. Selection as placard bearer, polka favor girl, flower girl, page, bride, and, of
course, king or queen indicated the high status of the mother within her
club. Still, when two seemingly equal queen candidates appeared on the
horizon, lineage could prove a tiebreaker. With honor of lineage came maintenance of the club.

In their early years the clubs could expect automatic and ecstatic acceptance by their choice for queen, but by the millennium this was no longer the
case. For one thing court participation typically required a significant commitment of time and money. In addition to the responsibility of hosting a

formal ball, there were clothes, gifts, and invitations to purchase, as well as out-of-town family and friends to entertain. Sometimes the honor was literally too expensive to accept.

For others different priorities lay behind the decision to decline. A prominent merchant in town reportedly turned down his daughter's invitation out of hand, despite being financially comfortable and owning an antebellum home in the area. According to dress designer and Pilgrimage Garden Club member Cynthia Whittington, "He said, 'She needs a car; she's going to school. And we're going to take $20,000 and do this? I don't think so.' The mother and daughter, so the story goes, cried for weeks."[50]

The honor also demanded the honorees' presence in Natchez for their two-week reign, a logistically daunting prospect for far-flung college students nearing the end of spring semester. The social season began in December and the parties did not stop until the pilgrimage ended in April. As a rite of passage, pilgrimage functioned as a debut in Natchez, an occasion for formally presenting certain young people of marriageable age to local society. In an earlier era, when a good marriage was the primary means of social and financial success for women, many a queen sat out a semester to reign at the pilgrimage; it was considered a smart investment. But as the millennium approached, young Natchez women no longer yearned to claim the crown. If earlier generations daydreamed about adding three little letters—"Mrs."—to their (changed) names, young women eligible for the court increasingly had their sights set on different letters like JD, MD, and PhD.[51] As a result, many viewed the prospect of serving as queen as an honor and, perhaps, an obligation—but not a necessity to social or professional success.

For those young women who accepted the invitation, however, the effort and expense were ultimately deemed worth it, as the queen's glory reflected on her extended family. Serving as queen of the Natchez Pilgrimage solidified her family's place in Natchez society for decades to come. Club members liked to claim that planning a wedding was a breeze compared with preparing a queen to reign over the Natchez Pilgrimage. But the similarities between the two rituals were striking. The king and queen of pilgrimage registered for china, silver, and other gifts, and a series of parties was thrown in the couple's honor. Like brides, second-generation queens honored the family by wearing heirloom garments.[52]

As with a wedding, when word got out about the queen's selection, friends and family members rushed to aid the honoree. "You usually have family and friends call and say, 'I can sew some beads,' or 'I can write your invitations for the [queen's] box,'" said Whittington. A dressmaker new in town was frowned upon when she forbade outside assistance in finishing the queen's gown.[53] Rallying around their own, upper-crust Natchezians were accustomed to constructing and displaying their class standing through pageant rituals of preparation and celebration.

An extensive wardrobe was required of the court. Members of the court assumed a new status in the community and assisted in perpetuating their class. Insider knowledge was paraded on the sleeve, and the ability to read these signs was proof of social place. Second- and third-generation queens took pains to incorporate bits of their mother's or grandmother's gown into their own ensemble, which then became a visible sign of lineage. Locals long familiar with the pageant could spot a "true Natchez dress" (with its specific cut, fabrics, and finishes) from across a crowded auditorium—as well as a fake.[54] Similarly, those in the know could identify the residences of former kings and queens by the royal flags hanging from their homes during pilgrimage. Former queens enjoyed additional honors—their signature scrawled on a wall at Magnolia Hall in perpetuity and an invitation to the annual martini luncheon of SPAM, the Society for the Preservation of Aged Monarchs.

With the pilgrimage's celebration of local lineage, it is small wonder that mothers were central to its scene. As sociologist Susan Ostrander notes, mothers are the driving force behind maintenance of the upper class. In "constructing class-exclusive social organizations and activities where upper-class boys and girls can meet one another," writes Ostrander, upper-class women "maximize opportunities for class marriages." The invitational nature of such activities is central to their meaning.[55] Through their structuring, maintenance, and policing of children's pilgrimage participation, Natchez mothers perpetuated their class.

At the start of the twenty-first century, pageant participants fell roughly into three camps: an older generation of club members quite serious about the pageant; an enthusiastic group of younger newcomers who saw the production as a ladder for social advancement; and a cohort of native baby boomers returned to Natchez for whom the pageant was a source of both nostalgia and discomfort. Some returnees reported feeling caught between familial expectations and representational politics. What had as a child seemed merely an occasion to wear an elaborate dress was to some a painfully obvious performance of race and class exclusion. Loathe to let their own children participate but reluctant to flat out refuse, the ambivalent often opted for limited participation, but this was easier said than done and an imperfect solution besides. Even inactive club members faithfully maintained their dues so that come summertime their children could swim in the club pool. As a result, they were vulnerable when the program committee came calling in search of cast members. Unwilling to take the one action that would free them from the pageant—relinquishing their garden club membership—they ultimately contributed to the continuity of the spectacle. In the end reluctant and willing participation were indistinguishable onstage and together produced the same result: a sugarcoated version of the past that simultaneously obscured the experience of African Americans, reinforced social hierarchies, and transported nostalgic spectators back to the days when the designation "southern" was largely understood to mean "White."[56]

Over the years the pageant angst of White Natchezians inspired numerous creative works. In his 2005 thriller, *Turning Angel*, Natchez writer Greg Iles characterizes the Confederate Pageant as both a "mark of social distinction" and "one of the most politically incorrect spectacles in the United States." Heather Marshall's short film *Water in Which I Swim (Memory Inside Out)* invites viewers into moments of time and images of Natchez's re-created antebellum South. Selah Saterstrom's 2004 novel *The Pink Institution* engages the pageant perhaps most directly. The title refers to the abundance of crape myrtle petals that fall like a pastel snow in Natchez in spring but also to the wraparound spell of nostalgia, violence, and silence that collude in casting White southern institutions as natural rather than as historically marginalizing forces. Juxtaposing haunting voices with photographic fragments from the 1938 Confederate Pageant program and generous visual and narrative gaps, Saterstrom, a Natchez native, addresses the decay and dysfunction obscured by tradition. In an interview the author recalled the garden clubs' presentation of "Dixie" as an innocent Eden existing before the Civil War. "Putting on the hoopskirt was a way of dreaming," noted Saterstrom. "And the *act* of that dreaming was offered. Slavery was not part of the dream narrative." Instead, the garden clubs offered "a history that of course left out vital narratives in exchange for a kind of public dreaming which very much felt to me like a public form of mass-numbing out. I began to consider how the ways in which history is framed is itself a mode of violence."[57]

Indeed, stereotypical renditions of Black life were a regular feature of early Confederate Pageant tableaux. From the passive, faithful servants of *The Serenade* (1938), *The Children's Party* (1939), and *Plantation Worship* (1948) to the four-part harmony of field hands singing "Swing Low, Sweet

Chariot" in *The Cotton Pickers* (late 1940s to early 1960s) and *Life on the Old Plantation* (1951), pageant performances provided caricatures of Black life for nostalgic White audiences.[58] But Blacks in Natchez put down their burlap sacks for good in the 1960s, never to pick cotton onstage again. Subservient pageant roles—butler, Mammy, cotton picker, watermelon eater—had gradually grown untenable as African Americans sought civil rights in their offstage lives.

In the years that followed, Black and White Natchezians conducted a halting conversation regarding the pageant. Garden club members lamented the lack of change, but rationalized it in terms of tradition; they claimed they *wished* the pageant could be different but did little to promote revision. Black Natchezians mostly just stayed away but also spoke bitterly about the lack of local media coverage of African American social events, including a local cotillion.[59] The result was a representational standoff, with African Americans doing their best to ignore the pageant, and garden club members continuing to perform the same gendered ritual that had reiterated race and class hierarchies in Natchez since the 1930s. In the end pageant custodians valued social privilege over an honest reckoning with history and so produced a version of the past that preserved it.

Even a significant script revision meant to transform the pageant ultimately failed to alter its central meaning. A 2007 rewrite intended to tell a more inclusive story about the city's past in the end proved more renovation than revolution. Several years prior Mimi Miller, cofounder of the Historic Natchez Foundation, had jumped at the Natchez Garden Club's request to refashion the script, foreseeing an alteration both radical and simple. It would be radical because the multiracial cast warranted by the new script would make obsolete the long-standing members-only performance policy or, more radical still, promote desegregation of the clubs. It would also be simplicity itself: inserting vignettes of local African American notables and deleting the racially exclusive Confederate court scene at the end, she would offer an account of Natchez's past that was credible, inclusive, *and* entertaining. What Miller remembered most about the assignment was how easy it was. Alas, her script was quietly shelved for several years, although some of her suggestions eventually came to light in the 2007 revised production.[60]

Miller's attempt to tell a truer Natchez story presented problems not so simply solved. Paramount among them was the practical matter of presentation: If the court scene were no more, where would the daughters of garden club members make their debut? History was all well and good, but heritage—what historian Michael Kammen called "history without guilt"—remained a better bet for spotlighting contemporary status and sustaining imagined connections to a cherished past.[61] In the end the prospect of dismantling the Confederate court scene was a bridge too far for garden club decision makers—it would have undermined the annual ritual of race and class display that remained the pageant's central premise.

The Southern Road to Freedom, a gospel production that tells the story of the local African American experience in narrative and song, was penned in direct response to the old Confederate Pageant. Mississippi native Ora Frazier, an educator and longtime leader in Natchez's African American community, first witnessed the Confederate Pageant around 1960. The stereotypical depiction of men and women happily singing while picking cotton had left Frazier infuriated—and determined to right the representational record. But it would be many years before she was presented with the opportunity. When her priest approached her about the possibility of Black people getting more involved with the pilgrimage, Frazier jumped at the chance. But she also had conditions. "I told him, 'Father, the only way this choir will do it is if we can tell our own story,'" recalled Frazier. "I said, 'We want people coming into Natchez to know the contribution of African Americans from pre–Civil War times to the present.'"[62] As a board member of the Historic Natchez Foundation, Frazier knew she had access to the materials, and she realized the stakes involved.

First staged in 1990, *The Southern Road to Freedom* attracted only a small band of curiosity seekers at first but gradually came to attract enthusiastic audiences of increasing size. It was considered a critical success. "One lady told me, 'I think you all are running them out of business!'" chuckled Frazier, although she claimed direct competition was never her intent.[63] Still, in illuminating the history of Black Natchezians, *The Southern Road to Freedom*, inevitably referenced White society in a way not reciprocated by the pageant.

For Frazier's part the pageant was both a source of social status ("You have *arrived* when you do anything in that pageant") and a way for White people to affirm certain ideas about their identity and the southern past.[64] As long as young parents continued putting their children in the pageant, she was pessimistic the production—and thus its meaning—would ever change. "I really don't see the pageant changing unless the membership changes," said Frazier. Members downplayed the exclusivity of the clubs, claiming practically anybody could join, so long as they were willing to work hard for the clubs. But in the early twenty-first century, such inclusivity remained unrealized; despite desegregation of the pageant cast and overtures of membership toward select African American women, the garden clubs remained segregated by race and (perhaps less obviously) by class.

Asked about the pageant's future, club members fondly repeated a local truism: "As long as there are mothers of little girls in Natchez, there will be a pageant."[65] But with Confederate symbols under scrutiny, the production's prospects appeared less certain. The popularity of *The Southern Road to Freedom*, seen alongside declining support for the pageant, pointed to a shift in public opinion regarding remembrance of the southern past. In many respects the garden clubs of Natchez appeared to have painted themselves into a representational corner—even as script revisions placed Black Natchezians onstage once more.

A historically accurate presentation of Natchez during the Confederacy would mean a decidedly different performance than the one many Natchezians had come to know and love and bank on. As one pageant insider, an aficionado of authentic period clothing, remarked after another evening at the auditorium, "The costumes are getting better. Now we've just got to work on the history."[66]

EPILOGUE

Resilient Routine

NEARLY TWO DECADES INTO THE TWENTY-FIRST CENTURY, THE RE-
christened Historic Natchez Tableaux appeared much as it had before. The
2018 series of musical sketches romanticized and celebrated the antebellum
White South while failing to depict slavery. The continuity was only worth
mentioning because, just a few years prior, the tableaux had broken it to tell
a more honest and balanced story about the city's past. Staple scenes from
past productions—*Little and Big Maypole, Polka, A Natchez Bride for Jefferson Davis*—had remained, but they were juxtaposed with others that told
the story of Black Natchezians before, during, and just after the Civil War.
One scene showed a ten-year-old and his mother clinging to each other just
before she is sold at the Forks of the Road, one the largest slave markets. In
another the son, now an adult Union soldier, took part in dismantling the infamous structure board by board, as a gospel choir harmonized in the background. In *The Home Front*, Black and White women sang mournful songs
while awaiting news of battle. Importantly, the final scene emphasized the
South's defeat.[1]

The changes could be traced to Madeline Iles, who, as queen-elect 2015,
had balked at the prospect of reigning over the traditional pageant depicting a fantasyland South. Persuading her father, best-selling novelist Greg
Iles, to rework the script, the Millsaps College history major affected a representational shift that had eluded many adults. Still, transformative change
remained elusive. African Americans did not breach the pilgrimage's inner
sanctum during Iles's reign: the royal debutante courts remained all-White.
A subsequent revision featured Black performers portraying enslaved per-

sons, a live African American choir singing the spiritual "Deep River," and a voice-over about the town's former slave market. But White audiences deemed slavery onstage a turnoff, and the local Black community chose not to attend. By late 2017 the Pilgrimage Garden Club had withdrawn from the joint production in favor of a new one, *A Royal Evening at Longwood*, citing artistic differences.[2]

In fact, across the South the landscape of gender performance remained largely unchanged. The southern beauty continued to show up on cue to enact race and region in predictable displays. On Southeastern Conference lawns, the tailgating still rivaled the gridiron action in form and finesse and at times surpassed it. In the Grove at Ole Miss, families and friends mingled in clubby tents featuring the sort of lavish spreads and formal accoutrement more typically found indoors. Against the sound of laughing children and clinking julep cups, men in sport coats and women in suits and sundresses caught up, performing and measuring southern gentility. Despite the bourbon and the barbecue, this was a showcase of the feminine arts, from adornment to hospitality. Across the region the scene was much the same. On the Capstone at Alabama and the Horseshoe at South Carolina, White southerners stepped back in time, communing with an earlier, imagined South.[3]

At sporting events, home and garden tours, commencement celebrations, and other rites of spring, predictable feminine displays served as markers of White southernness. Sometimes the message was legible from a distance. At the Kentucky Derby well-to-do women decorated the grandstands in splashy spring prints and pastel waves of composure. The derby was a sport of good breeding, and not all of it was found on the track. With their coordinated ensembles and signature hats, female spectators paid homage to the remembered southern past by enacting southern belles and ladies. The nostalgia peaked when all assembled rose to sing "My Old Kentucky Home."[4]

In Birmingham, Wilmington, and Mobile, fresh-faced teenagers in hoopskirts dotted the landscape as belles, azalea belles, and azalea trail maids, while at preparatory schools across the South, May Day rituals offered occasion for performing region. At Girls Preparatory School in Chattanooga, seniors in pastel gowns clutched fresh bouquets as they gathered on the lawn for presentation in the May court. The same rituals White southerners had once offered as evidence of their distinctive, aristocratic culture—first in the nineteenth century and again in the 1920s—continued to mark the season.[5]

The Chattanooga Cotton Ball, a debutante gala thrown since the Great Depression, held to tradition by crowning a local young woman queen and an older, male civic leader king to reign over pageantry that included presentation of belles from across the Southeast. With a strict requirement that the queen be local—rooted in Cotton Ball tradition through parents, grandparents, and cousins who had served on the court—the pageantry remained lily-White. Down in Laredo, Texas, the Society of Martha Washington presented richly garbed local debutantes—"the Marthas"—before a replica of Mount Vernon set against scrubby mesquite. Swathed in glittering gowns of voluminous velvet and charged with upholding more than a century of class standing, it was hard to say whether they were more weighted down by tradition or couture.[6]

Yet these scenes no longer took place without question. Sixth-generation Chattanoogan Mary Rebecca Gardner had taken the 2015 Cotton Ball Association to task in an open letter, in which she explained, "why I am ashamed of Chattanooga's proudest tradition" (and would be declining their invitation). "By holding on to traditions like the Cotton Ball, we hold on to the southern traditions of racism, classism, and sexism," wrote Gardner. "The Cotton Ball, in its name alone, maintains a deep racial divide in a community that is trying to heal." Gardner was not the first to reach this conclusion. "Cotton Ball is definitely racist," noted an earlier debutante to photographer Lauren Greenfield, whose 2002 book *Girl Culture* features images of the ritual. "We only have one Black girl. Maybe one Asian person. That's it. Everybody else is White. That's also part of the Southern tradition, you know, only having White girls. The Southern accent comes out a lot when you go to these types of things."[7]

Photographer Adair Rutledge addressed related concerns when she took the Azalea Trail Maids of her native Alabama as the subject of a body of work shown in 2018 at the Ogden Museum of Southern Art and in the *Fence*, one of the largest, juried outdoor traveling photography exhibitions in North America. Rutledge saw "a disconnect between what the dress historically represents and the multidimensional, multicultural, highly accomplished young women who wear it now," and her images highlighted this incongruity. What did it mean when young women of color donned brightly hued replicas of antebellum garb that would have been mostly unavailable to them in that era? What power dynamics were preserved when Azalea Trail Maids—accomplished young women selected on the basis of merit and an extensive interview process—wore costly, restrictive gowns in smiling silence?[8]

Some widely heralded changes failed to live up to their promise. After executives at the Miss America Organization were caught trash-talking past winners, the board installed Gretchen Carlson, Miss America 1989 and a former Fox News anchor, as chair in 2018. Carlson had been instrumental in the #MeToo anti–sexual harassment movement after suing her former boss, Fox News founder, Roger Ailes. The hope was that she would find a way to make the contest relevant again. Carlson wasted no time eliminating the swimsuit competition that had plagued the pageant's credibility for decades. But ultimately "Miss America 2.0"—touting social impact and empowerment but posing softball questions to self-effacing contestants—did not transform the pageant's reputation. Miss America had always promoted a model of womanhood that emphasized gender deference, humility, and positivity, and the revamped competition, though bikini-free, did not radically rewrite this script. Standards of acceptable femininity remained deeply engrained and decidedly raced, a fact made crystal clear when only twenty-four hours before the pageant tennis champion Serena Williams was penalized an entire game in the U.S. Open for smashing a racket and rebuking the ruling of an umpire. The bodies and behavior of women—especially non-White women—who defied standards of respectability and decorum were still deemed unruly and worthy of discipline.[9]

Outrage over the persistence of race and gender double standards sparked a digital backlash. When a spate of White women called police on Black people over trivial or nonexistent offenses in 2018, they were promptly ridiculed on social media. Following Beyoncé's 2016 lyric "Becky with the good hair," these social media comebacks deliberately paired old-school, stereotypically White names with the source of the dispute to call out White women ignorant of both their privilege and their prejudice. After Jennifer Schulte alerted Oakland, California, police that two African American men were using a charcoal grill in an area of a park not so designated, she became a hashtag and a viral meme: #BBQBecky. She was soon joined by #PermitPatty (who had complained about an eight-year-old girl selling bottled water), #PoolPatrolPaula (who had assaulted a teenager at a community pool), and #GolfCartGail (who had summoned police to a youth soccer match after seeing a father yell instructions to his son). The public shaming pushed back against the long-standing license of White women to criminalize Black bodies.[10]

In a similar vein ingrained assumptions about femininity, race, and place surfaced on social media in 2018 when Ed Meek, a former administrator at the University of Mississippi and benefactor of its Meek School of Journalism and New Media, posted photographs of two young African American women on the Oxford town square dressed in revealing party attire. Accompanying the photos were dire warnings to local Whites about declining enrollments and real estate values. Further investigation revealed an attempt by Meek to plant a story that prostitution and fights were hurting the city's reputation—implying that the women were sex workers. When the young women pictured turned out to be students at the university, Meek tried to walk it back, but the racism and misogyny inherent in his post were unmistakable. A 1961 Ole Miss graduate, Meek first made his mark as editor of the *Daily Mississippian*'s cheesecake photo feature, "Campus Cuties," published at the height of massive resistance. His name was hastily removed from the journalism building in a unanimous faculty decision.[11]

In the wake of Charleston and Charlottesville, Confederate symbols served as flash points in the contest over memory and history, with monuments and other signs coming down, if unevenly. In Richmond a statue of Confederate general Robert E. Lee was splattered with paint and the letters "BLM" painted on its base one week ahead of a White-nationalist rally set to take place in the District of Columbia. Washington and Lee University, in Lexington, Virginia, decided that Lee Chapel (where the Confederate general and founder of the school is buried) would remain a campus gathering space, but the Lee family crypt and recumbent statue of Lee would be closed off during school events so that participation did not suggest veneration of the Confederacy. In Winston-Salem, North Carolina, a small crowd cheered as a statue of an anonymous Confederate soldier left the grounds of the old courthouse on a flatbed truck, also headed for a historical cemetery. In Arlington, Virginia, the school board of Washington-Lee High School voted unanimously to drop the Confederate general's surname in favor of "Washington-Liberty"—but stopped short of adopting "Washington-Loving," which would have honored Richard and Mildred Loving's successful Supreme Court challenge of the state's ban on interracial marriage. Perhaps nowhere was the battle over collective memory more fraught than at the University of North Carolina, where protesters first toppled "Silent Sam"—a monument erected in 1913 to honor graduates who had died fighting for the Confederacy—then battled with university officials over the statue's fate (state law restricted what could be done with historical monuments). Even as Confederate monuments were removed or relocated across the region, they galvanized White nationalists, who saw in them not the past but symbols for a racist vision of the future. The Confederate flag too surged in popularity in the North and West, where, two years into the presidency of Donald Trump, disaffected White people displayed it as a sign of shared grievance and rebellion.[12]

Politicians claimed ignorance of racial symbols even as they demonstrated deep familiarity with them. In a Mississippi U.S. Senate race, Republican Cindy Hyde-Smith claimed victory over Democrat Mike Espy, a former Congress representative who is African American, in part by deploying racist tropes. Of a supporter Hyde-Smith noted, "If he invited me to a public hanging, I would be on the front row," a contentious choice of words given the state's history of lynching. Hyde-Smith might have been experiencing déjà vu; in 2014 she posed for photographs in Confederate garb, quipping, "Mississippi history at its finest." And as a teenager attending a segregation academy, she and other members of the cheerleading squad (southern beauties, all) posed for yearbook photos with a Confederate flag and mascot—a classic assemblage of White supremacist symbols. "Mississippi had the opportunity to show the country that it had become a state that has shaken off its image as a closed society," noted writer W. Ralph Eubanks of the race. "In the end, it was Mississippi's past that won the election rather than its future."[13]

The southern past—and their own—rushed back to haunt Virginia's top three elected officials when they were ensnared in scandals in 2019. When it was discovered that the 1984 medical school yearbook page of Gov. Ralph Northam, a Democrat, featured a photo of two young men, one in Blackface and the other in Klan robes, party officials wasted no time calling for his resignation. Northam responded in clunky and clueless fashion, first apologizing, then claiming that he was not pictured in the photo, then acknowledging that, well, he had once worn Blackface in a medical school–conference dance contest that he won by impersonating Michael Jackson, complete with moonwalk. In the maelstrom that erupted, Attorney General Mark Herring (D) stepped forward to admit that he too had donned Blackface, for a college party in 1980. Meanwhile, Justin Fairfax, the lieutenant governor of Virginia and descendant of slaves who had seemed so principled only days before when he declined to preside over speeches honoring Confederate general Robert E. Lee, faced multiple credible allegations of rape and sexual assault. All three refused to resign, inspiring widespread fury, but it was the response of Northam that cut the deepest. Taking responsibility for his racist actions but expressing a sheepish ignorance of their power to harm and to hurt, Northam spoke from a stance of race privilege as offensive as it was unconvincing. To African American Virginians in particular, it was a betrayal. Could the governor truly have been unaware of the historical role of Blackface in mocking and dehumanizing Black people? Northam's apologetic obliviousness was a textbook example of White fragility, the disbelieving defensiveness that White people exhibit when their complicity in the perpetuation of racism is pointed out. Which was more offensive, the Blackface or the not knowing, was a tough call, but reactions to both highlighted the racial divide over remembrance of the southern past. Northam's ignorance evidenced the success of the White southern nostalgia campaign led for decades by the southern beauty. As politicians and the press rushed to scour old yearbooks for depictions of Blackface (surprise!—there were lots), the southern past seemed to recede into a hazy distance for White culprits even as it surged to the forefront and into sharp focus for African Americans. Affecting amnesia about their Blackface performances, White elected officials made an art form of equivocation. One after another they downplayed their Blacking up as regrettable but innocent capers that they could scarcely even recall. The 1980s, after all, were "so long ago" and, perhaps most importantly, "A Much Different Time," as *Washington Post* humorist Alexandra Petri dubbed their preposterous claims. Meanwhile, African Americans had no trouble recalling events three decades and more earlier. Within two weeks and 125 miles of Northam's disgrace in Richmond, students and alumni gathered in Front Royal, Virginia, to mark Black History Month by remembering the 1959 desegregation of Warren County Schools. For the four of the original twenty-three African American students in attendance, the memory of walking up the long hill to the school with hostile Whites lining their path and calling them names was indelibly seared into their brains and hearts. It was impossible to forget.[14]

It is understandable that they did not consider the intervening years a much different time. After all, despite indisputable social and legal change, remnants of the past had routinely bubbled up, troubling narratives of progress. The southern beauty often figured prominently in these stories. Although negative publicity in the 1990s had sent Blackface capers deep underground, the same degradations continued to surface at Greek gatherings like "Golf Pros and Tennis Ho's," "White Trash Bash," and "Homeless Ball," where actives emphasized their own race and class privilege through crude caricature. A "Halloween in the 'Hood" fraternity party at Johns Hopkins University in 2006 attracted White students dressed as pimps, prostitutes, and slaves, while a "Tacos and Tequila" swap the same year at the University of Illinois enraged Latino students and their allies.[15] Such parties resonated strongly in the South, where Greek life remained starkly segregated by race and class.[16] At a Greek "Redneck Ball" in Virginia, guests in "gritty/ NASCAR themed clothes" enjoyed a bluegrass band, with the women issued bottles of Boone's Farm wine upon arrival. More than half a century after the Ole Miss Chi Os' "Down to Earth" party featured newspaper-covered walls, a hillbilly band, and refreshments in paper sacks, the performance remained unchanged.[17]

Two decades into the new century, gendered performances of race, region, and privilege persisted. Overtly racist acts now drew consequences, but the prospects of young White southerners proactively revising their repertoire to suggest an inclusive South remained mixed. In Mississippi three Ole Miss students were suspended from the Kappa Alpha Order, a fraternity known for its racist history, after an Instagram post emerged of them posing with guns and wide grins before a bullet-riddled plaque marking the spot where civil rights icon Emmett Till, a fourteen-year-old Black boy, was tortured and killed in 1955. The image, celebrating both White supremacy and lethal power, encapsulated a toxic but widely accepted understanding of White southern masculinity—the shadow of the southern beauty. In 2018, five years after the formal desegregation of Greek life at the University of Alabama, 92 Black or African American women (or 3.9 percent of 2,338 students total) were members of Alabama Panhellenic Association (APA) sororities, up from 10 in 2013; 2 had served their predominantly White sororities as chapter president. The representation of Asian and Latino women had also risen, and structural changes included diversity and inclusion officers in every APA sorority. Still, as some Black students saw it, APA sororities covertly discouraged African American students from rushing; a *Greek Chic* guide to recruitment featured few women of color and emphasized the steep financial obligation associated with membership. In 2015 Halle Lindsey, an African American woman in a predominantly White sorority, failed to receive the support of her own sorority in her run for homecoming queen because of members' fears that they would not be invited to fraternity parties. In 2018 New Jersey native Harley Barber was expelled from the University of Alabama and kicked out of Alpha Phi sorority after she posted a racist video on social media in which she repeatedly used the N-word. George Washington University student Alison Janega resigned from the presidency of Phi Sigma Sigma sorority after posting a photo on Snapchat of the exterior of a South Carolina plantation gift shop and the caption, "I wonder if they sell slaves." And in 2019 at the University of Oklahoma, where this tale

An image of George Floyd is projected on the Confederate general Robert E. Lee memorial in Richmond, Virginia. Dustin Klein and Alex Criqui lighting installations of Black historical figures drew people to renamed Marcus–David Peters Circle in the summer of 2020.
EVERGIB PHOTOGRAPH.

began, Delta Delta Delta ousted a member for filming and sharing a Blackface video that outraged students campus-wide.[18]

But the landscape of White nostalgia might have changed for good with the murder of George Floyd while in custody of Minneapolis police on May 25, 2020. The back-and-forth that had transpired after Charleston and Charlottesville—with activists affecting removal of some monuments to slavery and oppression but also meeting with legal stalling tactics and a waxing and waning of public interest—was replaced by a crescendo of renewed purpose. Floyd's killing after he was pinned to the asphalt under a White police officer's knee became a referendum on what it means to be Black in the United States of America, as millions of people took to the streets in historic protests. Across the nation people staged jubilee, freeing themselves of Confederate symbols in scenes of euphoric destruction. Urgency prevailed; it was no time to wait. Black Lives Matter activists and their allies avenged the recent deaths of Floyd, Ahmaud Arbery, and Breonna Taylor by obliterating

Confederate symbols in the streets. The battle over who owned history had reached a breaking point.[19]

In the nation's capital protesters jubilantly toppled the city's only outdoor Confederate statue—a tribute to Gen. Albert Pike—then set it on fire as District police watched but did not intervene. In Charlottesville, Virginia, people wearing Black Lives Matter shirts danced and families cheered as a Confederate soldier known as "At Ready" was taken down after 111 years of standing watch outside the county courthouse. The Maryland State House voted unanimously to remove a plaque sympathizing with the Confederacy that had been installed in 1964 at the height of the civil rights movement. A full 79 percent of the faculty of Washington and Lee University called for the removal of Robert E. Lee from the name of the university. In Fairfax County, Virginia, Robert E. Lee High School was renamed for the late Georgia Congress representative and civil rights leader John Lewis. In Mississippi state officials finally relented: the Confederate monument that had hovered over the heart of the University of Mississippi campus for more than a century could be relocated to a campus cemetery. In Richmond protestors pulled down a statue of Confederate president Jefferson Davis, then transformed the sixty-foot statue of Gen. Robert E. Lee that had towered over Monument Avenue for 130 years into a site of joyous protest. Residents and visitors gathered in renamed Marcus–David Peters Circle at the base of the graffiti-covered monument over several weeks to dance, sing, and testify in the name of hope and change. In this atmosphere other symbols of colonization also came crashing down. Minneapolis protesters toppled a statue of Christopher Columbus that had stood in front of the state capitol for nearly 90 years, while Boston demonstrators beheaded their figure of the Italian explorer. In Baltimore protesters celebrated Independence Day by tossing pieces of a Columbus statue into the Inner Harbor. At the Kentucky Derby in Louisville, the coronavirus emptied the stands but not the streets, where the annual performance of southern gentility was replaced by protests over the killing by police of local emergency-medical technician Breonna Taylor.[20]

The rising up inspired at least some southern beauties to consider their complicity in White supremacy. On the *Academy Stories* blog, alumni of all-White segregation academies contributed their reflections on attending the schools that sprouted up in thirteen states around 1970 to defy the ideal of racial equality. Women in particular recounted vague parental justifications that cloaked anxieties over interracial sex in terms of "getting a better educa-

Breonna Taylor mural by Future History Now, Annapolis, Maryland, 2020.
PHOTO BY MAURICE TAYLOR.

tion." In Alabama Emily Owen Mendelsohn started a Change.org petition, #nomorebelles, to put an end to the Birmingham Belles, a service organization that taps high school girls to do charitable work while dressed in replica hoopskirts, gloves, and hats. For the 120 girls inducted each year by invitation, selection by the Birmingham Belles is a status marker, and the presentation at Arlington Historic House—where 14 enslaved persons toiled—the pinnacle of the social season. "The fact that it is acceptable for 100+ young, southern women to dress up in antebellum regalia at Arlington House, a former PLANTATION home, is appalling," noted Mendelsohn, a former belle. "While volunteer work is a noble cause, Birmingham Belles needs to be seen for what it really is: an excuse for White women to 'play plantation' for a day." One year in more than 2,100 repentant belles had signed the petition. By 2020 the Cape Fear Garden Club had shuttered the Azalea Belles, following several years of discussion and a similar petition. The decision marked the end of a long era: the first class of Azalea Belles in 1969 are said to have worn dresses their mothers wore to the area's centennial Confederate Ball in 1962.[21]

But other belles used digital platforms to promote continuity, not change. A study of images posted to Instagram by students at the University of Georgia found a widespread practice of young White women posting gameday selfies that laid clear claim to the southern lady ideal. Employing photo-editing technologies and careful posing, calculated sartorial choices and romantic lighting, they reworked the traditional southern beauty performance for virtual space. Soft and flowy dresses set off by statement jewelry emphasized feminine curves without being revealing, while the manipulation of color saturations created a stark contrast between straight white teeth and pore-free skin and bright lipstick. The overall effect was exclusive—a hyperfeminine visage aligned with traditionally White, upper-middle-class standards of beauty. Like the sorority women "doing" southern lady on command during rush, these deliberate images magnified and pinned down events occurring in passing on Saturdays in Athens. It all amounted to a public pedagogy of femininity that reinforced classed and raced norms of beauty. But unlike the ephemeral moments of sorority rush, these gameday selfies circulated well beyond Athens, proliferating normalizing lessons about White southern femininity. Collectively they constituted nothing less than an insidious "disciplinary regime."[22]

Performance matters. Renovating the landscape of White southern remembrance will require more than removing monuments and renaming schools and streets. It will mean new motions and gestures, new rituals and productions. It will mean shuttering or rewriting the feminine performances central to White southern nostalgia. A shared southern future requires a reconciled past, and that will take radical honesty on the part of all White southerners but especially young women. What sort of trauma has their frivolity obscured? The power is theirs to alter the performance, share the memory, and change the South.

NOTES

PREFACE

1. Gusterson, "Studying Up Revisited," 114; Nader, "Up the Anthropologist," 289.
2. Morris, *North toward Home*, 319.

INTRODUCTION. *Power Play*

1. Associated Press, "Racist Oklahoma Video"; Dries, "Backlash Comes over UGA's Ban."

2. The vice president for student affairs, Victor Wilson, an African American alumnus of the university, had more than three decades of experience in student affairs leadership positions at the University of Georgia and other universities. Shearer, "Hoop Skirts Banned at UGA."

3. Workneh, "Bree Newsome, Activist"; Costa, Horwitz, and Wan, "Man Arrested in Charleston Killings"; Eugene Robinson, "Hope in Charleston"; Jenkins, "Erasing Ugly History"; David A. Graham, "Stubborn Persistence"; Jenkins, "On Confederate Symbols"; Jenkins, "Unraveling the Threads of Hatred"; Steinhauer, "Historical Symbols in Midst"; Krauthammer, "On Lowering the Flag"; Eugene Robinson, "150 Years Later, America"; Tucker, "Mississippi Flag Defenders"; John Woodrow Cox, "Defending Dixie"; Bauerlein, "Confederate Flag Removed"; Brumfield and Ellis, "New Orleans Votes to Remove"; Landrieu, "Why I'm Taking Down Confederate Monuments."

4. Thomas Chatterton Williams, "Why White America Insists"; O'Neil, "Jon Stewart on Racist Frat Song"; Loewen, "How Confederate Lore Survives"; Jenkins, "Unraveling the Threads of Hatred."

5. Fletcher and Ross, "Attack at Church"; Donadio, "Authors Tap into Mood"; Allen, "Trumpists' Party"; Staples, "Donald Trump"; Jenkins, "Unraveling the Threads of Hatred"; Eligon, "Black Students See"; Hartocollis and Bidgood, "Racial Discrimination Demonstrations Spread"; "University of Oklahoma SAE Racist Chant."

6. On the southern lady ideal, see Anne Firor Scott, *Southern Lady*; Jones, *Tomorrow Is Another Day*; Tartt, "Belle and the Lady"; and Diane Roberts, *Faulkner and Southern Womanhood*.

7. Young and Song, "Forum Introduction"; Ferguson, "Distributions of Whiteness."

8. Rodger Lyle Brown, *Ghost Dancing*, xxii.

9. Yaeger, *Dirt and Desire*, 99; Brundage, "No Deed but Memory," 12–13.

10. Yaeger, *Dirt and Desire*, 98–105; McRae, *Mothers of Massive Resistance*, 10, 14–15, 18–19, 105, 56.

11. Jones and Donaldson, *Haunted Bodies*, 16.

12. Coski, *Confederate Battle Flag*; Cobb, *Away Down South*; Cobb, *Redefining Southern Culture*; Martinez, Richardson, and McNinch-Su, *Confederate Symbols*; Prince, *Rally 'round the Flag*; King and Springwood, *Beyond the Cheers*; Barbee, *Race and Masculinity*. Notable exceptions include Craig, *Ain't I a Beauty Queen?*; Friend, *Southern Masculinity*; Falck, *Remembering Dixie*; Goldfield, *Still Fighting the Civil War*; Charlene M. Boyer Lewis, *Ladies and Gentlemen on Display*; McPherson, *Reconstructing Dixie*; Blain Roberts, *Pageants, Parlors, and Pretty Women*; Taylor, *Archive and the Repertoire*; Tice, *Queens of Academe*; Wallace-Sanders, *Mammy*; and Watts, *White Masculinity*.

13. Butler, *Gender Trouble*, 179; Ayers, "What We Talk About," 66–68.

14. On southern memory and its segregation, see Goldfield, *Still Fighting the Civil War*; Brundage, *Where These Memories Grow*; Brundage, *Southern Past*; Rubin, *Confederacy of Silence*; Horwitz, *Confederates in the Attic*; Cobb, *Away Down South*; Blight, *Race and Reunion*; Hobson, *But Now I See*; and Westen, "How Democrats Should Talk."

15. Ayers, "What We Talk About"; Cobb, *Redefining Southern Culture*, 148. W. Fitzhugh Brundage questions whether such commonality exists. "No Deed but Memory."

16. Goldfield, *Still Fighting the Civil War*, 3.

17. For the phrase "confederacy of silence," I am indebted to Richard Rubin, whose book by the same name chronicles the phenomenon in the late twentieth-century South. Rubin, *Confederacy of Silence*.

18. Associated Press, "Confederate Statue Removal"; Staples, "Donald Trump"; Graham, "Stubborn Persistence"; Appelbaum, "Why Is the Flag"; Lang, "Worse Than the Tea Party."

19. Gillis, "Memory and Identity," 3; Connerton, *How Societies Remember*, 36; Rosenzweig and Thelen, *Presence of the Past*, 10, 36, 115–16.

20. Anderson, *Imagined Communities*; Rosenzweig and Thelen, *Presence of the Past*, 54; Brundage, "No Deed but Memory," 5–6; Gillis, "Memory and Identity," 7; Connerton, *How Societies Remember*, 3; Kammen, *Mystic Chords of Memory*, 18.

21. Connerton, *How Societies Remember*, 3–4, 43–45.

22. Roach, *Cities of the Dead*, chap. 1.

23. Banner, *American Beauty*, 167; Rosenzweig and Thelen, *Presence of the Past*, 28–30; Goldfield, *Still Fighting the Civil War*, 55, 97; Brundage, "No Deed but Memory," 14.

24. Karen L. Cox, *Dixie's Daughters*, 60–61.

25. Cobb, *Away Down South*, 22, 42–45; Stampp, *Imperiled Union*, quoted in Cobb, *Away Down South*, 56.

26. Cobb, *Away Down South*, 22–23, 45; Banner, *American Beauty*, 251.

27. Banner, *American Beauty*, 251; Glassberg, *American Historical Pageantry*, 37; Savage, *Beauty Queens*, 20–21.

28. Jones, *Tomorrow Is Another Day*, 8–9.

29. Evans, "Women," 1353, quoted in Jones, *Tomorrow is Another Day*, 8; Goldfield, *Still Fighting the Civil War*, 108.

30. Anne Firor Scott, *Southern Lady*, 31–36.

31. Glymph, *Out of the House*, 6, 25–31.

32. Ibid., 7, 20, 76–77, 214.

33. Sommerville, *Rape and Race*, 231–43.

34. Bisher, "Landmarks of Power"; Hale, *Making Whiteness*, 94–106; Manring, *Slave in a Box*; Turner, *Ceramic Uncles and Celluloid Mammies*, 11, 25, 51; Casmier-Paz, "Heritage, Not Hate"; Goings, *Mammy and Uncle Mose*; Dilworth, "American Icons," 256; Dilworth, introd. to *Acts of Possession*; Theophano, *Eat My Words*, 54; Grubb, "House and Home," 170; "Jim Crow Museum"; "Southern Belle"; "What Were Coon Songs?"; "Historic American Sheet Music."

35. Goldfield, *Still Fighting the Civil War*, 25.

36. Ibid., 24, 25. The myth of the Lost Cause argued that states' rights, not slavery, was at the root of the Civil War and vigorously defended secession.

37. Kasson, *Rudeness and Civility*, 180; Beidelman, *Moral Imagination*, 61, quoted in Tice, *Queens of Academe*, 130.

38. Faust, "Living History," 45.

39. Boyd, "Southern Beauty," 22, 69, 79–80.

40. Savage, *Beauty Queens*, 11–21; Hamlin, "Bathing Suits and Backlash," 29–33, 43–45.

41. "About."

42. Blain Roberts, *Pageants, Parlors, and Pretty Women*, 128–36.

43. McLean, "Cotton Carnival," 99–101.

44. Franklin A. Robinson Jr., "Guide to the Maid"; Blain Roberts, *Pageants, Parlors, and Pretty Women*, 136–41.

45. Glassberg, *American Historical Pageantry*, 253–55. Midcentury commerce brochures for *Historic-Progressive Natchez, Mississippi*, for example, touted the city's Old South credentials and celebrations on one side and its up-to-the-minute electrification, industrialization, and agricultural diversification on the other. Subject file: Natchez Pilgrimage, circa 1940, Natchez Pilgrimage Pamphlets, Mississippi Department of Archives and History (hereafter cited as MDAH), Jackson.

46. "World Comes to Natchez"; Rosa Naomi Scott, "Natchez Pilgrimage"; New Orleans Spring Fiesta Association, "New Orleans Spring Fiesta"; "Come to Natchez"; Woodville Garden Club, *Woodville Garden Club Announces*; Garden Club of North Carolina, "North Carolina Garden Pilgrimage 1940," box 48: Resorts, Hotels, Travel, Ad Ephemera Collection, Duke Special Collections Library, Durham; "Pilgrims Travel to Mississippi"; Kimball, "Famed Mansions of 'Old South'"; Virginia Conservation

Commission, "Garden Week in Virginia, 1941," Ad Ephemera Collection, Special Collections Library, Duke University, Durham; Mississippi Gulf Coast Council, "1955 Annual Spring Pilgrimage," Pilgrimage Collection, Special Collections Library, University of Mississippi, Oxford; Garden Cub of South Carolina, "1957 Garden Pilgrimages," So-Car 367.05 G16p, South Caroliniana Library, Columbia.

47. Jessica Roberts, "Cypress Gardens." Thanks to Richard D. Mohr for calling Cypress Gardens to my attention.

48. Azalea Festival, programs, 1953–64, Wilmington, North Carolina, Duke University Archives, Durham.

49. May, *Homeward Bound*, 9; Palladino, *Teenagers*, 118–19, 52; Daniel, *Lost Revolutions*, 169.

50. Mary Ann Mobley and Lynda Lee Mead were Miss Americas 1959 and 1960, respectively. They are members of Chi Omega, Tau chapter.

51. University of Alabama, *Corolla*, 1940s–70s; University of Mississippi, *Ole Miss*; "Old South Architecture Charms New Buildings." The sorority houses of Louisiana State University were built together in the mid-1960s. "LSU Sororities Evoke Fond Memories"; Office of Greek Affairs, "Report on Sororities at LSU," Correspondence, Misc., 1956–64, Special Collections, Louisiana State University Libraries, Baton Rouge. Greek Village at the University of South Carolina is a twenty-house complex dating to 2001.

52. J. R. Colfield Collection, 00078_b02_f06_008, Special Collections, University of Mississippi Libraries; *Ole Miss* (1953), 189; *Ole Miss* (1953), 190, 202; "Stunt Nights," 197; *Garnet and Black* (1958), 269.

53. Tice, *Queens of Academe*, 57.

54. *Kappa Kappa Sigma*; "Harriett Dickert Crowned."

55. On the education of White southerners in segregation and massive resistance, see Woodward, *Strange Career of Jim Crow*; Silver, *Mississippi*; George Lewis, *Massive Resistance*; McRae, *Mothers of Massive Resistance*; Sokol, *There Goes My Everything*, 96–100, 10–13; and Maxwell and Shields, *Long Southern Strategy*, 10–11.

56. Maxwell and Shields, *Long Southern Strategy*, 8, 321; Spruill, *Divided We Stand*, 305; McRae, "Women behind White Power."

57. Spruill, *Divided We Stand*, 71–75, 86–92, 101; McRae, *Mothers of Massive Resistance*, 4; Maxwell and Shields, *Long Southern Strategy*, 13, 20.

58. McRae, "Women behind White Power"; Spruill, *Divided We Stand*, 256, 304–8.

59. Fred Davis, *Yearning for Yesterday*, 49; Kammen, *Mystic Chords of Memory*, 618.

60. Fred Davis, *Yearning for Yesterday*, 55, 31, 80.

61. Ibid., 14, 37; Tester, *Life and Times of Post-modernity*, 65.

62. Fred Davis, *Yearning for Yesterday*, 122.

63. Sokol, *There Goes My Everything*, introd. and chap. 2; McRae, *Mothers of Massive Resistance*, 166.

64. Sokol, *There Goes My Everything*, 8, 15.

65. Kammen, *Mystic Chords of Memory*, 539.

66. Rodger Lyle Brown, *Ghost Dancing*, x, 52, xi, xi–xxii; Hoelscher, *Heritage on Stage*, 17.

67. On the "Great White Switch," see Black and Black, *Rise of Southern Republicans*, 205.

68. Eichstedt and Small, *Representations of Slavery*, 12, 3, 12.

69. Yaeger, *Dirt and Desire*, 14.

CHAPTER 1. *Sister Act*

1. This chapter is based on ethnographic research on the historically White rush systems at the University of Mississippi and the University of Alabama. The observational material presented here was gathered during the August 1996 and October 1997 Panhellenic rush seasons at the University of Mississippi and during the 2002 Panhellenic rush at the University of Alabama. Recorded interviews were conducted between February 1997 and December 2006. Informants who requested anonymity in published works, although fully identified in the Rush Project papers and transcripts, are identified here as "Informant A," "Informant B," and so on. All recordings, papers, and transcripts are in the possession of the author. The moniker "Ole Miss" originally referenced the plantation mistress. Its continued use by the university is a source of contention, one largely split along racial lines. Jaschik, "U. of Mississippi Tries."

2. "Mississippi Quickfacts"; "Quick Facts."

3. Wuensch, "Examining Student Involvement."

4. Farnham, *Education of the Southern Belle*, 148–49.

5. Ibid., 150–51. Farnham's discussion of women's literary societies draws on records from clubs at southern schools, including the Carlisle Literary Society, Converse College, South Carolina; the Sigournian and the Philomathesian at Greensboro Female College, North Carolina; the Dialectic and Philanthropic Literary Societies, University of North Carolina; and the Sigourney Society of Limestone Springs Female High School, of Gaffney, South Carolina.

6. Farnham, *Education of the Southern Belle*, 151, 153.

7. Ibid., 152, 4–5, 127.

8. Ibid., 154. The rise of Greek letter societies outside the South is typically noted as corresponding to the expansion of U.S. higher education beginning in the 1880s, but with the period of most rapid expansion not occurring until the twentieth century. In many instances fraternities and sororities provided the housing and eating facilities for which rapidly growing universities had inadequate provision. Whereas there were 1,560 national fraternity and sorority chapters in 1912, the vibrant campus culture of the 1920s caused rolls to more than double by 1930, to 3,900. See Fass, *Damned and the Beautiful*; Horowitz, *Alma Mater*; Solomon, *In the Company*; and Gordon, *Gender and Higher Education*.

9. Farnham, *Education of the Southern Belle*, 154.

10. On the lady and the belle, see Tartt, "Belle and the Lady"; Faust, "Clutching the

Chains"; Hall, "Prong of Love"; Jones, "I Was Tellin It"; and Yaeger, "Race and the Cloud."

11. On symbolism at Ole Miss and on progress in race relations at the university, see Thornton, "Symbolism at Ole Miss"; Wilkie, "Region Apart"; and Sack, "Final Refrains of Dixie."

12. The Rebel Black Bear was replaced by Landshark Tony in 2018. Potter, "Wide-Ranging Reactions"; Robbie Brown, "Ole Miss Resolves"; Cayson, "Students Have Mixed Reaction"; West, "Ole Miss Announces"; Orman, "Colonel Reb Supporters Closer"; Kayleigh Webb, "Students Have Mixed Feelings."

13. On "hidden in plain sight," see Yaeger, "Race and the Cloud."

14. Informant F, interview.

15. On feminine intimacies, see Stacey, *Star Gazing*.

16. Rosanne Smith Robinson, "Great Sorority Swindle," 45.

17. Triplett, interview.

18. Burch, interview.

19. Informant B, interview.

20. Informant E, interview.

21. Burch, interview.

22. Triplett, interview.

23. Burch, interview.

24. Ibid.; Yow, interview.

25. Burch, interview; Yow, interview.

26. Burch, interview.

27. Yow, interview.

28. Payton, interview.

29. Alpha Omicron, skit-night party, August 1996, Oxford, Miss.

30. Triplett, interview.

31. Kappa Delta, skit-night party, August 1996, Oxford, Miss.

32. Ibid.

33. Pi Beta Phi, skit-night party, August 1996, Oxford, Miss.

34. Informant F, interview.

35. Ibid.

36. Chi Omega, skit-night party, August 1996, Oxford, Miss.

37. Overheard at Tri Delta, skit-night party, August 1996, Oxford, Miss. On gender proxy, see the H-Women listserv archives for a discussion thread about Takarazuka, the all-female Japanese dance troupe in which the women who play the male roles are wildly popular with female audiences. See also Robertson, *Takarazuka*; and Alpha Omicron Pi, skit-night party, October 1997, Oxford, Miss.

38. Tri Delta, skit-night party, August 1996, Oxford, Miss.; Kappa Kappa Gamma, skit-night party, October 1997, Oxford, Miss.; Purcell, *Rush*.

39. Triplett, interview.

40. Craft, "Rush Continues," 3A.

41. Zengerle, "Sorority Row"; Gettleman, "Sorority System in No Rush"; Eric Hoover, "New Scrutiny"; Lavey, "Twilley Cut from All Houses"; M. G. Lord, "Greek Rites of Exclusion."

42. Auchmutey, "Sister Who Spoke Up"; Doherty, "Greek Letters at a Price."

43. Hobsbawm and Ranger, *Invention of Tradition*; Hammons, "Diversity in the Greek Life."

44. Hammons, "Diversity in the Greek Life."

45. Phi Mu regional adviser, personal conversation.

46. Whittaker, "Phi-Mu Accepts African American Girl."

47. Ibid.; Auchmutey, "Sister Who Spoke Up"; Roche and Brice, "Blacks Need Not Apply"; Sanders, "Sorority Integrated Last Year"; Megan Nichols, "Sorority Integration Questioned."

48. Robertson and Blinder, "Sorority Exposes Its Rejection"; Blinder, "At Alabama, a Renewed Stand"; Luckerson, "University of Alabama"; Reeves, "At University of Alabama, Leaders"; Bidwell, "Following Controversy"; McBride, "How Student Reporters Ended Discrimination"; Grasgreen, "Segregated Sororities Not Limited."

49. Blinder, "Alabama"; Blinder, "Turnabout at Traditionally White Sororities"; Luckerson, "University of Alabama."

50. Hughey, "Paradox of Participation"; Grasgreen, "Segregated Sororities Not Limited"; Kaufman, "Curmudgeon Notes 10.2.2013"; Blinder, "At Alabama, a Renewed Stand."

51. Capriccioso, "Integration Later."

52. Triplett, interview.

53. Informant B, interview.

54. Informant D, interview.

55. Triplett, interview.

56. Henderson, interview.

57. Informant E, interview.

58. Triplett, interview.

59. Burch, interview.

60. Payton, interview.

61. Ibid.

62. Ibid.

63. Yow, interview.

64. Informant F, interview.

65. Informant B, interview.

66. Gray, "At Ole Miss, They Learned"; Zengerle, "Sorority Row"; Gettleman, "Sorority System in No Rush"; Weeks, "Ole Miss." Anne Goodwyn Jones's ruminations about the continued ideological power of the southern lady provided inspiration for this project. See Jones, *Tomorrow Is Another Day*, 3–50.

CHAPTER 2. *Miss Demeanor*

1. This depiction is drawn from ethnographic fieldwork conducted at the Miss University of Alabama 2007 pageant, held December 9, 2006, in Tuscaloosa.

2. Melinda Toole, of Birmingham, was Miss Alabama 2006.

3. On beauty pageantry as a strategy for Christian discipleship, see Tice, *Queens of Academe*.

4. Wilson, "Cult of Beauty"; Deford, *There She Is*; "Belles on Their Toes." When Miss South Carolina Kimberly Aiken, who is African American, became Miss America 1994, her parents declined their invitation to the Southern States party the following year. Noted her father, "We have an American flag in our home . . . a state flag, and that's it. We don't relate to the other flag." Associated Press, "Aiken's Parents Boycott Pageant Party."

5. Wilson, "Cult of Beauty," 145. Following Robert Bellah, Wilson defines civil religion as the religious dimension of a society through which it interprets its historical experience in the light of transcendent reality.

6. Blain Roberts, *Pageants, Parlors, and Pretty Women*, 119–221, 271–72; Banet-Weiser, *Most Beautiful Girl*, 18–21, 118–19, 154, 208.

7. Isaac, *Transformation of Virginia*, 58–114.

8. Banner, *American Beauty*, 250–54; Banet-Weiser, *Most Beautiful Girl*, 6–8, 254.

9. Charlene M. Boyer Lewis, *Ladies and Gentlemen on Display*, chap. 3.

10. Glassberg, *American Historical Pageantry*, 1, 18, 12–14, 122, 52, 26, 33.

11. Ibid., 4, 124; O. K. Williams Jr., "Spartanburg Centennial Celebration and Pageant," November 20, 1931, Spartanburg, South Caroliniana Library; "Plan Pageant to Depict Start."

12. Glassberg, *American Historical Pageantry*, 4–5, 132, 252–59, 269, 16, 18, 136, 139–45.

13. *The Making of South Carolina*, n.d., 378.75743 M28, South Caroliniana Library, 20–21.

14. Peter A. Brannon, ed., "The Pageant Book: Official Program of the Ceremonies and the Pageant in Celebration of Alabama Home Coming Week, May 5–6, 1926, Presenting *The Spirit of the South*," 1926, Montgomery, F 327 .B82, J. S. Hoole Special Collections Library, University of Alabama, Tuscaloosa; Glassberg, *American Historical Pageantry*, 252.

15. Glassberg, *American Historical Pageantry*, 114, 37, 64.

16. Banner, *American Beauty*, 253, 256–60.

17. Peiss, *Cheap Amusements*.

18. Nancie Martin, *Miss America*, 39.

19. On the early Miss America pageants, see Deford, *There She Is*; and Riverol, *Live from Atlantic City*.

20. Riverol, *Live from Atlantic City*, chap. 2.

21. Banet-Weiser, *Most Beautiful Girl*, 37; Savage, *Beauty Queens*, 76–77.

22. Banet-Weiser, *Most Beautiful Girl*, 37–39; Savage, *Beauty Queens*, 77–87.

23. Banet-Weiser, *Most Beautiful Girl*, 38–40; Savage, *Beauty Queens*, 77–87, 104.

24. On imagined communities, see Anderson, *Imagined Communities*, 7. On the Lost Cause, see Wilson, *Baptized in Blood*; Foster, *Ghosts of the Confederacy*; and Lumpkin, *Making of a Southerner*.

25. Wilson, *Baptised in Blood*; Foster, *Ghosts of the Confederacy*; Lumpkin, *Making of a Southerner*.

26. Boyd, "Southern Beauty," 79–80.

27. The classic treatment of massive resistance remains Bartley, *Rise of Massive Resistance*. See also Clive Webb, *Massive Resistance*; and George Lewis, *Massive Resistance*.

28. Boyd, "Southern Beauty," 80–81; Blain Roberts, *Pageants, Parlors, and Pretty Women*, 194.

29. Boyd, "Southern Beauty," 81; Blain Roberts, *Pageants, Parlors, and Pretty Women*, 204–8.

30. "Gumbo Beauty Ball"; "Bama Day Features"; Smithey, "O'Flynn Wins"; Phil Smith, "Bama Beauties Score"; "20 Southern Belles"; "Lynda Meade Visits Capstone"; *Garnet and Black*, 1955; *Garnet and Black*, 1963; *Ole Miss*, 1949–61.

31. *Ole Miss*, 1951; Bill Smith, "Boone Will Select"; *Ole Miss*, 1957; "Gumbo Beauty Ball."

32. "Cotton Maid, Alice Corr."

33. "20 Southern Belles Reign"; Phil Smith, "Bama Beauties Score"; "Beauty Queens to Spare."

34. "Photos Have Public Relations Value"; Boyd, "Southern Beauty," 81–82.

35. Virtually every history of the U.S. civil rights movement describes the integration crisis at Ole Miss, in which James Meredith's desegregation of the university in September 1962 under federal protection sparked riots. For accounts written soon after the event, see Silver, *Mississippi*; and Walter Lord, *Past That Would Not Die*.

36. Weeks, "Ole Miss"; Gray, "At Ole Miss, They Learned."

37. Boyd, "Southern Beauty"; Tice, *Queens of Academe*; Blain Roberts, *Pageants, Parlors, and Pretty Women*.

38. Banet-Weiser, *Most Beautiful Girl*, 207, 150–51.

39. Savage, *Beauty Queens*, 1–9.

40. Banet-Weiser, *Most Beautiful Girl*, 16–18.

41. Ibid.; M. G. Lord, "Greek Rites of Exclusion."

42. Boyd, "Southern Beauty," 87. On minstrelsy, see Lott, *Love and Theft*; Cockrell, *Demons of Disorder*; Lhamon, *Raising Cain*; Toll, *Blacking Up*; and Bean, Hatch, and McNamara, *Inside the Minstrel Mask*.

43. Press, "Private Faces, Public Lives."

44. Kirby, *Media-Made Dixie*; Karen L. Cox, *Dreaming of Dixie*.

45. Lavenda, "Minnesota Queen Pageants," 170. In my participant observation of twice weekly coaching sessions held to prepare Miss Houston and Miss Magnolia 1996

for that year's Miss Mississippi Pageant, the contestants were repeatedly, if gently, persuaded to tone down or rephrase answers and attitudes not in keeping with community attitudes. Such "touchy" issues included abortion access, prayer in public schools, school vouchers, and same-sex marriage.

46. Lavenda, "Minnesota Queen Pageants," 170–71.

47. Ibid., 169–73.

48. Ibid., 170–71; "Controversial Spectator Sport"; Wilson, *Judgment and Grace in Dixie*, 151.

49. Boyd, "Southern Beauty," 87.

50. Craig, *Ain't I a Beauty Queen?*, 30–35; Tiffany M. Gill, *Beauty Shop Politics*, 105–6; Tice, *Queens of Academe*, 35, 43–45; Hine, "In the Kingdom of Culture."

51. Craig, *Ain't I a Beauty Queen?*, 66–77; Tice, *Queens of Academe*, 43–44, 50–51; Lillian Smith, *Killers of the Dream*, 89, 121–23, 169–70; Early, "Waiting for Miss America."

52. McQuary, interview.

53. Lindsay, interview.

54. Clinton, *Tara Revisited*, 204.

55. Jon-Benet Ramsey was sexually assaulted and murdered in her Boulder, Colorado, home on Christmas night, 1996.

56. King, *Confessions*.

57. I witnessed this phenomenon at virtually every pageant rehearsal I attended. Pageant contestants were likewise quick to downplay their chances, denigrate their good looks and talent, and point out their physical flaws. This behavior was in stark contrast to their confident performance onstage.

58. Advertisement for Dr. Suman Das, 1996 Miss Mississippi Scholarship Pageant program book, Miss Mississippi Corporation, Vicksburg.

59. Michelle Meyer, "Expertise, Cost Create Arkansas Glamour."

60. Dodson, "Fifty Years without a Winner," 90.

61. "Miss America Losers Ponder Question."

62. Flowers, interview.

63. Holley, interview.

64. Michelle Meyer, "Here He Comes."

65. Ibid.

66. Temple, "Miss Alabama Ashley Davis"; Temple, "Miss Alabama Courtney Porter"; Michelle Meyer, "Here He Comes."

67. Reality television shows trading in southern stereotypes include *Toddlers and Tiaras* (TLC, 2009–13); *Southern Belles: Louisville* (Soapnet, 2009); *Sweet Home Alabama* (CMT, 2011); *Here Comes Honey Boo Boo* (TLC, 2012–17); *Duck Dynasty* (A&E, 2012–17); and *Southern Charm* (Bravo, 2014–).

68. Lowry, "Born to Preen," 28.

69. Cochran, "Official Quits." Magness was alleged to have made lewd and sugges-

tive remarks to contestants and to have had them model swimsuits for him in his home, unchaperoned.

70. Aitkin, "Crowning Touch of Richard Guy"; Gamboa, "Turning Misses into Hits"; "No More Apple Pie"; "Keys to Mississippi's Winning Miss."

71. Chu, "His Fair Ladies"; Haas, "Auburn Alumnus Star"; Devadanam, "Coaching King of Pageant Queens."

72. Lowry, "Born to Preen," 30.

73. Under the Clinton administration's "Don't ask, don't tell" policy, members of the armed services were to neither offer nor inquire about the sexual orientation of enlisted persons.

74. Lowry, "Born to Preen," 30.

75. The concept of a woman's physical appearance as a manifestation of her true inner nature has a long history in U.S. prescriptive literature. For examples of the genre, see Paralee Nichols, *How to Achieve Inner Beauty*; and Tice, *Queens of Academe*, 164, 71–73, 81.

76. Chu, "His Fair Ladies."

77. "Keys to Mississippi's Winning Miss."

78. Given the variety of pageant types (from well-organized national systems to one-off competitions that appear, disappear, and reappear from year to year), a definitive count of pageants is probably impossible. But the preliminary competitions of the Miss America Organization provide a gauge. The southern states routinely held many more prelims than their more populous nonsouthern states, partially accounting for their competitive status. For example, in 2018 the Miss Mississippi program held forty-nine preliminaries to the state pageant; Miss Alabama, fifty; Miss South Carolina, fifty-two; Miss Louisiana, thirty-three; Miss Georgia, forty-three; and Miss Texas, fifty-two. Miss Massachusetts, meanwhile, a highly populous state, held twenty-seven preliminaries; Miss New York, twenty-four; Miss Illinois, twenty-three; and Miss Maine, seven. For many years the Miss Maine program held no preliminaries. "Miss America."

79. Flowers, interview.

80. "Miss Kansas Is Crowned."

81. "Miss America Losers Ponder Question."

82. Lowry, "Born to Preen," 30.

83. Dodson, "Fifty Years without a Winner," 183.

84. Connerton, *How Societies Remember*, 11.

85. Miss Magnolia contestants, interviews.

86. Courtney Williams, interview.

87. "Around Town."

88. Wilson, "Cult of Beauty."

89. "Kari Litton Crowned Miss Mississippi."

90. Tice, *Queens of Academe*, 70.

91. Kuperinsky, "Miss America Organization Responds."

92. Tice, *Queens of Academe*, 83; Flowers, interview.

93. Louwerens, interview; Wallace, "Victory Is Sweet"; Frank, "Currier Junior Wins Pageant."

94. Mueller, "Magoffin Closing Schools."

95. Green, "Pre-pageant Fashion Show."

96. Holley, interview.

CHAPTER 3. *Hoop Dreams*

1. My depiction of the pageant's opening scenes, or "prologue," is based on my observation of the production in 1998 and 2000 and on Danny Duncan Collum's and June Newman Graham's accounts of witnessing the 2002 and 2010 productions, respectively. These performances continued to use the prologue script first penned in 1932. The joint production of the Natchez Garden Club and the Pilgrimage Garden Club was known as the Confederate Pageant from 1932 to 2000; as the Historic Natchez Pageant from 2001 to 2009; and as the Historic Natchez Tableaux beginning in 2010. Collum, *Black and Catholic*, 19–29; June Newman Graham, "Social Graces."

2. *Confederate Pageant*, performances, 1998, 2000, Natchez, Mississippi; *Confederate Pageant*. Originally the home of the Natchez Indians, the area was claimed in succession by France, England, Spain, the United States, and the Confederate States of America.

3. *Confederate Pageant*, performances, 1998, 2000; *Confederate Pageant*.

4. Democrat Editorial Board, "New Cast at Pageant"; Mickens, "Organizers Tweak Historic Tableaux"; Mickens, "Pageant Continues"; June Newman Graham, "Social Graces," 141. For discussions of race, performance, and public memory in Natchez in the twentieth century, see Hoelscher, "Making Place, Making Race"; Jack Emerson Davis, "Struggle for Public History"; Jack Emerson Davis, *Race against Time*; and Falck, *Remembering Dixie*.

5. Gandy, "Young Takes Solo"; Ronald L. F Davis, *Black Experience in Natchez*, 143.

6. Historical pageants using revised scripts included the circa 1970 *Cotton Palace Pageant* of Waco, Texas (revised 2010) and *Unto These Hills . . . a Retelling*, the story of the Cherokee of North Carolina, first performed in their namesake town in 1950 (revised 2006). Carl Hoover, "Cotton Palace Pageant Looks"; Teachout, "History under the Stars."

7. MacNeil, interview.

8. Confederate Pageant, 2000.

9. Connerton, *How Societies Remember*.

10. Whittington, interview.

11. Confederate Pageant, 2000.

12. The tale of "the late freeze" was widely circulated locally. Natchez Garden Club, *Natchez Garden Club*, 6; Blankenstein, interview.

13. McWhite, "Natchez Is a Fairy Story."

14. Harlow, "Annual Natchez Pilgrimage."

15. On club members using traditional understandings of "a woman's place" to venture outside the domestic sphere and into larger cultural and political arenas, see Blair, *Clubwoman as Feminist.*

16. Natchez Garden Club, *Natchez Garden Club.*

17. "'Impractical' Dream for Pilgrimage"; article, subject file: Natchez Pilgrimage, 1934–50, MDAH.

18. Cohn, "Natchez Was a Lady," 15.

19. Natchez Garden Club, *Natchez Garden Club.*

20. "Pilgrimage Celebrates 50 Years."

21. Natchez Garden Club, *Natchez Garden Club*; "Petticoat Peace Quiets Quarreling Natchez."

22. Shaffer, *See America First*; Karen L. Cox, *Dreaming of Dixie*; Falck, *Remembering Dixie*, 153–210.

23. Robert Meyer Jr., "Spring's Parade of Festivals"; Suzanne, "Madame Chairman."

24. American Express, display advertisement.

25. "Enjoy the South This Spring."

26. Alabama State Planning Commission, display advertisement.

27. On pilgrimage, see Ray, *Highland Heritage*, 140–41; Kushner, *Sound and Spirit*, 533.

28. Mrs. James Bland Martin, *Follow the Green Arrow*, vii, 20. See also Yuhl, *Golden Haze of Memory.*

29. Cohn, "Natchez Was a Lady," 15.

30. Wyatt Moore, "Monteigne."

31. "Elgin Place, Typical Plantation Home," 8.

32. Wyatt Moore, "Natchez Pilgrimage 'Pink Edition.'"

33. George Nealy, of the *Times Picayune*, penned the tourism slogan for the first pilgrimage in April 1932. The Natchez Garden Club paid him seven dollars for his work. Shemanski, *Guide to Fairs and Festivals*, 102.

34. *Glamorous Natchez*, pamphlet, 1939, subject file: Natchez Pilgrimage, 1934–50, MDAH; "Mississippi Pilgrimages Began"; Katherine Grafton Miller, "Scrapbook."

35. Boatner, "Scrapbook"; McLeod, "Radio's Forgotten Years"; Patterson, "Ingenious Methods Used as Advertising"; "Promoting Pilgrimage Was Hard"; Parks, "Pilgrimage Publicity Film Delights Audience."

36. Boatner, "Scrapbook." On automobile touring and the construction of national identity, see Shaffer, *See America First.*

37. Gueymard, "Natchez to Welcome Pilgrims."

38. "Pilgrims Travel to Mississippi," 1.

39. Patterson, "Ingenious Methods Used as Advertising"; Cook, "Famous Humorist and Publisher Toured"; "Newspaper, Mag. Writers, Photo Men."

40. Boatner, "Scrapbook"; Patterson, "Ingenious Methods Used as Advertising."

41. Knabb-Lane Studio, "Pilgrimage Photographs"; Patton, "Mammy"; Katherine Grafton Miller, "Pilgrimage to Dixieland"; Gueymard, "Natchez to Welcome Pilgrims"; "'Impractical' Dream for Pilgrimage"; Peterson, "Old South Lives Again!"

42. "Wright to Make States Rights Speech"; "State Rights Meetings"; "Mrs. Kendall Issues Call"; "Here for the Natchez Pilgrimage"; "Governor Will Speak"; Lambert, "Natchez Belles Invite Governor."

43. Hass, *Carried to the Wall*, especially chap. 4; Dilworth, introd. to *Acts of Possession*; Stewart, "Death and Life," 204.

44. "Pilgrims Travel to Mississippi"; Iovine, "Where Nothing Is Gone"; Peterson, "Old South Lives Again!"

45. Iovine, "Where Nothing Is Gone"; Tolf, "Natchez"; Pope, "Natchez Pilgrimage"; Suzi Parker, "Amid Linen and Lace."

46. Iovine, "Where Nothing Is Gone"; Hudson, "Beyond Moonlight and Magnolias"; Northway, "Natchez Mississippi."

47. Iovine, "Where Nothing Is Gone"; Bowman, "Performing Southern History," 152–54; Warren, *Legacy of the Civil War*, 54, 59–60.

48. Pope, "Natchez Pilgrimage"; Tolf, "Natchez"; Seebohm, "Enshrining the Old South."

49. Stokes, interview; Whittington, interview.

50. Whittington, interview.

51. McGehee and McGehee, interview.

52. Edwards, "China Business Picks Up."

53. Whittington, interview.

54. Ibid.

55. Ostrander, *Women of the Upper Class*, 88–90.

56. Pilgrimage Garden Club member, interview. On the equation of southernness with Whiteness, see Cobb, *Redefining Southern Culture*; Cobb, *Away Down South*, 212–13; Thadious Davis, "Expanding the Limits"; and Hale, *Making Whiteness*, 3–11.

57. Saterstrom, *Pink Institution*; "Interview with Selah Saterstrom"; Saterstrom, "Pink Institution"; Iles, *Turning Angel*; Marshall, "Water in Which I Swim." The pilgrimage and Natchez provided fodder for numerous novels, most notably Stark Young's ode to plantation gentility, *So Red the Rose*. Natchez native and Natchez Garden Club member Alice Walworth Graham set much of her romantic fiction on local plantations, with the creation of the pilgrimage a plot line in her novel, *The Natchez Woman*.

58. *The Pilgrimage Garden Club Presents the Confederate Ball Tableaux*, 1938; *Confederate Ball, Eighth Annual Pageant of the Original Natchez Garden Club*, 1939; Confederate Pageant program, 1948; *The Confederate Pageant*, 1963, subject file, Natchez Pilgrimage, 1950–70; *The Confederate Tableaux, Annual Pageant of the Natchez Pilgrimage*, 1951, all in Historic Natchez Foundation, box 1, Natchez Pilgrimage Collection, MDAH.

59. Wheatley, interview.

60. Miller and Miller, interviews.

61. Kammen, *Mystic Chords of Memory*, 688.

62. Frazier, interview; Collum, *Black and Catholic*, 158–63.

63. Frazier, interview.

64. Ibid.

65. Garden club members repeated this maxim numerous times in interviews conducted in April 2000, in Natchez, Mississippi.

66. Remark made to the author by the sister-in-law of Anne MacNeil at the 2000 Confederate Pageant.

EPILOGUE. *Resilient Routine*

1. McCann, "Tableaux Debuts New Play Format"; Amy, "Author Iles Reworks Natchez Pageant"; Hillyer, "Changes Planned for Tableaux."

2. Amy, "Author Iles Reworks Natchez Pageant"; Hillyer, "PGC Pulls out of Tableaux"; Grant, *Deepest South of All*, 41, 78–79, 84–85, 252–55, 72. On progressive attempts to rescript the production to document a more inclusive past, see also Falck, *Remembering Dixie*, 239–42.

3. Frederick, "Good Day to Be Here"; Hamilton, "At Ole Miss, the Tailgaters."

4. Remington Smith, *Derby*; Harrah-Conforth, "Landscape of Possibility," 229–30.

5. "GPS Celebrates May Day 2018."

6. Pierce, "Chattanooga Cotton Ball King"; Colloff, "'Beldades' of the Ball"; "Photos."

7. Gardner, "Rethinking Chattanooga Tradition"; Greenfield, *Girl Culture*.

8. Rutledge, "Azalea Trail Maids";

9. Kathleen Parker, "Queen Carlson Wins Again"; Yahr, "Miss America 2019"; Hesse, "'New' Miss America"; Argetsinger, "Miss America's New Face."

10. Farzan, "BBQ Becky, Permit Patty."

11. Johnson, "Big Donor's Facebook Photos"; Ganucheau, "Protect the Values"; Meek, "Top Stories of 2017."

12. Armus, "Robert E. Lee Statue Vandalized"; Svrluga, "Washington and Lee Renames Buildings"; Associated Press, "City Dismantles Confederate Statue"; Associated Press, "Civil War Plaque to Be Removed"; Truong, "Va. School Shifts from Lee"; Svrluga, "UNC in Turmoil"; Svrluga, "All Signs of Silent Sam"; Karen L. Cox, "What Changed in Charlottesville"; Sellers, "Flying the Colors."

13. Lartey and Jacobs, "Cindy Hyde-Smith Wins"; Eubanks, "Mississippi's Past, Not Its Future."

14. Vozzella, Morrison, and Schneider, "Gov. Ralph Northam Admits"; Portnoy et al., "Second Woman Accuses"; Vozzella, "Tribute to Lee Inspires Sit-Out"; Vozzella and Schneider, "Gov. Northam Refuses"; Martin, Eligon, and Robertson, "He's Not

There Yet"; Waldman, "Sociologist Examines the 'White Fragility'"; Barnes, "Baseball, Apple Pie, Blackface"; Petri, "Amazing Thing about the '80s"; Bahrampour, "Remembering Massive Resistance."

15. "Party Themes"; Bartlett, "Ugly Tradition Persists"; Kantor, "Quad Protest Targets"; Cassie, "Johns Hopkins Fraternity Suspended." Greek Blackface parties in the 1990s included Pi Kappa Alpha's "Party in the Projects" at Texas Tech University; Kappa Delta's "Who Rides the Bus?" mixer at the University of Alabama; and Sigma Alpha Epsilon's "Jungle Party" at Texas A&M. The campus climate at the University of Illinois appears to have regressed since 1951, when the student body elected Black coed Clarice Clotilde Davis, a member of Alpha Kappa Alpha sorority, homecoming queen. *Time*, November 19, 1951, Clyde S. Johnson Fraternity Collection, series 41/2/50, box 2.

16. Auchmutey, "Sister Who Spoke Up"; Zengerle, "Sorority Row"; Robbins, "Joining the Systems."

17. "Party Themes."

18. Mathias, "Outrage at Ole Miss"; *Greek Chic*; Crain, "Alabama Sororities Desegregated"; Joshua Rhett Miller, "Sorority Sister Speaks Out"; Mintz and Mallard, "Officials Working to Address"; Bacon, "Oklahoma Sorority Sister Booted."

19. Ahmaud Arbery, a twenty-five-year-old Black man, was shot dead in February 2020 after being chased by armed White residents in a neighborhood outside Brunswick, Georgia. Blackistone, "As Monuments Fall, Don't Overlook"; Bailey, "Community at a Crossroads"; Fisher, "Unending Civil War Flares Anew."

20. Stein, Williams, and Hermann, "D.C.'s Sole Outdoor Confederate Statue"; Schneider, "Crowds Cheer Removal"; Cox and Wiggins, "State House to Lose Plaque"; Svrluga, "Washington and Lee Faculty Vote"; Sullivan, "Moment of Reckoning in Va."; Svrluga, "Prominent Confederate Statue"; Berkowitz and Blanco, "Confederate Monuments Are Falling"; Schneider, "Untouchable No More, Lee Statue"; Kolenich, "Space around the Lee Statue"; Hilton, "As Columbus Statues Fall"; "Protesters Fill Streets."

21. Riley, "'Better' Education"; Clark, "We Said the Sheriff's Name"; Mendelsohn, "#nomorebelles"; Elizabeth Anne Brown, "In Alabama, a Debate"; Ingram, "Azalea Belles No More."

22. Schmeichel, Kerr, and Linder, "Selfies as Postfeminist Pedagogy." On "disciplinary regime," the authors cite Rosalind Gill, "Culture and Subjectivity."

BIBLIOGRAPHY

"20 Southern Belles Reign as Top Corolla Beauties." *Crimson-White*, November 10, 1953, 1.

"About." Buc Days. Accessed November 5, 2006. https://bucdays.com/about/.

Aitkin, Lee. "The Crowning Touch of Richard Guy and Rex Holt Shapes Texas Teens into Lovelies Who Just Can't Lose." *People*, May 4, 1987. http://www.people.com /people/archive/article/0,,20096191,00.html.

Alabama State Planning Commission. Display advertisement. *Chicago Daily Tribune*, January 7, 1940.

Allen, Danielle. "The 'Trumpists' Party." *Washington Post*, September 6, 2015, A19.

American Express. Display advertisement. *Chicago Daily Tribune*, n.d.

Amy, Jeff. "Author Iles Reworks Natchez Pageant." *Jackson (Miss.) Clarion Ledger*, April 5, 2015. https://www.clarionledger.com/story/news/2015/04/05/author-iles -reworks-natchez-pageant/25338913/.

Anderson, Benedict. *Imagined Communities: Reflections on the Origin and Spread of Nationalism*. London: Verso, 1991.

Appelbaum, Yoni. "Why Is the Flag Still There?" *Atlantic*, June 21, 2015. http://www .theatlantic.com/politics/archive/2015/06/why-is-the-flag-still-there/396431/.

Argetsinger, Amy. "Miss America's New Face." *Washington Post*, September 7, 2018, C1, 3.

Armus, Teo. "Robert E. Lee Statue Vandalized with Paint." *Washington Post*, August 6, 2018, B3.

"Around Town." *Jackson (Miss.) Clarion-Ledger*, July 8, 1996, B1.

Associated Press. "Aiken's Parents Boycott Pageant Party over Flag." *Press of Atlantic City*, September 21, 1994, A1.

———. "City Dismantles Confederate Statue." *Washington Post*, March 13, 2019, A3.

———. "Civil War Plaque to Be Removed from Capitol." *Washington Post*, January 12, 2019, A2.

———. "Confederate Statue Removal in New Orleans Turns Nasty." Nola. March 25, 2016. https://www.nola.com/politics/2016/03/confederate_statue_removal_in.html.

———. "Racist Oklahoma Video Leads to Hoop Skirt Ban on Ga. Campus." March 18, 2015. http://www.gpb.org/news/2015/03/18/racist-oklahoma-video-leads-hoop -skirt-ban-on-ga-campus.

———. "Woman Says She Broke Sorority Race Bar." *New York Times*, September 9, 2001, sec. 1, p. 28.

Auchmutey, Jim. "The Sister Who Spoke Up: Ali Davis Loved Her Life in Alpha Gamma Delta at the University of Georgia: Then a Black Student Came through Sorority Rush and Everything Changed." *Atlanta Journal and Constitution*, February 10, 2002, A1.

Ayers, Edward L. "What We Talk about When We Talk about the South." In *All over the Map: Rethinking American Regions*, edited by Edward L. Ayers, Patricia Nelson Limerick, Stephen Nissenbaum, and Peter S. Onuf, 62–82. Baltimore: Johns Hopkins University Press, 1996.

B, Informant. Interview by Elizabeth Boyd. February 27, 1997. Oxford, Miss.

Bacon, John. "Oklahoma Sorority Sister Booted after Posting Blackface Video." *USA Today*, January 20, 2019. https://www.usatoday.com/story/news/nation/2019/01/20/blackface-video-sorority-sister-booted-senseless-act-racism/2631162002/.

Bahrampour, Tara. "Remembering Massive Resistance: Black Students Who Integrated a Va. High School Recall Their Role in History." *Washington Post*, February 15, 2019. https://wapo.st/2SS5gt4?tid=ss_mail&utm_term=.84df21f8d254.

Bailey, Holly. "Community at a Crossroads over Future of Floyd Tribute." *Washington Post*, October 16, 2020, A3.

"Bama Day Features Politics and Beauty." *Crimson White*, March 20, 1956, 10.

Banet-Weiser, Sarah. *The Most Beautiful Girl in the World: Beauty Pageants and National Identity*. Berkeley: University of California Press, 1999.

Banner, Lois. *American Beauty*. New York: Knopf, 1983.

Barbee, Matthew Mace. *Race and Masculinity in Southern Memory: History of Richmond, Virginia's Monument Avenue, 1948–1996*. Lanham, Md.: Lexington Books, 2013.

Barnes, Rhae Lynn. "Baseball, Apple Pie, Blackface." *Washington Post*, February 10, 2019, B1.

Bartlett, Thomas. "An Ugly Tradition Persists at Southern Fraternity Parties." *Chronicle of Higher Education*, November 30, 2001, 33.

Bartley, Numan V. *The Rise of Massive Resistance: Race and Politics in the South during the 1950's*. Baton Rouge: Louisiana State University Press, 1969.

Bauerlein, Valerie. "Confederate Flag Removed from South Carolina Statehouse." *Wall Street Journal*, July 10, 2015. http://www.wsj.com/articles/confederate-flag-removed-from-south-carolina-statehouse-1436538782.

Bean, Annemarie, James V. Hatch, and Brooks McNamara, eds. *Inside the Minstrel Mask: Readings in Nineteenth-Century Blackface Minstrelsy*. Hanover, N.H.: Wesleyan University Press, 1996.

"Beauty Queens to Spare." *Life*, August 25, 1961, 58–64.

Beidelman, Thomas O. *Moral Imagination in Kaguru Modes of Thought*. Washington, D.C.: Smithsonian, 1993.

"Belles on Their Toes." *Coast Magazine*, July 1995, 39–47.

Berkowitz, Bonnie, and Adrian Blanco. "Confederate Monuments Are Falling, but Hundreds Still Stand." *Washington Post*, June 21, 2020, A6.

Bidwell, Allie. "Following Controversy, University of Alabama Sororities Accept Minority Students." *U.S. News and World Reports*, September 23, 2013. https://www .usnews.com/news/articles/2013/09/23/following-controversy-university-of -alabama-sororities-accept-minority-students.

Bisher, Catherine W. "Landmarks of Power: Building a Southern Past in Raleigh and Wilmington, North Carolina, 1885–1915." In Brundage, *Where These Memories Grow*, 139–68.

Black, Earl, and Merle Black. *The Rise of Southern Republicans*. Cambridge, Mass.: Harvard University Press, 2002.

Blackistone, Kevin B. "As Monuments Fall, Don't Overlook Activist's Athletic Act of Protest." *Washington Post*, July 13, 2020, C11.

Blair, Karen J. *The Clubwoman as Feminist: True Womanhood Redefined, 1868–1914*. New York: Holmes and Meier, 1980.

Blankenstein, Kathie. Interview by Elizabeth Boyd. April 3, 2000. Natchez, Miss.

Blight, David. *Race and Reunion: The Civil War in American Memory*. Cambridge: Belknap, 2001.

Blinder, Alan. "Alabama: Sororities Told to Increase Diversity." *New York Times*, September 17, 2013, A15.

———. "At Alabama, a Renewed Stand for Integration." *New York Times*, September 19, 2013, A18.

———. "A Turnabout at Traditionally White Sororities, in Nine Days at Alabama." *New York Times*, September 21, 2013, A10.

Boatner, Lillie Vidal. *Scrapbook*. Natchez, Miss., 1932.

Bowman, Michael. "Performing Southern History for the Tourist Gaze." In *Exceptional Spaces: Essays in Performance and History*, edited by Della Pollack, 142–58. Chapel Hill: University of North Carolina Press, 1998.

Boyd, Elizabeth Bronwyn. "Southern Beauty: Performing Femininity in an American Region." PhD diss., University of Texas at Austin, 2000.

Brown, Elizabeth Anne. "In Alabama, a Debate over Rewriting or Merely Righting History." *Washington Post*, August 21, 2020, C1–2.

Brown, Robbie. "Ole Miss Resolves One Mascot Controversy and Creates Another." *New York Times*, October 15, 2010, A17.

Brown, Rodger Lyle. *Ghost Dancing on the Cracker Circuit: The Culture of Festivals in the American South*. Jackson: University Press of Mississippi, 1997.

Brumfield, Ben, and Ralph Ellis. "New Orleans Votes to Remove Confederate, Civil War Monuments." CNN. December 17, 2015. http://www.cnn.com/2015/12/17/us /new-orleans-confederate-monuments-vote/.

Brundage, W. Fitzhugh. "No Deed but Memory." In Brundage, *Where These Memories Grow*, 1–28. Chapel Hill: University of North Carolina Press, 2000.

———. *The Southern Past: A Clash of Race and Memory*. Cambridge, Mass.: Harvard University Press, 2005.

———. *Where These Memories Grow: History, Memory, and Southern Identity*. Chapel Hill: University of North Carolina Press, 2000.

Burch, Lauren. Interview by Elizabeth Boyd. December 7, 2006. Tuscaloosa, Ala.

Butler, Judith. *Gender Trouble: Feminism and the Subversion of Identity*. New York: Routledge, 1990.

Capriccioso, Rob. "Integration Later." *Inside Higher Ed*, February 6, 2006. https://www.insidehighered.com/news/2006/02/06/integration-later.

Casmier-Paz, Lynn. "Heritage, Not Hate? Collecting Black Memorabilia." *Southern Cultures*, Spring 2003, 43–61.

Cassie, Ron. "Johns Hopkins Fraternity Suspended after Racially Themed Halloween Party." *Washington Examiner*, October 31, 2006. https://www.washingtonexaminer.com/johns-hopkins-fraternity-suspended-after-racially-themed-halloween-party.

Cayson, Leah. "Ole Miss Fans' Reception of Rebel the Black Bear Mixed." *Daily Mississippian*, September 12, 2011. https://issuu.com/dailymississippian/docs/09132011-small.

———. "Students Have Mixed Reaction to Rebel Black Bear." *Daily Mississippian*, September 12, 2011.

Chu, Jeff. "His Fair Ladies." *New York Times Magazine*, July 20, 2014, 31.

Clark, Courtney. "We Said the Sheriff's Name. But What about Emmett Till's?" *Academy Stories*. 2020. https://www.theacademystories.com/post/we-said-the-sheriff-s-name-but-what-about-emmett-till-s.

Clinton, Catherine. *Tara Revisited: Women, War, and the Plantation Legend*. New York: Abbeville, 1995.

Cobb, James C. *Away Down South: A History of Southern Identity*. New York: Oxford University Press, 2005.

———. *Redefining Southern Culture: Mind and Identity in the Modern South*. Athens: University of Georgia Press, 1999.

Cochran, Mike. "Official Quits after Miss America Threat to Bar Texas." *Montgomery (Ala.) Advertiser*, November 22, 1990, 4A.

Cockrell, Dale. *Demons of Disorder: Early Blackface Minstrels and Their World*. Cambridge: Cambridge University Press, 1997.

Cohn, David L. "Natchez Was a Lady." *Atlantic Monthly*, January 1940, 13–19.

Colloff, Pamela. "'Beldades' of the Ball." *Texas Monthly*, April 2006. https://www.texasmonthly.com/articles/beldades-of-the-ball/.

Collum, Danny Duncan. *Black and Catholic in the Jim Crow South: The Stuff That Makes Community*. New York: Paulist, 2006.

"Come to Natchez: Where the Old South Still Lives." Natchez, Miss.: Pilgrimage Garden Club, 1938.

The Confederate Pageant. Vidalia, La.: Bruce Video, 1999.

Connerton, Paul. *How Societies Remember*. Cambridge: Cambridge University Press, 1989.

"A Controversial Spectator Sport." *Newsweek*, September 17, 1984, 58.

Cook, Audrey. "Famous Humorist and Publisher Toured, Fêted during Short Visit to Natchez." *Natchez Democrat*, February 5, 1948, 4.

Coski, John M. *The Confederate Battle Flag: America's Most Embattled Emblem*. Cambridge, Mass.: Belknap Press of Harvard University Press, 2005.

Costa, Robert, Sari Horwitz, and William Wan. "Man Arrested in Charleston Killings." *Washington Post*, June 19, 2015, A1, 13.

"Cotton Maid, Alice Corr, Says Good to Be Back at Bama." *Crimson-White*, June 29, 1954, 7.

Cox, Erin, and Ovetta Wiggins. "State House to Lose Plaque Sympathetic to Confederacy." *Washington Post*, June 16, 2020, B6.

Cox, John Woodrow. "Defending Dixie." *Washington Post*, June 28, 2015, C1, 5.

Cox, Karen L. *Dixie's Daughters: The United Daughters of the Confederacy and the Preservation of Confederate Culture*. Gainesville: University Press of Florida, 2003.

———. *Dreaming of Dixie: How the South Was Created in American Popular Culture*. Chapel Hill, N.C.: University of North Carolina Press, 2011.

———. "What Changed in Charlottesville." *New York Times*, August 12, 2019, A23.

Craft, Emily. "Rush Continues: Twilley Called Back for Second Round of Rush." *Crimson White*, September 5, 2001, 1.

Craig, Maxine Leeds. *Ain't I a Beauty Queen? Black Women, Beauty, and the Politics of Race*. Oxford: Oxford University Press, 2002.

Crain, Abbey. "Alabama Sororities Desegregated, but Has Anything Changed?" AL. August 30, 2018. https://www.al.com/news/birmingham/2018/08/alabama_sororities_desegregate.html.

D, Informant. Interview by Elizabeth Boyd. March 26, 1998. Oxford, Miss.

Daniel, Pete. *Lost Revolutions: The South in the 1950s*. Chapel Hill: University of North Carolina Press, 2000.

Davis, Fred. *Yearning for Yesterday: A Sociology of Nostalgia*. New York: Free Press, 1979.

Davis, Jack Emerson. *Race against Time: Culture and Separation in Natchez since 1930*. Baton Rouge: Louisiana State University Press, 2001.

———. "A Struggle for Public History: Black and White Claims to Natchez's Past." *Public Historian* 22, no. 1 (2000): 45–63.

Davis, Ronald L. F. *The Black Experience in Natchez, 1720–1880*. Denver: U.S. Department of the Interior, National Park Service, 1993.

Davis, Thadious. "Expanding the Limits: The Intersection of Race and Region." *Southern Literary Journal* 20, no. 2 (1988): 3–11.

Deford, Frank. *There She Is: The Life and Times of Miss America*. New York: Penguin Books, 1971.

Democrat Editorial Board. "New Cast at Pageant Is Right Step." *Natchez Democrat*, April 3, 2007.

Devadanam, Steven. "The Coaching King of Pageant Queens." *Houstonia Magazine*, January 5, 2016. https://www.houstoniamag.com/articles/2016/1/5/king-of-queens -pageant-jj-smith-january-2016.

Dilworth, Leah, ed. *Acts of Possession: Collecting in America*. New Brunswick: Rutgers University Press, 2003.

———. "American Icons: Photographs by Carrie Mae Weems." In Dilworth, *Acts of Possession*, 255–66.

———. Introduction to Dilworth, *Acts of Possession*, 3–15.

Dodson, James. "Fifty Years without a Winner." *Yankee*, September 1987, 86–91, 178–83.

Doherty, Risa C. "Greek Letters at a Price." *New York Times*, October 28, 2014.

Donadio, Rachel. "Authors Tap into Mood of a France 'Homesick at Home.'" *New York Times*, January 9, 2015, A4.

Dries, Kate. "Backlash Comes over UGA's Ban on Hoop Skirts at Greek Functions." *Jezebel*, March 25, 2015. http://jezebel.com/backlash-comes-over-ugas-ban-on-hoop -skirts.

E, Informant. Interview by Elizabeth Boyd. March 4, 1997. Oxford, Miss.

Early, Gerald. "Waiting for Miss America." *Antioch Review* 42, no. 3 (1984): 291–305.

Edwards, Jennifer. "China Business Picks Up during Pageant." *Natchez Democrat*, February 28, 2010. https://www.natchezdemocrat.com/2010/02/28/china-business -picks-up-during-pageant-season/.

Eichstedt, Jennifer L., and Stephen Small. *Representations of Slavery: Race and Ideology in Southern Plantation Museums*. Washington, D.C.: Smithsonian Institutions Press, 2002.

"Elgin Place, Typical Plantation Home of Early Days, Old Fashioned Gallery Feature, Builder Was a Horticulturalist of Wide Note." *Natchez Democrat*, February 29, 1948.

Eligon, John. "Black Students See a Campus Riven by Race." *New York Times*, November 12, 2015, A1.

"Enjoy the South This Spring." *Natchez Democrat*, February 4, 1948.

Eubanks, W. Ralph. "Mississippi's Past, Not Its Future, Won the Election." CNN. November 28, 2018. https://www.cnn.com/2018/11/28/opinions/mississippi-cindy-hyde -smith-senate-eubanks-opinion/index.html.

Evans, Sara M. "Women." In *The Encyclopedia of Southern History*, edited by David C. Roller and Robert W. Twyman, 1353–55. Baton Rouge: Louisiana State University Press, 1979.

F, Informant. Interview by Elizabeth Boyd. February 28, 1997. Oxford, Miss.

Falck, Susan T. *Remembering Dixie: The Battle to Control Historical Memory in Natchez, Mississippi, 1865–1941*. Jackson: University Press of Mississippi, 2019.

Farnham, Christie Anne. *The Education of the Southern Belle: Higher Education and Student Socialization in the Antebellum South.* New York: New York University Press, 1994.

Farzan, Antonia Noori. "BBQ Becky, Permit Patty and Cornerstore Caroline: Too 'Cutesy' for Those White Women Calling Police on Black People?" *Washington Post*, October 19, 2018. https://wapo.st/2S1WDcf?tid=ss_mail&utm_term= .docaf03528ea.

Fass, Paula. *The Damned and the Beautiful: American Youth in the 1920s.* New York: Oxford University Press, 1977.

Faust, Drew Gilpin. "Clutching the Chains That Bind: Margaret Mitchell and *Gone with the Wind.*" *Southern Cultures* 5, no. 1 (1999): 6–19.

———. "Living History." *Harvard Magazine*, May–June 2003, 39–46, 82–83.

Ferguson, Ronald A. "The Distributions of Whiteness." *American Quarterly* 66, no. 4 (2014): 1101–106.

Fisher, Marc. "Unending Civil War Flares Anew, Now over Confederate Statues." *Washington Post*, June 12, 2020, A1, A22.

Fletcher, Michael, and Janell Ross. "Attack at Church Evokes Dark Days from Nation's Past." *Washington Post*, June 19, 2015, A1, 14.

Flowers, Megan. Interview by Elizabeth Boyd. February 25, 2000. Oxford, Miss.

Foster, Gaines M. *Ghosts of the Confederacy: Defeat, the Lost Cause, and the Emergence of the New South, 1865–1913.* Baton Rouge: Louisiana State University Press, 1987.

Frank, Stephen E. "Currier Junior Wins Pageant." *Harvard Crimson*, March 12, 1992. https://www.thecrimson.com/article/1992/3/12/currier-junior-wins-pageant-pa -currier/.

Frazier, Ora. Interview by Elizabeth Boyd. August 2002. Natchez, Miss.

Frederick, Charles R. "A Good Day to Be Here: Tailgating in the Grove at Ole Miss." PhD diss., Indiana University, 1999.

Friend, Craig Thompson, ed. *Southern Masculinity: Perspectives on Manhood in the South since Reconstruction.* Athens: University of Georgia Press, 2009.

Gamboa, Suzanne. "Turning Misses into Hits: Beauty Queen Makers' Crowning Success Leads to Fame and Lawsuits in El Paso." *Houston Chronicle*, June 30, 1991, 4.

Gandy, Joan. "Young Takes Solo in 'Ol' Man River.'" *Natchez Democrat*, April 2, 2007. https://www.natchezdemocrat.com/2007/04/02/young-takes-solo-in-ol-man-river/.

Ganucheau, Adam. "'Protect the Values We Hold Dear': A Closer Look inside the Ed Meek, Ole Miss Race Controversy." *Mississippi Today*, October 18, 2018. https:// mississippitoday.org/2018/10/18/protect-the-values-we-hold-dear-a-closer-look-inside -the-ed-meek-ole-miss-race-controversy/.

Gardner, Mary Rebecca. "Rethinking Chattanooga Tradition." *I've Been Thinking* (blog). April 1, 2015. https://maryrgardner.wordpress.com/2015/08/01/rethinking -chattanooga-tradition/.

Gettleman, Jeffrey. "Sorority System in No Rush to Integrate." *Los Angeles Times*, September 10, 2001, A1.

Gill, Rosalind. "Culture and Subjectivity in Neoliberal and Postfeminist Times." *Subjectivity* 25, no. 1 (2008): 432–45.

Gill, Tiffany M. *Beauty Shop Politics: African American Women's Activism in the Beauty Industry*. Women in American History. Urbana: University of Illinois Press, 2010.

Gillis, John R. "Memory and Identity: The History of a Relationship." In *Commemorations: The Politics of National Identity*, edited by John R. Gillis, 3–24. Princeton: Princeton University Press, 1994.

Glassberg, David. *American Historical Pageantry: The Uses of Tradition in the Early Twentieth Century*. Chapel Hill: University of North Carolina Press, 1990.

Glymph, Thavolia. *Out of the House of Bondage: The Transformation of the Plantation Household*. Cambridge: Cambridge University Press, 2008.

Goings, Kenneth W. *Mammy and Uncle Mose: Black Collectibles and American Stereotyping*. Bloomington: Indiana University Press, 1994.

Goldfield, David. *Still Fighting the Civil War: The American South and Southern History*. Baton Rouge: Louisiana State University Press, 2002.

Gordon, Lynn D. *Gender and Higher Education in the Progressive Era*. New Haven: Yale University Press, 1990.

"The Governor Will Speak from an Appropriate Setting." *Natchez Democrat*, March 20, 1948, 4.

"GPS Celebrates May Day 2018." *News*. Girls Preparatory School. April 25, 2018. https://www.gps.edu/page/news-detail?pk=1179984.

Graham, Alice Walworth. *The Natchez Woman*. New York: Doubleday, 1950.

Graham, David A. "The Stubborn Persistence of Confederate Monuments." *Atlantic*, April 26, 2016. http://www.theatlantic.com/politics/archive/2016/04/the-stubborn -persistence-of-confederate-monuments/479751/.

Graham, June Newman. "Social Graces: The Natchez Garden Club as a Literacy Sponsor." PhD diss., Louisiana State University and Agricultural and Mechanical College, 2011.

Grant, Richard. *The Deepest South of All: True Stories from Natchez, Mississippi*. New York: Simon and Schuster, 2020.

Grasgreen, Allie. "Segregated Sororities Not Limited to Alabama, Experts Say." *Inside Higher Ed*, September 19, 2013. https://www.insidehighered.com/news/2013/09/19 /segregated-sororities-not-limited-to-alabama-experts-say.

Gray, Jerry. "At Ole Miss, They Learned to Play Hardball." *New York Times*, June 2, 1996, A1.

Greek Chic. University of Alabama. June 26, 2015. https://issuu.com /alabamapanhellenic/docs/ua_greek_chic_2015.

Green, Nancy. "Pre-pageant Fashion Show." *Kosciusko (Miss.) Star-Herald*, July 2, 1998, B1.

Greenfield, Lauren. *Girl Culture*. San Francisco: Chronicle Books, 2002.

Grubb, Alan. "House and Home in the Victorian South: The Cookbook as Guide." In *In Joy and in Sorrow: Women, Family, and Marriage in the Victorian South, 1830–1900*, edited by Carol Bleser, 154–75. New York: Oxford University Press, 1991.

Gueymard, Ernest A. "Natchez to Welcome Pilgrims." *Advocate*, 1937.

"Gumbo Beauty Ball." *Gumbo*, 1956.

Gusterson, Hugh. "Studying Up Revisited." *PoLAR* 20, no. 1 (2008): 114–19.

Haas, Katherine. "Auburn Alumnus Star of New TLC Reality Show, 'Coach Charming.'" *Opelika-Auburn News*, October 31, 2015. https://www.oanow.com/news/auburnuniversity/auburn-alumnus-star-of-new-tlc-reality-show-coach-charming/article_9341e28a-803d-11e5-9cac-1faf11731132.html.

Hale, Grace Elizabeth. *Making Whiteness: The Culture of Segregation in the South, 1890–1940*. New York: Random House, 1998.

Hall, Jacquelyn Dowd. "The Prong of Love." *Southern Cultures* 5, no. 1 (1999): 44–48.

Hamilton, William L. "At Ole Miss, the Tailgaters Never Lose." *New York Times*, September 29, 2006, F1.

Hamlin, Kimberly A. "Bathing Suits and Backlash: The First Miss America Pageants, 1921–1927." In *"There She Is, Miss America": The Politics of Sex, Beauty, and Race in America's Most Famous Pageant*, edited by Elwood Watson and Darcy Martin, 27–52. New York: Palgrave, 2004.

Hammons, Rachel. "Diversity in the Greek Life." *JOUR102sec.4sp11* (blog). May 8, 2011. http://jour102sec4sp11.blogspot.com/2011/05/diversity-in-greek-system_09.html.

Harlow, Jeanerette. "Annual Natchez Pilgrimage Helps Make City Well Known." *Jackson (Miss.) Clarion-Ledger*, May 8, 1970, A10.

Harrah-Conforth, Jeanne. "The Landscape of Possibility: An Ethnography of the Kentucky Derby." PhD diss, Indiana University, 1992.

"Harriett Dickert Crowned Queen of the May." *Garnet and Black*, 1957.

Hartocollis, Anemona, and Jess Bidgood. "Racial Discrimination Demonstrations Spread at Universities across the U.S." *New York Times*, November 12, 2015, A16.

Hass, Kristin Ann. *Carried to the Wall: American Memory and the Vietnam Veterans Memorial*. Berkeley: University of California Press, 1998.

Henderson, Honea. Interview by Elizabeth Boyd. February 26, 1997. Oxford, Miss.

"Here for the Natchez Pilgrimage." *Natchez Democrat*, March 21, 1948.

Hesse, Monica. "The 'New' Miss America and the Trap of Ladylike Expectations." *Washington Post*, September 10, 2018. https://www.washingtonpost.com/lifestyle/style/the-new-miss-america-and-the-trap-of-ladylike-expectations/2018/09/10/94793eb2-b525-11e8-a7b5-adaaa5b2a57f_story.html?utm_term=.6a650e955216.

Hillyer, Ben. "Changes Planned for Tableaux to Tell Entire Natchez Story." *Natchez Democrat*, February 15, 2015. https://www.natchezdemocrat.com/2015/02/15/changes-planned-for-tableaux-to-tell-entire-natchez-story/.

———. "PGC Pulls out of Tableaux." *Natchez Democrat*, October 6, 2017. https://www.natchezdemocrat.com/2017/10/06/pgc-pulls-out-of-tableaux/.

Hilton, Jasmine. "As Columbus Statues Fall, Some Aim to Rename Ohio City." *Washington Post*, July 8, 2020, A3.

Hine, Darlene Clark. "'In the Kingdom of Culture': Black Women and the Intersection of Race, Gender, and Class." In *Lure and Loathing: Essays on Race, Identity, and the Ambivalence of Assimilation*, edited by Gerald Early, 346. New York: Penguin Books, 1993.

"Historic American Sheet Music." Duke University Libraries. Accessed November 6, 2021. https://repository.duke.edu/dc/hasm.

Hobsbawm, Eric, and Terence Ranger, eds. *The Invention of Tradition*. Cambridge: Cambridge University Press, 1983.

Hobson, Fred. *But Now I See: The White Southern Racial Conversion Narrative*. Baton Rouge: Louisiana State University Press, 1999.

Hoelscher, Steven D. *Heritage on Stage: The Invention of Place in America's Little Switzerland*. Madison: University of Wisconsin Press, 1998.

———. "Making Place, Making Race: Performances of Whiteness in the Jim Crow South." *Annals of the Association of American Geographers* 93, no. 3 (2003): 657–86.

Holley, Leila. Interview by Elizabeth Boyd. December 5, 2006. Tuscaloosa, Ala.

Hoover, Carl. "Cotton Palace Pageant Looks to Waco's Future." *Waco Tribune*, April 22, 2010. https://www.wacotrib.com/entertainment/accesswaco/cotton-palace-pageant-looks-to-waco-s-future/article_bc0774b8-2f32-5575-a52b-4dcccco673c8.html.

Hoover, Eric. "New Scrutiny for Powerful Greek Systems." *Chronicle of Higher Education*, June 8, 2001, A35–A37.

Horowitz, Helen Lefkowitz. *Alma Mater: Design and Experience in the Women's Colleges from Their Nineteenth-Century Beginnings to the 1930s*. Amherst: University of Massachusetts Press, 1984.

Horwitz, Tony. *Confederates in the Attic: Dispatches from the Unfinished Civil War*. New York: Vintage, 1999.

Hudson, Patricia L. "Beyond Moonlight and Magnolias." *Americana*, February 1992, 25–30.

Hughey, Matthew W. "A Paradox of Participation: Nonwhites in White Sororities and Fraternities." *Social Problems* 57, no. 4 (2010): 653–79.

Iles, Greg. *Turning Angel*. New York: Scribner, 2005.

"'Impractical' Dream for Pilgrimage Makes Natchez Famous City." *Jackson Daily News*, June 22, 1949.

Ingram, Hunter. "Azalea Belles No More: Cape Fear Garden Club Ends N.C. Azalea Festival Tradition." *Wilmington Star-News*, October 7, 2020. https://www.starnewsonline.com/story/news/local/2020/10/07/azalea-belles-n-c-azalea-festival-tradition-canceled/5909592002/.

"Interview with Selah Saterstrom." *Avant-Women Writers: A Conversation*. April 21, 2008. http://avantwomenwriters.blogspot.com/2008/04/interview-with-selah-saterstrom_21.html.

Iovine, Julie V. "Where Nothing Is Gone with the Wind." *New York Times*, November 13, 1997, F1.

Isaac, Rhys. *The Transformation of Virginia, 1740–1790*. New York: Norton, 1982.

Jaschik, Scott. "U. of Mississippi Tries New Approach to Its History with Race—and Faces Criticism." *Inside Higher Ed*, August 4, 2014. http://www.insidehighered .com/print/news/2014/08/04/u-mississippi-tries-new-approach-its-history-race-and -faces-criticism.

Jenkins, Sally. "Erasing Ugly History Isn't a Cure." *Washington Post*, June 28, 2015, A19.

————. "On Confederate Symbols: Which Ones Should Stay and Which Ones Should Go?" *Washington Post*, June 26, 2015. https://www.washingtonpost.com /opinions/the-confederacys-ugly-history-cannot-be-painted-over/2015/06/26 /f4443a8e-1c28-11e5-bd7f-4611a60dd8e5_story.html?utm_term=.aff9a234c518.

————. "Unraveling the Threads of Hatred, Sewn into a Confederate Icon." *Washington Post*, June 20, 2015. https://www.washingtonpost.com/opinions/unraveling-the -threads-of-hatred-sewn-into-a-confederate-icon/2015/06/20/aa6a73f4-1775-11e5-9518 -f9e0a8959f32_story.html?utm_term=.7428d0ab103d.

"Jim Crow Museum of Racist Memorabilia." Ferris State University. Accessed November 6, 2021. https://www.ferris.edu/jimcrow/.

Johnson, Steven. "Big Donor's Facebook Photos of 2 Black Students Unsettle Ole Miss." *Chronicle of Higher Education*, September 20, 2018. https://www.chronicle .com/article/Big-Donor-s-Facebook-Photos/244590.

Jones, Anne Goodwyn. "'I Was Tellin It': Race, Gender, and the Puzzle of the Storyteller." *Southern Cultures* 5, no. 1 (1999): 29–43.

————. *Tomorrow Is Another Day: The Woman Writer in the South, 1859–1936*. Baton Rouge: Louisiana State University Press, 1981.

Jones, Anne Goodwyn, and Susan V. Donaldson, ed. *Haunted Bodies: Gender and Southern Texts*. American South. Charlottesville: University Press of Virginia, 1997.

Kammen, Michael. *Mystic Chords of Memory*. New York: Knopf, 1991.

Kantor, Susan. "Quad Protest Targets Racial Stereotyping." *Daily Illini*, November 1, 2006, A1.

Kappa Kappa Sigma Proudly Presents the Coronation of the May Queen. Columbia: University of South Carolina, 1956.

"Kari Litton Crowned Miss Mississippi." *Pontotoc (Miss.) Progress*, July 18, 1996, A1.

Kasson, John F. *Rudeness and Civility: Manners in Nineteenth-Century America*. New York: Hill and Wang, 1990.

Kaufman, Ben L. "Curmudgeon Notes 10.2.2013." *Cincinnati City Beat*, October 2, 2013. https://www.citybeat.com/voices/on-second-thought/article/13006521 /curmudgeon-notes-1022013.

"The Keys to Mississippi's Winning Miss." *Southern Living*, April 1986, 130.

Kimball, Kendrick. "Famed Mansions of 'Old South' Restored and Opened to Pilgrims as Natchez Turns Back the Clock." *Detroit News*, February 23, 1941.

King, C. Richard, and Charles Fruehling Springwood. *Beyond the Cheers: Race as Spectacle in College Sport*. Sport, Culture, and Social Relations. Albany: State University of New York Press, 2001.

King, Florence. *Confessions of a Failed Southern Lady*. New York: Bantam Books, 1986.

Kirby, Jack Temple. *Media-Made Dixie: The South in the American Imagination*. Baton Rouge: Louisiana State University Press, 1978.

Knabb-Lane Studio. "Pilgrimage Photographs." *Natchez Democrat*, February 29, 1948, 7.

Kolenich, Eric. "Space around the Lee Statue Has Been Informally Named for a Black Man Who Lost His Life at the Hands of Police." *Richmond Times-Dispatch*, June 26, 2020. https://richmond.com/news/local/space-around-the-lee-statue-has -been-informally-named-for-a-black-man-who-lost/article_1b48d63f-e932-5edc-8d0b -0e3289ac71bb.html.

Krauthammer, Charles. "On Lowering the Flag." *Washington Post*, June 26, 2015, A21.

Kuperinsky, Amy. "Miss America Organization Responds to John Oliver's Segment on Pageant." NJ. September 25, 2014. https://www.nj.com/entertainment/tv/2014/09 /miss_america_john_oliver_scholarships_1.html.

Kushner, Ellen. *Sound and Spirit: From Canterbury to Graceland*. Boston: WGBH Radio, 2000.

Lambert, James W. "Natchez Belles Invite Governor, State Legislators to Pilgrimage." *Natchez Democrat*, March 17, 1948, 1–4.

Landrieu, Mitch. "Why I'm Taking Down Confederate Monuments in New Orleans." *Washington Post*, May 14, 2017, B2.

Lang, Nico. "'Worse Than the Tea Party': 'Confederate Spring' Ushers in Wave of Hate." *Rolling Stone*, May 3, 2016, http://www.rollingstone.com/politics/news /worse-than-the-tea-party-confederate-spring-ushers-in-wave-of-hate-20160503.

Lartey, Jamiles, and Ben Jacobs. "Cindy Hyde-Smith Wins Mississippi Senate Seat in Special Election." *Guardian*, November 27, 2018. https://www.theguardian.com /us-news/2018/nov/27/cindy-hyde-smith-wins-mississippi-senate-seat-in-special -election.

Lavenda, Robert. "Minnesota Queen Pageants: Play, Fun, and Dead Seriousness in a Festive Mode." *Journal of American Folklore* 101, no. 400 (1988): 168–75.

Lavey, Megan. "Twilley Cut from All Houses." *Crimson-White*, September 10, 2001, 1.

"Legislator Pushes Bill to Restore Colonel Reb as Ole Miss Mascot." CNN. January 28, 2011. http://www.cnn.com/2011/US/01/28/mississippi.school.mascot/index .html?eref=rss_us.

Lewis, Charlene M. Boyer. *Ladies and Gentlemen on Display: Planter Society at the Virginia Springs, 1790–1860*. Charlottesville: University Press of Virginia, 2001.

Lewis, George. *Massive Resistance: The White Response to the Civil Rights Movement*. London: Arnold, 2006.

Lhamon, William Taylor, Jr. *Raising Cain: Blackface Performance from Jim Crow to Hip Hop*. Cambridge, Mass.: Harvard University Press, 1998.

Lindsay, Leslie. Interview by Elizabeth Boyd. March 16, 1996. Houston, Miss.

Loewen, James W. "How Confederate Lore Survives." *Washington Post*, July 5, 2015, B1, 4.

Lord, M. G. "The Greek Rites of Exclusion." *Nation*, July 4, 11, 1987, 10–13.

Lord, Walter. *The Past That Would Not Die*. New York: Harper and Row, 1965.

Lott, Eric. *Love and Theft: Blackface Minstrelsy and the American Working Class*. New York: Oxford University Press, 1993.

Louwerens, Monica. Interview by Elizabeth Boyd. March 16, 1996. Houston, Miss.

Lowry, Beverly. "Born to Preen: Why Southern Girls Dominate Beauty Contests." *Southern Magazine*, September 1987, 26–33, 88–89.

"LSU Sororities Evoke Fond Memories." Louisiana State University Libraries. Accessed May 17, 2002. http://www.lib.lsu.edu/special/oh/newsletters/ohnewsleter4 .html#sororities.

Luckerson, Victor. "University of Alabama Integrates Sororities." *Time*, September 20, 2013. https://nation.time.com/2013/09/20/university-of-alabama-integrates -sororities/.

Lumpkin, Katharine Du Pre. *The Making of a Southerner*. Rev. ed. Athens: University of Georgia Press, 1974.

"Lynda Meade Visits Capstone." *Crimson-White*, November 8, 1962, 1A.

MacNeil, Anne. Interview by Elizabeth Boyd. April 4, 2000. Natchez, Miss.

Manring, Maurice M. *Slave in a Box: The Strange Career of Aunt Jemima*. Edited by Edward Ayers. Charlottesville: University Press of Virginia, 1998.

Marshall, Heather. *Water in Which I Swim (Memory Inside Out)*. Philadelphia: Crinoline, n.d.

Martin, Jonathan, John Eligon, and Campbell Robertson. "'He's Not There Yet': Embattled Governor Seeks Forgiveness from Black Virginians." *Washington Post*, February 14, 2019, https://www.nytimes.com/2019/02/14/us/ralph-northam-black -virginians.html.

Martin, Mrs. James Bland. *Follow the Green Arrow: The History of the Garden Club of Virginia, 1920–1970*. Richmond: Dietz, 1970.

Martin, Nancie. *Miss America through the Looking Glass: The Story behind the Scenes*. New York: Messner Books, 1985.

Martinez, J. Michael, William D. Richardson, and Ron McNinch-Su, eds. *Confederate Symbols in the Contemporary South*. Gainesville: University Press of Florida, 2000.

Mathias, Christopher. "Outrage at Ole Miss over White Students Posing with Bullet-Riddled Emmett Till Sign." *Huffington Post*, August 1, 2019. https://www.huffpost .com/entry/ole-miss-emmett-till-guns-sign_n_5d42fe86e4b0ca604e2e69ed.

Maxwell, Angie, and Todd Shields. *The Long Southern Strategy: How Chasing White*

Voters in the South Changed American Politics. New York: Oxford University Press, 2019.

May, Elaine Tyler. *Homeward Bound: American Families in the Cold War Era*. New York: Basic Books, 1988.

McBride, Kelly. "How Student Reporters Ended Discrimination among University of Alabama Sororities." *Poynter*, October 2, 2013. https://www.poynter.org/reporting-editing/2013/how-two-student-reporters-ended-discrimination-among-university-of-alabama-sororities/.

McCann, Nita. "Tableaux Debuts New Play Format." *Natchez Democrat*, March 8, 2015. https://m.natchezdemocrat.com/2015/03/08/tableaux-debuts-new-play-format/.

McGehee, Rebecca, and Anna Catesby McGehee. Interview by Elizabeth Boyd. August 2002. Natchez, Miss.

McLean, Robert Emmett. "Cotton Carnival and Cotton Makers Jubilee: Memphis Society in Black and White." Master's thesis, George Mason University, 1994.

McLeod, Elizabeth. "Radio's Forgotten Years: Tuning Thru the Great Depression." Wayback Machine. Accessed October 4, 2010. https://web.archive.org/web/20070209024336/http://www.midcoast.com/~lizmcl/rfy.html.

McPherson, Tara. *Reconstructing Dixie*. Durham: Duke University Press, 2003.

McQuary, Carol. Interview by Elizabeth Boyd. September 16, 1996. Houston, Miss.

McRae, Elizabeth Gillespie. *Mothers of Massive Resistance: White Women and the Politics of White Supremacy*. New York: Oxford University Press, 2018.

———. "The Women behind White Power." *New York Times*, February 2, 2018. https://www.nytimes.com/2018/02/02/opinion/sunday/white-supremacy-forgot-women.html.

McWhite, Leigh. "'Natchez Is a Fairy Story': Examining the Origins of the Natchez Pilgrimage." Paper presented at the Historic Natchez Conference, February 2000.

Meek, Ed. "Top Stories of 2017: 'Campus Cuties' Made Ed Meek UM's Big Man on Campus." *HottyToddy*, January 1, 2018. https://www.hottytoddy.com/2018/01/01/reflections-cheesecake-campus-cuties-made-big-man-campus-58/.

Mendelsohn, Emily Owen. "#nomorebelles." Change.org. June 2020. https://www.change.org/p/birmingham-belles-nomorebelles/.

Meyer, Michelle. "Expertise, Cost Create Arkansas Glamour." *Memphis Commercial Appeal*, September 15, 1989, C2.

———. "Here He Comes with Miss America." *Memphis Commercial Appeal*, September 15, 1989, C1–2.

Meyer, Robert, Jr. "Spring's Parade of Festivals Gets Underway." *New York Times*, March 1958.

Mickens, Cassandra. "Organizers Tweak Historic Tableaux." *Natchez Democrat*, April 1, 2010. https://www.natchezdemocrat.com/2010/04/01/organizers-tweak-historic-tableaux/.

———. "Pageant Continues to Bring Natchez Story to Life." *Natchez Democrat*,

March 23, 2010. https://www.natchezdemocrat.com/2010/03/23/pageant
-continues-to-bring-natchez-story-to-life/.

Miller, Joshua Rhett. "Sorority Sister Speaks Out on Racist Videos That Got Her
Booted from College." *New York Post*, January 17, 2018. https://nypost.com/2018
/01/17/sorority-sister-booted-for-posting-profanity-laced-racist-videos/.

Miller, Katherine Grafton. *A Pilgrimage to Dixieland in the Deep South*. Natchez,
Miss., n.d.

———. *Scrapbook*. Natchez, Miss.: Historic Natchez Foundation, 1932.

Miller, Mimi, and Ron Miller. Interviews by Elizabeth Boyd. July 18, 19, 2002. Natchez, Miss.

Mintz, Lizzie, and Shannon Mallard. "Officials Working to Address Racist Snapchat
Post from Sorority President's Account." *GW Hatchet*, September 4, 2019. https://
www.gwhatchet.com/2019/09/04/officials-working-to-address-racist-snapchat-post
-from-sorority-presidents-account/.

"Miss America." Miss America Organization. Accessed May 6, 2018. http://www
.missamerica.org.

"Miss America Losers Ponder Question: Who's the Fairest of Them All?" *Jackson
(Miss.) Clarion-Ledger*, September 17, 1986, 1A.

"Mississippi Pilgrimages Began as a Dream." *Helping Build Mississippi*, 1977, 12–14.

"Mississippi Quickfacts from the U.S. Census Bureau." U.S. Census Bureau. November 22, 2013. http://quickfacts.census.gov/qfd/states/28000.html.

"Miss Kansas Is Crowned Miss America." *Vickburg (Miss.) Evening Post*, September
15, 1996, A1.

Miss Magnolia contestants. Interviews by Elizabeth Boyd. March 16, 1996. Houston,
Miss.

Morris, Willie. *North toward Home*. Oxford, Miss.: Yoknapatawpha/Houghton Miff-
lin, 1967.

"Mrs. Kendall Issues Call for State-Wide Mass Meet of Women." *Natchez Democrat*,
April 2, 1948, 1–4.

Mueller, Lee. "Magoffin Closing Schools for Miss America Contest." *Lexington
Herald-Leader*, August 9, 1988, 1.

Nader, Laura. "Up the Anthropologist: Perspectives Gained from Studying Up." In
Reinventing Anthropology, edited by Dell H. Hymes, 284–311. New York: Pantheon
Books, 1969.

Natchez Garden Club. *The Natchez Garden Club: A Brief History*. Natchez, Miss.,
1995.

New Orleans Spring Fiesta Association. *New Orleans Spring Fiesta*. N.p., 1938.

"Newspaper, Mag. Writers, Photo Men Pouring In." *Natchez Democrat*, March 17,
1948, 1–4.

Nichols, Megan. "Sorority Integration Questioned." *Crimson-White*, September 24,
2003. http://now.dirxion.com/Crimson_White/library/Crimson_White_9_24_2003
.pdf. Accessed September 9, 2006.

Nichols, Paralee. *How to Achieve Inner Beauty and Outer Charm*. New York: Hearthside, 1961.

"No More Apple Pie." *Time*, March 13, 1989, 85.

Northway, Martin. "Natchez Mississippi: A History Runs through It." *Endless Vacation*, March–April 1999, 61–65.

"Old South Architecture Charms New Buildings." *Crimson-White*, October 25, 1962, 20.

O'Neil, Lorena. "Jon Stewart on Racist Frat Song: There Is a 'Deep, Problematic Racial Divide in Our Nation.'" *Hollywood Reporter*, March 12, 2015. https://www .hollywoodreporter.com/news/jon-stewart-racist-frat-song-780941.

Orman, Shelley. "Colonel Reb Supporters Closer to Bringing Back the Mascot." 2011. abc24.com.

Ostrander, Susan. *Women of the Upper Class*. Philadelphia: Temple University Press, 1986.

Palladino, Grace. *Teenagers: An American History*. New York: Basic Books, 1996.

Parker, Kathleen. "Queen Carlson Wins Again." *Washington Post*, January 3, 2018, A15.

Parker, Suzi. "Amid Linen and Lace, Antebellum Legacy Thrives." *Christian Science Monitor*, November 20, 2002. https://www.csmonitor.com/2002/1120/p02s02-ussc .html.

Parks, Marty. "Pilgrimage Publicity Film Delights Audience." *Natchez Democrat*, January 9, 1981.

"Party Themes for Sorority/Fraternity Mixers/Switches." *GreekChat*, June 23, 2000. http://www.greekchat.com/gcforums/archive/index.php/t-2476.html.

Patterson, Suzannah. "Ingenious Methods Used as Advertising." *Natchez Democrat*, March 12, 1982, 3A.

———. "Promoting Pilgrimage Was Hard." *Natchez Democrat*, March 12, 1982, 2A.

Patton, Phil. "Mammy: Her Life and Times." *American Heritage* 44, no. 5 (1993): 78–87.

Payton, Jobie. Interview by Elizabeth Boyd. December 7, 2006. Tuscaloosa, Ala.

Peiss, Kathy. *Cheap Amusements: Working Women and Leisure in Turn-of-the-Century New York*. Philadelphia: Temple University Press, 1986.

Peterson, Elmer T. "The Old South Lives Again!" *Better Homes and Gardens*, n.d.

Petri, Alexandra. "The Amazing Thing about the '80s Is They Were Much Longer Ago Than You Realize." *Washington Post*, February 7, 2019. https://www .washingtonpost.com/opinions/2019/02/06/amazing-thing-about-s-is-they-were -much-longer-ago-than-you-realize/?utm_term=.e3ce72e5e1f6.

"Petticoat Peace Quiets Quarreling Natchez." *American Weekly*, August 16, 1942, 8.

Phi Mu regional adviser. Personal conversation with Elizabeth Boyd. October 1997. Oxford, Miss.

"Photos: Martha's Ball Features Debutantes during Laredo's Washington Birthday Celebration." *Laredo Morning Times*, February 25, 2019. https://www.lmtonline.com /local/slideshow/Photos-Martha-s-Ball-features-debutantes-during-190320.php.

"Photos Have Public Relations Value." *Crimson-White*, March 18, 1958, 4.

Pierce, Susan. "Chattanooga Cotton Ball King and Queen Announced." *Times Free Press*, July 29, 2018. https://www.timesfreepress.com/news/breakingnews/story /2018/jul/29/chattanooga-cotton-ball/475931/.

"Pilgrimage Celebrates 50 Years." *Natchez Democrat*, March 6, 1982, 2.

Pilgrimage Garden Club member. Interview by Elizabeth Boyd. August 2002. Natchez, Miss.

"Pilgrims Travel to Mississippi to View Deep South of Yesterday." *Motor News*, February 1940, 1–7.

"Plan Pageant to Depict Start of Miss. Territory." *Natchez Democrat*, February 24, 1948, 5.

Pope, John. "The Natchez Pilgrimage: A Hoop-Skirted Time Warp." *Washington Post*, April 3, 1977, M1.

Portnoy, Jenna, Gregory S. Schneider, Neena Satija, and Laura Vozzella. "Second Woman Accuses Va. Lt. Gov. Justin Fairfax of Sexual Assault." *Washington Post*, February 8, 2019. https://www.washingtonpost.com/local/virginia-politics/second -woman-accuses-va-lt-gov-justin-fairfax-of-sexual-assault/2019/02/08/19e6bb6c-2bdf -11e9-b011-d8500644dc98_story.html?utm_term=.a1d29955acb2.

Potter, Davis. "The Wide-Ranging Reactions to Ole Miss' New On-Field Mascot." *Oxford Eagle*, August 11, 2018. https://www.oxfordeagle.com/2018/08/11/the-wide -ranging-reactions-to-ole-miss-new-on-field-mascot/.

Press, Nancy. "Private Faces, Public Lives: The Women of the Downtown Group of Charleston, South Carolina." In *Women in the South: An Anthropological Perspective*, edited by Holly F. Matthews. Athens: University of Georgia Press, 1989.

Prince, K. Michael. *Rally 'round the Flag, Boys!* Columbia: University of South Carolina Press, 2004

"Promoting Pilgrimage Was Hard." *Natchez Democrat*, March 12, 1982, 2A.

"Protesters Fill Streets Outside Kentucky Derby, Calling for Justice for Breonna Taylor." *Louisville Courier-Journal*, September 5, 2020. https://www.courier-journal .com/story/news/local/breonna-taylor/2020/09/05/louisville-breonna-taylor -protesters-fill-streets-outside-kentucky-derby-2020/3454750001/.

Purcell, Evelyn. dir. *Rush*. P. Bottom Pictures, 1980.

"Quick Facts." University of Mississippi. Accessed November 22, 2013. http://www .olemiss.edu/aboutum/quickfacts/.

Ray, Celeste. *Highland Heritage: Scottish Americans in the American South*. Chapel Hill: University of North Carolina Press, 2001.

Reeves, Jay. "At University of Alabama, Leaders Tread Lightly on Segregation in Greek System." *Washington Post*, September 22, 2013. https://www.washingtonpost .com/politics/at-university-of-alabama-leaders-tread-lightly-on-segregation-in-greek -system/2013/09/22/eedb4f48-239f-11e3-b75d-5b7f66349852_story.html?utm_term= .c145ec6a976b.

Riley, Harriet. "A 'Better' Education." *Academy Stories*. 2020. https://www .theacademystories.com/post/a-better-education.

Riverol, Armando R. *Live from Atlantic City: The History of the Miss America Pag-*

eant before, after, and in Spite of Television. Bowling Green: Bowling Green State University Popular Press, 1992.

Roach, Joseph. *Cities of the Dead: Circum-Atlantic Performance*. New York: Columbia University Press, 1996.

Robbins, Linda. "Joining the Systems: Years after the Schoolhouse Stand, Greeks Still Practice 'Separate but Equal' Policies." In *Corolla*, edited by Rena Havner, 106:173. Tuscaloosa: University of Alabama, 1998.

Roberts, Blain. *Pageants, Parlors, and Pretty Women: Race and Beauty in the Twentieth-Century South*. Chapel Hill: University of North Carolina Press, 2014.

Roberts, Diane. *Faulkner and Southern Womanhood*. Athens: University of Georgia Press, 1994.

Roberts, Jessica. "Cypress Gardens: Florida's 1st Tourist Attraction." Visit Central Florida, Accessed October 14, 2021. https://visitcentralflorida.org/blog/cypress -gardens-was-floridas-first-tourist-attraction/.

Robertson, Campbell, and Alan Blinder. "Sorority Exposes Its Rejection of Black Candidate." *New York Times*, September 13, 2013, A14.

Robertson, Jennifer. *Takarazuka: Sexual Politics and Popular Culture in Modern Japan*. Berkeley: University of California Press, 1998.

Robinson, Eugene. "150 Years Later, America Is Still Battling the Confederate Mentality." *Washington Post*, June 25, 2015. https://www.washingtonpost.com/opinions /the-confederate-state-of-mind-remains/2015/06/25/58bf34f6-1b79-11e5-93b7 -5eddc056ad8a_story.html?utm_term=.14e133a24b26.

———. "Hope in Charleston." *Washington Post*, June 28, 2015, A21.

Robinson, Franklin A., Jr. *Guide to the Maid of Cotton Records, 1939–1993*. Washington, D.C.: National Museum of American History, 2012.

Robinson, Rosanne Smith. "The Great Sorority Swindle." *Look*, June 5, 1951, 40–48.

Roche, Timothy, and Leslie Everton Brice. "Blacks Need Not Apply." *Time*, June 11, 2000, 104.

Rosenzweig, Roy, and David Thelen. *The Presence of the Past: Popular Uses of History in American Life*. New York: Columbia University Press, 2000.

Rubin, Richard. *Confederacy of Silence: A True Tale of the New Old South*. New York: Atria, 2002.

Rutledge, Adair Freeman. "Azalea Trail Maids." *Photoville Fence*. 7th ed. Photography exhibition. 2018. https://fence.photoville.com/azalea-trail-maids/.

Sack, Kevin. "The Final Refrains of Dixie." *New York Times*, November 1, 1998, sec. 4A, pp. 20–35.

Sanders, Chris. "Sorority Integrated Last Year without Fanfare." *Crimson-White*, September 7, 2001.

Saterstrom, Selah. *The Pink Institution*. Minneapolis: Coffee House, 2004.

———. "The Pink Institution: An Interview with Author Selah Saterstrom." Avant-Women Writers. April 21, 2008. http://avantwomenwriters.blogspot.com/2008/04 /interview-with-selah-saterstrom.html.

Savage, Candace. *Beauty Queens: A Playful History*. New York: Abbeville, 1998.

Schmeichel, Mardi, Stacey Kerr, and Chris Linder. "Selfies as Postfeminist Pedagogy: The Production of Traditional Femininity in the US South." *Gender and Education* 32, no. 3 (2020): 363–81.

Schneider, Gregory S. "Crowds Cheer Removal of Confederate Statue in Charlottesville." *Washington Post*, September 13, 2020, C1, C12.

———. "Untouchable No More, Lee Statue at Center of Civic Outpouring." *Washington Post*, June 16, 2020, B1, B4.

Scott, Anne Firor. *The Southern Lady: From Pedestal to Politics, 1830–1930.* 25th Anniversary ed. 1970. Reprint, Charlottesville: University Press of Virginia, 1995.

Scott, Rosa Naomi. "The Natchez Pilgrimage: A New Spring Tour." *AAA Travel*, March 1935, 6–7.

Seebohm, Caroline. "Enshrining the Old South." *New York Times*, February 10, 1991, sec. 5, p. 15.

Sellers, Frances Stead. "Flying the Colors for Racial Grievance." *Washington Post*, October 23, 2018, A1, 20.

Shaffer, Marguerite S. *See America First: Tourism and National Identity, 1880–1940.* Washington, D.C.: Smithsonian Institution Press, 2001.

Shearer, Lee. "Hoop Skirts Banned at UGA Following Oklahoma Frat Video." *Athens Banner-Herald*, March 18, 2015. http://onlineathens.com/uga/2015-03-17/hoop -skirts-banned-uga-following-Oklahoma-frat-video.

Shemanski, Frances. *A Guide to Fairs and Festivals in the United States.* Westport, Conn.: Greenwood, 1984.

Silver, James W. *Mississippi: The Closed Society.* New York: Harcourt, Brace and World, 1963, 1964.

Smith, Bill. "Boone Will Select Top Corolla Beauty." *Crimson-White*, December 11, 1956, 1.

Smith, Lillian. *Killers of the Dream.* New York: Norton, 1994.

Smith, Phil. "Bama Beauties Score with Judges." *Crimson-White*, May 17, 1956, 3.

Smith, Remington. *The Derby.* Louisville, Ky.: FilmSmith Productions, 2019.

Smithey, Waylon. "O'Flynn Wins 'Miss Venus'; ODK Taps Student Leaders." *Crimson White*, April 23, 1959, 1.

Sokol, Jason. *There Goes My Everything: White Southerners in the Age of Civil Rights, 1945–1975.* New York: Knopf, 2006.

Solomon, Barbara Miller. *In the Company of Educated Women: A History of Women and Higher Education in America.* New Haven: Yale University Press, 1985.

Sommerville, Diane Miller. *Rape and Race in the Nineteenth-Century South.* Chapel Hill: University of North Carolina Press, 2004.

"Southern Belle." Ruby Lane Group. Accessed November 6, 2021. https://www .rubylane.com/a&c?f_itemtype=Vintage&lane=a%26c&q=southern%20belle.

Spruill, Marjorie J. *Divided We Stand: The Battle over Women's Rights and Family Values That Polarized American Politics.* New York: Bloomsbury, 2017.

Stacey, Jackie. *Star Gazing: Hollywood Cinema and Female Spectatorship.* London: Routledge, 1994.

Stampp, Kenneth. *The Imperiled Union: Essays on the Background of the Civil War*. New York: New York: Oxford University Press, 1980.

Staples, Brent. "Donald Trump and Reconstruction-Era Politics." *New York Times*, March 3, 2016, A22.

"State Rights Meetings for 82 Counties." *Natchez Democrat*, March 19, 1948, 2.

Stein, Perry, Clarence Williams, and Peter Hermann. "D.C.'s Sole Outdoor Confederate Statue Is Toppled, Set on Fire." *Washington Post*, June 21, 2020, C1, C7.

Steinhauer, Jennifer. "Historical Symbols in Midst of a 'Purge Moment.'" *New York Times*, September 1, 2015. http://nyti.ms/1Q70CQ9.

Stewart, Susan. "Death and Life, in That Order, in the Works of Charles Willson Peale." In *The Cultures of Collecting*, edited by John Elsner and Roger Cardinal, 204–23. Cambridge, Mass.: Harvard University Press, 1994.

Stokes, Sandra. Interview by Elizabeth Boyd. August 14, 2002. Natchez, Miss.

"Stunt Nights, Concerts, and Dance Highlight Greek Week." *Garnet and Black*, 1957.

Sullivan, Patricia. "Moment of Reckoning in Va." *Washington Post*, July 26, 2020, C1, C5.

Suzanne. "Madame Chairman." *New York Times*, n.d.

Svrluga, Susan. "All Signs of Silent Sam Are Gone, and Soon, UNC's Chancellor Will Be, Too." *Washington Post*, January 16, 2019, A4.

———. "Prominent Confederate Statue at Ole Miss Will Go." *Washington Post*, June 20, 2020, A3.

———. "UNC in Turmoil over Silent Sam, the Confederate Monument Toppled by Protestors." *Washington Post*, December 13, 2018. https://www.washingtonpost.com/education/2018/12/13/unc-turmoil-over-silent-sam-confederate-monument-toppled-by-protesters/.

———. "Washington and Lee Faculty Vote for Name Change." *Washington Post*, July 6, 2020, B4.

———. "Washington and Lee Renames Buildings, Replaces Military Portraits of Its Namesakes." *Washington Post*, October 11, 2018. https://www.washingtonpost.com/education/2018/10/11/washington-lee-renames-buildings-replaces-military-portraits-its-namesakes/.

Tartt, Donna. "The Belle and the Lady." *Oxford American*, March–May 1999, 94–105.

Taylor, Diana. *The Archive and the Repertoire: Performing Cultural Memory in the Americas*. Durham: Duke University Press, 2005.

Teachout, Terry. "History under the Stars." *Wall Street Journal*, July 6, 2007, W5.

Temple, Chandra. "Miss Alabama Ashley Davis Will Dress to Impress at the Miss America Pageant." AL. January 9, 2011. http://blog.al.com/living-news/.

———. "Miss Alabama Courtney Poter Gets Her Wardrobe Ready for the Miss America Pageant." AL. January 8, 2012. http://blog.al.com/living_impact/.

Tester, Keith. *The Life and Times of Post-modernity*. London: Routledge, 1993.

Theophano, Janet. *Eat My Words: Reading Women's Lives through the Cookbooks They Wrote*. New York: Palgrave, 2002

Thornton, Kevin Pierce. "Symbolism at Ole Miss and the Crisis of Southern Identity." *South Atlantic Quarterly* 86, no. 3 (1987): 254–68.

Tice, Karen Whitney. *Queens of Academe: Beauty Pageantry, Student Bodies, and College Life*. New York: Oxford University Press, 2012.

Tolf, Robert W. "Natchez, 'Where the Old South Still Lives,' Proves It Each Spring." *New York Times*, March 5, 1978, sec. Travel, p. 6.

Toll, Robert C. *Blacking Up: The Minstrel Show in Nineteenth-Century America*. New York: Oxford University Press, 1974.

Triplett, Tana. Interview by Elizabeth Boyd. March 19, 1997. Oxford, Miss.

Truong, Debbie. "Va. School Shifts from Lee to Liberty." *Washington Post*, January 12, 2019, B1.

Tucker, Neely. "Mississippi Flag Defenders Dig In." *Washington Post*, August 19, 2015, A1, 8.

Turner, Patricia. *Ceramic Uncles and Celluloid Mammies: Black Images and Their Influence on Culture*. Charlottesville: University of Virginia Press, 2002.

"University of Oklahoma SAE Racist Chant." YouTube video. March 8, 2015. https://www.youtube.com/watch?v=GBq4_A9nQvw.

Vozzella, Laura. "Tribute to Lee Inspires Sit-Out." *Washington Post*, January 19, 2019, B1.

Vozzella, Laura, Jim Morrison, and Gregory S. Schneider. "Gov. Ralph Northam Admits He Was in 1984 Yearbook Photo Showing Figures in Blackface, KKK Hood." *Washington Post*, February 1, 2019. https://www.washingtonpost.com/local/virginia-politics/va-gov-northams-medical-school-yearbook-page-shows-men-in-blackface-kkk-robe/2019/02/01/517a43ee-265f-11e9-90cd-dedb0c92dc17_story.html.

Vozzella, Laura, and Gregory S. Schneider. "Gov. Northam Refuses to Step Down, Despite Flood of Calls for His Resignation over Racist Photo." *Washington Post*, February 2, 2019. https://www.washingtonpost.com/local/virginia-politics/northam-mum-about-his-plans-after-a-flood-of-calls-for-his-resignation-for-racist-and-offensive-photo/2019/02/02/5883402a-26e9-11e9-90cd-dedb0c92dc17_story.html?utm_term=.5f25f5d0ead2.

Waldman, Katy. "A Sociologist Examines the 'White Fragility' That Prevents White Americans from Confronting Racism." *New Yorker*, July 23, 2018. https://www.newyorker.com/books/page-turner/a-sociologist-examines-the-white-fragility-that-prevents-white-americans-from-confronting-racism.

Wallace, Phil. "Victory Is Sweet for Honey East." *Jackson (Miss.) Clarion-Ledger*, March 12, 1992.

Wallace-Sanders, Kimberly. *Mammy: A Century of Race, Gender and Southern Memory*. Ann Arbor: University of Michigan Press, 2009.

Warren, Robert Penn. *The Legacy of the Civil War*. 1961. Reprint, Lincoln: University of Nebraska Press, 1998.

Watts, Trent, ed. *White Masculinity in the Recent South*. Baton Rouge: Louisiana State University Press, 2008.

Webb, Clive, ed. *Massive Resistance: Southern Opposition to the Second Reconstruction*. Oxford: Oxford University Press, 2005.

Webb, Kayleigh. "Students Have Mixed Feelings on Col. Reb Legislation." *Daily Mis-*

sissippian, February 1, 2011. https://issuu.com/dailymississippian/docs/daily
missississippiano20111.

Weeks, Linton. "Ole Miss: Gateway to Power." *Washington Post*, January 7, 1999, C1.

West, Phil. "Ole Miss Announces Its New Mascot-Rebel Black Bear." *Commercial Appeal*, October 14, 2010.

Westen, Drew. "How Democrats Should Talk about Racism." *Washington Post*, March 23, 2014, B3.

"What Were Coon Songs?" Ferris State University. May 2005. https://www.ferris.edu/HTMLS/news/jimcrow/question/2005/may.htm.

Wheatley, Shirley. Interview by Elizabeth Boyd. August 2002. Natchez, Miss.

Whittaker, Andrew C. "Phi-Mu Accepts African American Girl; Ole Miss in Disarray." *Andrew C. Whittaker* (blog). March 4, 2011. https://acwhittaker.wordpress.com/2011/03/04/phi-mu-accepts-african-american-girl-ole-miss-in-disarray/.

Whittington, Cynthia. Interview by Elizabeth Boyd. August 2002. Natchez, Miss.

Wilkie, Curtis. "A Region Apart." *Boston Globe Magazine*, September 14, 1997, 14–22.

Williams, Courtney. Interview by Elizabeth Boyd. March 1996. Oxford, Miss.

Williams, Thomas Chatterton. "Why White America Insists on Its Racial Innocence." *Washington Post*, July 12, 2015, B1, 5.

Wilson, Charles Reagan. *Baptized in Blood: The Religion of the Lost Cause, 1865–1920*. Athens: University of Georgia Press, 1980.

———. "The Cult of Beauty." In Wilson, *Judgment and Grace in Dixie*, 144–58.

———. *Judgment and Grace in Dixie: Southern Faiths from Faulkner to Elvis*. Athens: University of Georgia Press, 1995.

Woodville Garden Club. *The Woodville Garden Club Announces Its Second Annual Pilgrimage*. Woodville, Miss., 1939.

Woodward, C. Vann. *The Strange Career of Jim Crow*. Commemorative ed. Oxford: Oxford University Press, 2002.

Workneh, Lilly. "Bree Newsome, Activist Who Took Down Confederate Flag, Says She Refused 'to Be Ruled by Fear.'" *Huffington Post*, June 30, 2015. https://www.huffpost.com/entry/bree-newsome-speaks-out_n_7698598.

"World Comes to Natchez, 38 States Send Visitors, Ancient City Ready for 25,000." *Jackson Daily News*, March 27, 1935.

"Wright to Make States Rights Speech." *Natchez Democrat*, March 16, 1948, 1.

Wuensch, Chris. "Examining Student Involvement in Greek Life on SEC Campuses." *Princeton Review*, 2015. https://www.saturdaydownsouth.com/sec-football/greek-life-involvement-sec-schools/.

Wyatt Moore, Edith. "Monteigne, One of the Most Beautiful Show Places, Former Home of Gen. William T. Martin of Natchez, Rich in Period Furnishings." *Natchez Democrat*, February 29, 1948.

———. "Natchez Pilgrimage 'Pink Edition.'" *Natchez Times*, 1939.

Yaeger, Patricia. *Dirt and Desire: Reconstructing Southern Women's Writing, 1930–1990*. Chicago: University of Chicago Press, 2000.

————. "Race and the Cloud of Unknowing in *Gone with the Wind*." *Southern Cultures* 5, no. 1 (1999): 21–28.

Yahr, Emily. "Miss America 2019: The Best, Worst and Weirdest Moments from the Swimsuit-Free Competition." *Washington Post*, September 10, 2018. https://www .washingtonpost.com/news/arts-and-entertainment/wp/2018/09/10/miss-america -2019-the-best-worst-and-weirdest-moments-from-the-swimsuit-free-pageant/?utm _term=.040763fc989d.

Young, Cynthia A., and Min Hyoung Song. "Forum Introduction: Whiteness Redux or Redefined?" *American Quarterly* 66, no. 4 (2014): 1071–76.

Young, Stark. *So Red the Rose*. New York: Scribner's, 1934.

Yow, Miranda. Interview by Elizabeth Boyd. December 8, 2006. Tuscaloosa, Ala.

Yuhl, Stephanie E. *A Golden Haze of Memory: The Making of Historic Charleston*. Chapel Hill: University of North Carolina Press, 2005.

Zengerle, Jason. "Sorority Row." *New Republic*, February 4, 2002, 19–23.

INDEX